Ahead of

JD Kirk is the author of the multi-million bestselling DCI Logan series, set in the Highlands of Scotland. He also does not exist. Instead, JD is the pen name of former children's author and screenwriter, Barry Hutchison, who was born and raised in Fort William. He still lives in the Highlands with his wife and children. He has no idea what the JD stands for.

Also by JD Kirk

DCI Logan Crime Thrillers

JD KIRK

AHEAD
OF THE
GAME

CANELO CRIME

First published in the United Kingdom in 2021 by Zertex Crime

This edition published in the United Kingdom in 2024 by

Canelo
Unit 9, 5th Floor
Cargo Works, 1-2 Hatfields
London SE1 9PG
United Kingdom

A CIP catalogue record for this book is available from the British Library.

Paperback ISBN 978 1 80436 824 4

Cover design by Tom Sanderson

Cover images © Alamy, Shutterstock

Look for more great books at www.canelo.co

Printed and bound in Great Britain by Clays Ltd, Elcograf S.p.A.

Chapter 1

It had seemed like a good idea at the time, this self-employment lark.

Working for yourself. Setting your own hours. No boss breathing down your neck. Just you, the open road, and an endless cavalcade of tourists lining up to hang on your every word.

That was the theory, at least. That was how Ernie Woodcock had imagined it, and how he'd sold the idea to his wife when he'd first suggested jacking in his perfectly adequate, reasonably paid job of eleven years.

It hadn't worked out quite as well as he'd hoped. Not by a long shot, in fact.

There was so much to do. That was the first problem he'd come across. There was always another Facebook ad to set up, another query to respond to, another fire to put out, both metaphorically and—on one occasion, when someone had sparked up a crafty Lambert & Butler at the back of the minibus—literally.

And then there was the tax stuff. Most of it was well beyond his understanding, and he couldn't afford to even think about an accountant at this stage. Fortunately, he'd made approximately fuck-all in the six weeks he'd been in business, so he wasn't too bothered about it yet.

Mostly, though, the big issue with running a tourist-related business of one's own was that tourists, by and large, were all arseholes.

Oh sure, there was the odd one or two who were decent. The occasional odd-one-out who didn't put their feet on the seats, or talk all the way through his carefully-scripted narration, or loudly complain when he overtook some dawdling old bugger in a camper van right before a blind corner.

These heroes—these rare gems—were few and far between, though. Mostly, it was wall-to-wall arseholes, and because he was still establishing his Tripadvisor rating, he could only nod and smile and bend over backwards to accommodate the loathsome bastards and their idiotic requests.

Not a problem, Madam. I'll clean that up. No bother. I hope poor wee Johnny feels better soon. No, don't you worry about a thing.

Wankers.

Still, it had to be done. A few bad Tripadvisor reviews could spell disaster for a fledgling tourism business. Just look at what happened with that theatre cruise company from Fort Augustus a year or two back. A string of bad reviews, and bankrupt within months.

He wondered what had happened to the owners of that in the end, as he scrunched up the tinfoil he'd wrapped his tuna sandwich in, formed it into a little ball, then stuffed it back into his lunch bag next to his flask.

The punters were eating at the coffee shop across the road. Three of them. South African couple in their forties, and a teenage son.

And him with a bus built for twelve.

He felt guilty for inflicting them on the folks who owned the place over the road. The Loch Oich Food Company was a family-run coffee shop and takeaway that had been on the market for about a year now, but with no takers. Hard to believe someone hadn't bitten their hands off yet, given how ideal a spot they were in—right on the A82, a thirty-second walk away from the loch, and slap bang next to one of the more interesting landmarks on Ernie's tour.

They'd owned the place for years. He didn't know why they were selling. Probably just wanted out of the tourist business. He'd imagine they'd had quite enough of dealing with the bastards.

And now he'd gone and inflicted three more on them. And an awful bloody shower they were, too.

The husband—frankly, an absolute dildo of a man, who seemed to have modelled his facial hair on any or all of the Three Musketeers—had questioned almost every part of Ernie's narration, from when the Caledonian Canal was built (1804 to 1822), to the length of Loch Ness (twenty-two and a half miles.) Ernie knew for a bloody *fact* that those were both correct, because he'd checked Wikipedia.

The wife, on the other hand, had not engaged with the tour in the slightest. Instead, she'd talked on her phone the whole way, jabbering away to some shrill-voiced harridan on the other end of the line, snorting, and laughing, and giving it, 'Oh, I know. I know. I *know*,' every three minutes.

During the call, she'd been less than complimentary about the tour, and had made no attempt to be even the slightest bit subtle about it. Which was a bloody cheek, considering she hadn't listened to a word of anything that Ernie had said.

The teenage son had mostly just slumped up the back in silence, except to twice ask, 'Are we there, yet?'

Only Ernie's 'Remember Tripadvisor!' Post-it Note on the dash had stopped him pointing out to the dour-faced little shit that he'd know when they were there, because 'there' would be back at the hotel where they'd all been picked up at seven o'clock that bloody morning.

Scowling at the thought of another two hours with the family, Ernie folded the top of his lunch bag closed and tucked it into the passenger footwell.

'Bastards, the lot of them,' he announced for the benefit of nobody but himself.

He caught himself sighing heavily as the front door of the cafe opened and the three familiar figures emerged. The wife was still talking on the bloody phone. Surely, she hadn't done that all through their lunch? She'd been non-stop wittering on the thing since the back of seven that morning. What was she trying to do, get her name in the record books?

The husband strode purposefully down the steps at the front of the building and gave Ernie a wave like he was hailing a cab.

'Aye, I see you fine, ya bellend,' Ernie muttered through a fixed rictus of a smile. 'I'm a tour bus, no' a bloody taxi service.'

He opened the driver's door and stepped down, if only to emphasise the fact that he had no intention whatsoever of driving across the main road to pick them up.

He savoured the moustache-twitch of irritation from the husband, then waited for them to join him by the minibus.

'You all right there?' he asked, booming out the question in his best 'affable host' manner. 'Get something nice to eat?'

'It was fine,' the husband said, shrugging to highlight quite how indifferent he was to the whole experience. He shivered, despite his heavy coat. 'Are we getting back in? It's freezing.'

Ernie sniffed in a deep breath that filled his lungs with the scents of springtime. 'You think this is cold? You should've been here a few months back. Snow covering the place. This is border-line tropical. And it isn't raining, which is a miracle in and of itself.'

'I wish we'd just gone to Florida again,' the son said, and Ernie caught himself nodding in agreement. He wished they had, too.

'Right, well, I've got a treat in store for you,' he said, setting off towards a tall, roughly triangular monument that stood by the edge of the road. 'And believe me, you won't get this at Disneyland.'

'Are those… heads?' asked the husband, when they stopped by the monument.

This was just the latest in his long line of stupid bloody ques-tions, as far as Ernie was concerned. The sculpture at the top of the monument clearly showed seven heads, all neatly severed, and clutched by a carved stone hand at the top.

'Correct! Seven of them,' Ernie said. 'It's the Well of the Seven Heads.'

'Wow. How original!' the son remarked, and his father let out a gleeful little snort that put Ernie's nose right out of joint.

Bad reviews, he thought. *Can't get bad reviews.*

Rising above the remark, he began to recite his well-rehearsed spiel about the history of the well.

4

1663.

Letters of 'Fire and Sword'

'Ample and summary vengeance.'

Blah, blah, blah.

He led them down the banking as he spoke, saving the good bits until they were huddled by the mouth of the passageway that led beneath the monument itself.

'Seven murderers,' he whispered, the echo of the passageway adding gravitas and drama. 'All beheaded. Washed right here on this spot, before being presented to—'

'What the hell is that?'

Ernie turned, surprised by the question. Or rather, surprised by who it came from. The wife had finally managed to unglue the phone from her ear and was angling the screen into the tunnel mouth, trying to use its dim glow to push back the shadows.

'What's what?' Ernie asked.

She tutted and sighed like a surly teenager, told whoever she was on the phone to that she would call them back, then hung up and activated the torch function with a couple of indignant thumb presses.

As soon as the light kicked in, Ernie saw them.

Feet.

Two of.

Wearing trainers.

'What the fuck?' the son ejected.

'Give me that,' said the husband, taking the phone from his wife. He stepped forward and the torchlight drove the darkness further back.

'Is this part of the tour?' asked the wife. 'If it is, it's horrible. It's sick!'

Ernie didn't hear her. He was too focused on the contents of the passageway.

Past the feet, he saw legs. Hips. Arms. Shoulders.

The light revealed more of the passageway, but there the body ended.

5

'The head. Where the hell's his head gone?' Ernie wondered aloud, surprisingly calmly, given the circumstances.

But as the screaming started behind him, Ernie had a horrible sinking feeling that this was *really* going to affect his Tripadvisor score.

Chapter 2

DCI Jack Logan stood surrounded by the smell of death. He'd love to be able to say this was unusual, but it was pretty much par for the course by this point in a long, and not particularly glamorous, polis career.

The particular aroma of death that lingered in this place was far from fresh. The building had once been a butcher's shop. It stood tucked away just off Shore Street—barely a stone's throw from the Burnett Road station he was based at—and had mostly served local restaurants until it had shut down a year or so back.

The stench of dead animal flesh had permeated the fabric of the building, but that was just background olfactory noise. Much more overpowering was the rancid reek of the human remains that had been discovered in the big walk-in freezer through the back of the shop.

The property owner had made the grisly discovery back in February, when he'd come up from the south of England to prep the place for sale. The smell hadn't hit him until he'd opened the freezer door, and months of stale warm air had come cascading out.

Once he'd finished throwing up, he'd got straight on to 999. To Logan's immense relief, he'd been pulled out of a strategy meeting with Detective Superintendent Mitchell and a couple of the higher-ups from the central belt, and the whole rigmarole of murder investigation had kicked off once again.

It wasn't hard to identify a suspect, of course. The remains had lain there decomposing since whoever had been paying the electric bill had stopped doing so, but cause of death was organ failure due to extreme cold temperatures. Logan had guessed that, even before the post-mortem.

The Iceman, it seemed, had left one final surprise.

They'd investigated, of course. Checked with the power company that had previously been supplying energy to the place. The name on the bill had actually been one of the Iceman's original victims, which was a nicely macabre little touch, Logan thought.

The bills hadn't been paid in December or January, and the supply had been cut. It wasn't like home electricity, where the company had an obligation to help you keep the heating on. With commercial supply, there was no such requirement. Two strikes and you were out. No heating. No lights. And certainly no big power-guzzling, walk-in freezer.

And so the freezer's contents had begun to thaw.

The case wouldn't technically be closed for a while yet. The paperwork would see to that. But for all intents and purposes, it was off Logan's plate.

And yet…

He shoved his hands deep into the pockets of his overcoat and turned on the spot, taking in the room around him. The windows were still boarded up, and the only light came from the open door. The shop had been picked clean by Geoff Palmer's Scene of Crime team. There had been very little to discover this side of the freezer door.

But what there had been—a metal pipe and a spray of blood on the floor—didn't fit with the rest of the Iceman murders. Not exactly. Not quite.

The rest of Logan's team had told him he was overthinking it, but those two slight incongruities dangled like loose threads from the case file. He tried to ignore them, but kept circling back around.

A metal pipe.

A spray of blood.

Two pieces of a puzzle that didn't *quite* fit.

8

His phone rang in his pocket. He stole another quick glance around at the shop's interior, then stepped outside to take the call.

The name that was emblazoned on the screen made him hesitate.

'Vanessa,' he said, pulling the shop door closed behind him. 'To what do I owe the pleasure?'

His ex-wife's tone had more of a chill to it than the mid-morning air. This was not exactly a surprise. She had demonstrated very little warmth towards him since…

Well, for a very long time.

'Jack. How have you been?' she asked. Although 'asked' wasn't quite the right word. 'Asked' implied the expectation of an answer. The words had been spoken out of habit, though. A verbal tic. He knew she couldn't care less. That wasn't what this was about.

'What's up?' he asked. 'What's happened?'

'What makes you think something's happened?' Vanessa asked.

'Because you're phoning me.'

Logan locked the door to the shop, replaced the cordon tape across it, then marched back in the direction of the station. It was only a couple of minutes' walk if he cut across the back way. If past experiences were anything to go by, Vanessa would've hung up on him long before he got there.

'Yes. Well,' she said, and Logan could picture her shifting around uncomfortably on her big expensive couch. 'I just… I thought you should know.'

'Know what?'

'It's Maddie.'

Logan slowed his pace at the mention of his daughter's name. He swapped the phone from one ear to the other. 'What's wrong? Is she all right? What's happened?'

'She's fine. She's better than fine, actually,' Vanessa said. There was an inhalation from the other end of the line. A silent holding of breath. A building up to something.

'Vanessa—'

'She got married.'

Logan stopped halfway across a side-road. A van honked at him, and he continued to the pavement before responding.

'Married? What do you mean "she got married"?'

'I mean she got married.'

'When? To who?'

'To her boyfriend. Anderson.'

Logan's lips drew back in a sneer. 'Anderson? Who the fuck is Anderson when he's at home?'

'He's your son–in–law. As of three weeks ago.'

'Three weeks?!' Logan spat. 'She marries some arsehole with a last name for a first name three fucking weeks ago, and I'm only finding out about it now?'

'She didn't want you finding out about it at all,' Vanessa said, her voice rising to match his. 'And he's not an arsehole. He's lovely. Kind. Considerate. He works in banking.'

'Oh, does he? *Does he?*' Logan asked. Like Vanessa's, this wasn't a real question. Unlike him, she went ahead and answered it, anyway.

'Yes. He's got a house just outside London. She moved in at the start of the year.'

'She's married and living with a banker she's only just met in *London*?' Logan practically shrieked down the microphone.

'They've been seeing each other for a year and a bloody half, Jack. They've hardly "only just met".'

'And what do you mean she didn't want me finding out about it?' Logan demanded.

Vanessa replied with the bluntness he'd come to expect from her.

'Are you being deliberately difficult about this? She didn't want you knowing because, right now, she doesn't want you in her life. After everything that happened.'

Logan remained silent at that. He had no real defence to offer. Given what she'd gone through, he couldn't blame her for never taking his calls. The truth of it was, he'd stopped trying months ago, after a single text had come through from her late one night.

Leave me alone.

'She's happy, Jack. She's genuinely happy for the first time in… God. I don't even know. She'll probably kill me for telling you, but I just… I thought you should know.'

Logan leaned his back against a fence and leaned the elbow of his phone arm on a post. From where he stood, he could see the Burnett Road Police Station looming just beyond the skip hire place and the Scotbake bakery. At a good clip, it was a one-minute walk away. Right now, though, his legs weren't up for moving.

'I just… I always thought… even with everything…' Logan began. He didn't finish, though. He didn't know how.

'I know,' Vanessa said, and for the first time in a long while, there was a slight softening of her tone. 'But she's happy. And that's the main thing. Right?'

Logan grimaced—not because he disagreed, but because she was right. Annoyingly, she was right.

'Aye. That's the main thing,' he agreed. 'So, how—?'

'I have to go, Jack.'

She didn't bother to offer an explanation. She had no obligation to do so, and he had no right to ask for one.

Instead, he just nodded and forced a smile into his voice. 'Aye. Right you are. Well, thanks for letting me know.'

'You won't tell her I told you?'

'Tell her? No. Like she'd talk to me, anyway.'

There was a pause then. An awkward little blip of silence.

'She'll come around, I'm sure. Give her time.'

'Aye,' Logan said. 'I'm sure. Thanks again. You take care.'

'And you.'

The line went quiet as Vanessa ended the call. Logan immediately opened his contacts, found his daughter's name, and tapped it with his thumb.

It rang twice, and went to voicemail halfway through the third.

He waited for the beep, spent far too long trying to work out what to say, then hung up without leaving a message.

'Fucking *Anderson*,' he muttered, stuffing the phone back into his pocket.

He had barely gone a few steps when the mobile rang. His heart leapt into his throat as he reached into the pocket again, then the nervous excitement fizzled away when he saw that the name on-screen wasn't Maddie's.

'Tyler,' he said, putting the phone to his ear. 'I'm almost back at the office, what's up?'

DC Neish's voice was partly drowned out by the rumble of an engine and the sound of traffic, suggesting he was calling from his car. 'Just got word, boss. There's been a body found down near Invergarry,' he said. 'And by all accounts, it's an absolute belter!'

Chapter 3

'What time did you call that last night?'

Three hours before Ernie Woodcock's tour had made its grisly discovery, Bennet Lennon looked up from his bowl of cereal to find his dad, Clyde, standing in the kitchen doorway. It was rare to see him up and about this early, and he had the look about him of someone who had fallen far short of their required sleep quota.

'Sorry?' Bennet asked, shooting a glance into the hallway behind his dad in the hope his mum might be there to offer support. She was still upstairs getting ready for work, though. Bennet was on his own.

'I'll fucking "sorry" you,' Clyde spat. His eyes were ringed with red, but seemed to bulge with barely contained rage. 'Half-past bloody midnight you and that bastard were still playing your wee fucking games. I'd a good mind to come in there and skelp the pair of you.'

'We were quiet,' Bennet protested. Not too forcefully, though. The last thing he wanted to do was set his old man off. He was on a short fuse at the best of times. This early in the morning? After being kept awake late into the night? It didn't bear thinking about.

'Quiet, were you? Fucking quiet? You call this quiet?' He raised his voice into a monotone shout and mimed pressing the buttons of a video game controller. 'Shoot him! Watch out! Blow it up!' Clyde dropped his hands to his side and scowled at the seventeen-year-old at the kitchen table. 'Does that sound fucking quiet to you?'

'We were playing *FIFA*,' Bennet countered. He dropped his eyes and looked into the half-finished bowl of cereal, no longer hungry. 'Sorry. It won't happen again.'

'Too fucking true. You don't need to tell me that. Your wee games stop at ten from now on, or I'll come in there and put my foot up your fucking arse. I don't care who's in, you'll get fucking leathered. All right?'

There was no point in trying to negotiate. You couldn't hold a debate with his dad. If you tried, it became an argument.

And Clyde Lennon was a big man. He knew the most effective way to end an argument.

'And next time, tell him not to rev his engine when he's driving away. What a fucking racket that was. And fix your fucking tie. You're not going to school looking like that. You're a disgrace.'

Bennet didn't know what was wrong with his tie, but he adjusted it anyway. His dad grunted some form of begrudged approval, then headed for the fridge and took out a can of Strongbow.

'What?' he asked, when he caught the look from Bennet. 'It's my day off, isn't it?'

'I didn't say anything,' Bennet replied, rising from the table, cereal bowl in hand.

'No. Make sure you don't.' Clyde cracked open the ring-pull, took a drink, then swirled the cider around like mouthwash before swallowing it down. He watched his son rinsing out his bowl, then shook his head in disgust. 'Don't you stand there fucking judging me.'

'I wasn't,' Bennet said, not looking back.

'I work flat-out putting food on the table. The table that I fucking built, I might add. I deserve to enjoy a day off now and again. Or don't I? Should I just work my fingers to the fucking bone? That keep you happy?'

Bennet finished washing his bowl and set it on the draining board. He was tempted to point out that his mum was the main breadwinner, and that Clyde spent half his time at the pub, spending most of the income his business brought in.

He'd been out for a big chunk of the previous evening, for example, and had returned home about twenty minutes before Bennet's mate, Lachlan, had set off back to the staff accommodation of the hotel they both worked at. Clyde's complaints about them making too much noise were bullshit, Bennet knew, but he daren't say that to his face.

Not if he wanted to make it to school.

'You do deserve time off. You work really hard. Thanks,' Bennet said, carefully stripping any trace of sarcasm from the sentence. He indicated the door with a nod. 'I'd, um, I'd better get going. Don't want to be late.'

Clyde clenched and unclenched his jaws, his gaze fixed on the boy like it was laser-guided. Then, with a burp and a wave of his hand, he sent him on his way.

'Fuck off, then,' he said to Bennet's back. 'And tell your mother to make sure she picks something up for dinner on the way home this time.' He burped again, gave his can a swirl, and said the next part to the empty room. 'I'm sick to the back teeth of having to do everything around here.'

—

The drive from Roy Bridge to Lochaber High School was just a little over ten miles. At this time of year, before the campers and caravans came along to clog the route, Bennet barely noticed the journey passing. A couple of miles south to Spean, a left turn onto the A82, then a quick shoot down the road. One last right turn at the roundabout on the way into Fort William, and they were practically there.

Today, though, it seemed to be taking longer than usual. He gazed out the side window, watching the trees trundle past. They were just about to pass the turn-off for the Nevis Range ski resort.

Just over halfway there, then.

He'd hoped he'd pass his test before he finished Sixth Year, but with barely a month until his final exams started, and his driving test still not even booked, it looked like he'd have to settle for lifts with his mum.

Or 'Mrs Lennon', as he had to call her at school. That was the depute headteacher's suggestion, not hers. Mrs Robertson had come round the house specifically to discuss the matter before Bennet had started high school. He didn't remember ever seeing his mum looking more uncomfortable as she had when her boss was sitting there in the front room with her husband. Something about those two worlds colliding had made her deeply uneasy.

It wouldn't do for Bennet to call her 'Mum' in class, the depute head had said. It would *undermine her authority*.

Clyde had enjoyed that remark. 'Authority?' he'd snorted. 'What fucking authority?'

Bennet felt his ears burn red at the thought of it, even all these years later. The look on his mum's face. The shame of it. The tears he'd heard her shed in the bathroom later as he'd stood on the other side of the door, wishing he could think of the right thing to say.

Wishing he could make his dad disappear from their lives for good.

'You're quiet.'

Bennet turned his attention from the passing trees. His mum, Lana, was giving him a sideways look through the thick lenses of her glasses, her eyes flitting back and forth between him and the road ahead.

'Am I? Sorry.'

'No need to apologise,' Lana said. He watched her testing out a few sentences in her head before she spoke again. 'You should try to ignore him. I mean… don't *ignore* ignore him. He hates that. Just… don't let him bother you too much.'

Ah, so it was this conversation again, was it? How many times had they been over this before? Apparently, it was their job not to provoke him, and not his own responsibility to keep his temper in check.

Just watch what you say.

Just mind where you put things.

Just agree. It's easier.

Whether it was her intention or not, all her advice always put the blame squarely on Bennet's shoulders. His father's outbursts were Bennet's fault, apparently, because he'd said or done the wrong thing at the wrong time.

'Why do you always make excuses for him?' Bennet asked.

'I don't always make excuses.'

Bennet turned further in his chair so he was fully facing his mother in the driver's seat. They were passing the turn-off to Inverlochy Castle Hotel now, where Bennet had a part-time weekend job, carrying suitcases, running errands, and generally doing whatever he was told by rich people dressed in outfits he'd never be able to afford.

'You do so make excuses,' he insisted. 'Every time. You say he's tired, or he's having a hard time of things lately, or… I don't know… some bullshit about his childhood.'

'He did have a tough childhood.'

'See? You're doing it again! Fuck's sake, Mum!'

'Benny!'

'Well!'

He threw himself around in his seat and went back to the window. Over six years of driving this road almost every weekday, he and his mum had a little running… joke, he supposed, about the trees. It had started on his first day, when he'd sat anxiously hunched in the front passenger seat, dread filling his belly like a dodgy curry.

'Oh look, the trees are waving you off, Benny,' she'd said.

And with a bit of imagination, they had been. The leafy branches had been swaying side-to-side on the breeze, creaking and groaning as they'd moved back and forth.

He'd known they weren't really waving, of course, but it had made him feel a little better. They'd watched out for it every day since, waving back whenever the wind was high enough to animate the branches.

Now, the trees stood stoic and still. They didn't wave him off to school. Not today.

'Let's make a deal, all right?' Lana began.

'Does it involve you finally kicking him out?' Bennet asked, his gaze still fixed on the world blurring by outside.

'Let's both decide we're going to have a good day. We're going to go into school, and we're going to love every bloody minute of it.'

'I've got double Higher Maths.'

Lana winced. 'Oof. OK, how about *I* love every bloody minute of it, and you love every bloody minute of it with the obvious exception of the hundred minutes of Maths, which you are free to hate? How does that sound?'

Bennet shrugged, then he jumped when his mum prodded him in the ribs.

'Boop. How does that sound? Is that a plan? Boop. Boop!'

'Argh! Quit that!' Bennet yelped, as her finger jabbed at him again. A smirk tugged at the corners of his mouth, despite his best efforts to hold it back.

'I'm not going to stop until you agree. Boop.'

'All right! Fine!' he ejected, blocking another finger-poke before it could reach him. 'You win!'

'Do we have a deal?' Lana asked, wiggling her finger back and forth like a snake. 'Are you going to love every bloody minute?'

'Except Maths.'

'Obviously.'

'Fine. We have a deal.'

He sat up a little straighter, and watched as a police car went tearing up the road past them, lights flashing and siren wailing.

'Someone's in a hurry,' Lana remarked, as she always did on occasions such as these.

Bennet watched in the wing mirror until the car disappeared.

Outside, a breeze had begun to blow, and ten thousand trees waved him on his way.

Chapter 4

Logan timed his arrival perfectly. DC Sinead Bell handed him a takeaway coffee cup almost as soon as he'd pulled into the car park on the shore of Loch Oich and got out of the car.

And it was a *proper* car he was driving, these days. By which he meant, it was not a Ford Fiesta. After the collision that had written that bloody thing off, he'd stood his ground with Detective Superintendent Mitchell, and she'd finally agreed to give him the keys to something that wasn't built for someone two-thirds his height and half his width.

Nowadays, when he climbed behind the wheel, it was of a shiny black BMW X5. It marked him out as polis from a mile away, but he didn't care. He was able to get in and out of the driver's seat without the risk of slipping a disc, and he didn't have to shoogle back and forward in the seat to try to give the vehicle an additional burst of speed whenever he went uphill. He'd take those over a loss of anonymity, any day.

'Morning, sir,' Sinead said, once he'd taken the coffee cup from her. 'Journey all right?'

'A bloody dream,' Logan said, giving the bonnet of the Beamer a loving stroke. He took a drink of his coffee, winced as it burned his lips, then gestured with the cup to where a knot of white suits was assembled around the base of some sort of obelisk. 'What's the story, then?'

'Male. No ID yet. Group from a tour bus found him just before eleven this morning. Or, most of him.'

'Aye. Tyler mentioned,' Logan said. He took another experimental sip of his coffee, but more carefully this time. It was still like molten lava against his lips. 'He sounded quite excited.'

'Not every day we get a headless one, I suppose,' Sinead remarked.

'No. Thankfully not,' Logan said.

He let his gaze drift away from the throng of activity around the monument, first to the wide, flat water of Loch Oich on the right, then back across the road to a large white and green building that stood almost directly across from where the SOC team were beavering away.

'What's that?' he asked.

'Loch Oich Food Company. Coffee shop.'

'Big for a coffee shop,' Logan remarked.

'Think it's a house, too,' Sinead said. 'Owners live there. Maybe B&B. I'm not sure.'

'They see anything?'

'No. Nothing. Tyler's getting statements from them, but I'd be surprised if they know anything.' Sinead took a drink from her own cup, then recoiled and hurriedly licked her lips.

'Take it yours is as hot as the bloody sun, too, then?' Logan asked.

'You can say that again,' Sinead replied.

They both prised off the plastic lids of the cups. Two clouds of trapped steam rose up like ghosts fleeing the grave.

'Is Geoff Palmer in amongst that lot?' Logan asked, nodding over at the largely indistinguishable figures in the paper suits.

'Afraid so, sir,' Sinead confirmed.

Logan tutted. As if the day hadn't been going badly enough. Now, he'd have to have a conversation with that bulbous-nosed gobshite.

Still, at least there was one bright spot.

'Shona Maguire's on her way down,' he said, risking another go at the coffee. Taking the lid off had lowered the temperature of the liquid by a couple of degrees, but it still burned his lips, while the steam practically scalded his sinuses.

'Is she?' Sinead asked, making no attempt to hide her smirk. 'Did you ask her yet?'

'Not yet,' Logan said, avoiding her gaze. 'Building up to it.'

'The wedding's in less than a fortnight,' the DC pointed out. 'You've not got a lot of building room left.'

'We're... taking things slow.'

'That's a bloody understatement,' Sinead said. Logan shot her a look, and she smiled back at him. 'Sir.'

'Aye. That's more like it, Detective Constable. Bit of respect,' Logan said. He turned his attention back to the activity around the monument. 'I'll ask her tonight.'

'Or you could ask her this morning, if she's coming down the road.'

Logan looked back at her. 'Hardly the most romantic venue in the world, huddled around a bloody corpse.'

Sinead shrugged. 'Isn't that more or less how you met, though?'

Logan let out a little hmpf. Not quite a laugh, but not far off. 'You've a point there, right enough.'

The DC shifted her weight from foot to foot, building up to the next question. 'And you're still all right with it? Giving me away? Doing the speech, and everything?'

'Christ. Speech. Aye, I should get on that, too,' Logan said. 'And yes. Of course, I'm still all right with it. I'm more than all right with it. I'm delighted.' He breathed in deeply through his nose, then released all the air again as a sigh. 'Speaking of weddings, Vanessa phoned me this morning.'

'Your ex? What, is she getting remarried or something?'

Logan shook his head. 'No. Maddie.'

'Oh,' said Sinead. She was more aware than most of the team of how complicated Logan's relationship with his daughter was, and so was equally aware of the minefield she was stepping into. 'That'll be nice.'

'I'm sure it was,' Logan replied.

'Was?'

'Happened three weeks ago. She didn't want me there. Doesn't even want me to know.'

Sinead winced. 'Ah. Bugger. I'm sorry.'

'Not to worry. Two weddings in as many months? Who's got time for that?'

He blew on his coffee to signal he was getting back to business, chanced the briefest of sips, then put the lid back on. There was no more avoiding it. The time had come.

'Right then,' he said with a heavy sigh, and a heavier heart. 'I suppose we should go and talk to Geoff Palmer.'

—

When it came to being a detective, it didn't pay to deal in absolutes. Not until you'd built enough evidence to get a solid conviction, at least. And even then, the world had many more shades of grey than it had lines drawn in black and white.

DCI Logan had told Tyler that himself once. Maybe not word for word, but that was the general gist of it.

Here and now, though, DC Neish was prepared to go out on a limb and state for the record that this was *absolutely* the best cinnamon bun he'd ever eaten, no two ways about it. Warm, gooey, sweet, with just the right hint of spice. It really was a treat to be—

'Detective Constable, did you hear what I just said?'

Tyler paused mid-chew, and looked across the table to where the South African couple and their teenage son sat watching him.

He swallowed the half-chewed bite of bun with some difficulty, forced it down with a glug of tea, then wiped his hands on a little paper napkin.

'Sorry. Missed breakfast,' he explained. 'You were telling me about finding the body.'

The woman on the other side of the table rolled her eyes. 'I knew it. He wasn't even listening. We *told* you about finding the body. We were asking when we could go.'

Tyler sat up, wiped his mouth with the back of his hand, then cleared his throat in a manner he hoped sounded suitably go-getting and businesslike. 'Right. Aye. Sorry, Mrs…' he glanced at his notes, '…Blomkamp. Can I just…? If we could quickly go over it again, that would be useful. So, you came out of here and crossed the road…'

'The driver took us down to look at a hole in a wall, we found a dead body, we called the police, the end,' Mrs Blomkamp replied, her South African accent made thicker by her annoyance. 'There's not exactly a lot to report, and we'd like to get back to our holiday, if you don't mind?'

Tyler hadn't had a lot of experience of dealing with white South Africans. His only real exposure to them had been one fleeting conversation in a pub a few years back, and the bad guy in *Lethal Weapon 2*. He was well aware, though, of the stereotype that they were all horrible racist bastards.

He was also well aware that you shouldn't put too much stock in stereotypes, but he was definitely getting both 'horrible' and 'bastard' vibes off the family sitting across from him. Their racism, or lack thereof, remained an unknown quantity at this stage in the proceedings.

'And the head was missing when you got there?' Tyler asked.

'Well, of course, it was!' Mrs Blomkamp said.

'What, you think we took it as a souvenir or something?' her husband chipped in.

'Ugh. When can we *go*?' demanded their son, throwing himself back in his chair and folding his arms across his chest.

Tyler channelled his inner Logan and fixed them all with a stern glare. 'Maybe you've forgotten, but a man has died. An innocent man has lost his life here,' he said. 'So, I'd appreciate it if you dropped the attitude, answered my questions, and started to take this a bit more seriously.'

The family returned his glare. After a moment, Mrs Blomkamp pointed to his top lip. 'You've got icing there,' she told him.

Instinctively, Tyler stuck out his tongue and licked the cinnamon-flavoured blob from his philtrum. For reasons he couldn't explain, but which would likely keep him awake wondering about on some sleepless night months from now, he maintained unwavering eye-contact with Mrs Blomkamp while doing so.

She regarded him with a sort of fascinated horror until he cleared his throat, tapped his notebook, and announced, 'Actually, I've probably got enough to be going on with, for now.'

–

There was something about Geoff Palmer's face that made Logan think of a cartoon. Not all the time—mostly, Palmer's face just made the DCI think how much he'd enjoy punching it. But when it was encased inside the white paper hood of forensics gear, with the elastic forming a misshapen circle around his features, there was definitely a cartoonish quality about it.

And not a good cartoon, either. Not *Pixar* or *Disney*. No, his was a face that belonged in a cheap Saturday morning kids' cartoon, put together frame by frame in some animation sweatshop that could never quite get the flesh tones right, and didn't know how to make eyes look all the way human.

'Oh. It's you,' Palmer said, forcibly exhaling when he made his way up from the well's entrance to find Logan standing by the monument.

'Always a pleasure to see you too, Geoff,' Logan said. He considered this to be the end of their small talk, and got down to business. 'What have we got?'

'Ninety percent of a human body, give or take a pound or two,' Palmer replied. 'We'll have to wait for Shona to check it over and do her stuff, but I can say with some certainty that someone's had his head off.'

'No sign of it?'

'My guess? Someone chucked it in the loch. We'll need to bring the divers in.'

Logan gave Sinead a quick nod and she retreated, already reaching for her mobile.

'Confident this one wasn't natural causes?' he asked.

Palmer scowled. 'Christ, not this again. I don't attend one murder scene. *One*. In ten years. And I'll never hear the bloody end of it.'

'I didn't say anything, Geoff,' Logan said, holding his hands out like a magician revealing he had nothing up his sleeves. 'I just asked if you were confident that—'

'Yes! I'm confident it wasn't natural causes,' Palmer spat. 'All right? Not unless his head just fucking... I don't know... disintegrated, or floated away.'

Logan looked doubtful. 'I mean... is that likely? You being the expert and everything.'

'Oh, shut up,' Palmer muttered. 'I already know what you're going to ask, so write this down. He wasn't killed at the scene. No blood spray, and marks on the ground suggest he was dragged from that lay-by there, down this ramp, then dumped in the... whatever it is. *Passageway* under the well.'

'Well?'

Palmer gestured to the monument. His expression, confined as it was by the circle of elastic, took on the look of a disappointed teacher. 'Yes. That's what this is. The Well of the Seven Heads. You'll have heard of it.'

Logan considered the obelisk. Carvings of severed heads adorned the top of it. Seven of them, presumably. A hand was holding them all by the hair, while also clutching a long, slender knife. As decoration went, it was a particularly macabre example.

'Oh. Aye. I've heard of it,' Logan said, which was partly true. He'd heard, or maybe seen, the name in passing at some point, but that was the extent of his knowledge. Fortunately, Google and Wikipedia were never far away, and he made a mental note to do some reading when he got back to the office.

Logan's gaze traced the route that Palmer had laid out. A minibus sat at the far end of the lay-by, almost directly across the road from the coffee shop. Assuming the killer had parked as close as possible to the monument, he'd have had to drag the body a good twenty feet along the side of one of the busiest roads in the

West Highlands, right in front of a building with—he counted quickly—eleven windows.

Bold, then, whoever they were. Even if they'd done it in the dead of night, which he was assuming would be the case, there was traffic going up and down the A82 at all hours. Moving a body even a short distance along it would've been risky.

'We've found no fingerprints on the handrails, and the walls of the passageway are porous rock, so we're unlikely to get anything off them, even if there was something to find, which I doubt,' Palmer continued.

Logan nodded his agreement. A handrail at a popular tourist site—even before the season had really kicked in—would generally be a *Who's Who* of fingerprints. The fact that the SOC team had drawn a blank told him the killer had done a thorough job of wiping them clean.

'We've got the opposite problem with footprints,' Geoff continued, indicating the muddy lay-by 'Too many of the bloody things, all piled up on top of each other. And that's before the bloody bus tour trampled through it.'

'Anything corresponding to the drag marks you found?' Logan asked.

'I'll have to double-check with the team, but I wouldn't hold my breath if I were you. There was rain last night. Even if we get something, it's unlikely to be clear enough to be useful.'

Logan ran his hand down his face. This was not a great start to an investigation. 'What about the shore? Anything closer to the water?'

'We haven't done a full and thorough search yet,' Palmer replied. 'But there's nothing jumping out at us, no.'

Logan looked past the monument to where the waters of Loch Oich lapped against the land. A rough stone wall ran around the back of the obelisk at around knee-height. From there to the water was a good twenty to thirty feet through weeds and bracken.

'How far could you chuck a head, do you think?' he wondered.

Palmer followed his gaze, running his tongue across the front of his yellowing teeth as he considered the question. 'Underarm or overarm?'

'Either one. Just in general.'

'I mean, it depends on the hair, doesn't it?'

Logan turned to the other man, a frown troubling his brow. 'The hair?'

Palmer sighed. It was loud and theatrical, and done solely for the purpose of trying to make Logan feel stupid. It didn't work. It would be a cold day in Hell before Logan let anything Geoff Palmer had to say impact his self-esteem.

'Yes. *Obviously*,' Palmer said. 'If the head has short hair, you've got a limited number of ways to hold it. You could try shot-putting it from the shoulder, but then its face is right next to your face, eyeball to eyeball, and what sort of nutter wants that?'

'The sort of nutter that tries to shot-put a severed head into a loch?' Logan guessed, but Palmer ignored him.

'You could try bowling it, but that's not going to get you very far. Overarm lob would be too unpredictable, and would probably give you too much height when what you want is distance. With long hair, though, you've got a handle. You can get a grip on it, and really welly the bastard. Really swing it.'

He mimed twirling something at his side, like a cowboy with a lasso, then released his imagined grip and watched an invisible human head go sailing through the air.

'You could put some real distance on it that way,' he continued. 'Yeah, I reckon you'd reach the water no problem, if you had long hair to work with. Easy. That's what I'd do, anyway.'

Logan regarded him for a moment, then raised his eyebrows and gave a little shake of his head. 'Well, that was both enlightening and frankly quite concerning, Geoffrey. I thought you might say "ten yards" or something, but thanks for the detailed assessment.'

He turned at the sound of a car engine passing through one side of the cordoned area that currently blocked the main road in both directions. Shona Maguire gave a wave from the driver's seat, then followed the pointed directions of a uniformed constable that guided her to the car park a little further on.

Without looking, Logan could feel the intensity of Geoff Palmer's glare on the back of his head. He'd had his sights on Shona for some time, long before Logan came along. He'd even tried to warn the DCI off 'his lady' at one point, which had gone about as well for him as might reasonably be expected.

'Best let you get back to it, Geoff,' Logan said. 'Dr Maguire and I will be along together shortly. Maybe best if you don't mention the head-twirling, though,' he suggested with a grim smile. 'She thinks you're creepy enough as it is.'

Chapter 5

Bennet arrived a few minutes late for his first lesson of the day. PE. Not his favourite subject. Not by a long shot.

The only reason he'd even taken the class was because he needed to fill up his timetable in his last year at school, and PE was the only thing that didn't clash with his other choices. Well, it was that or Drama. Both involved jumping around making a dick of yourself, but only one had you doing so in front of a large audience, and so the choice had been an easy one.

Actually, none of that was quite true. Yes, PE had been one of a limited number of choices available to him, but the main reason for choosing the class had been the teacher. Mr Forsyth was relatively new to the school—he'd arrived when Bennet was in Second Year—and was less than a decade older than everyone from Fourth Year and up.

Unlike most of the teachers—Bennet's mum included—he was a good laugh. All the students loved him. Everyone had a really good relationship with him, and Bennet most of all.

After quickly getting changed into his shorts and t-shirt, Bennet followed the echoing thwack of bouncing basketballs and began a breathless apology as he raced into the hall.

'Sorry, Fergus, I was—'

He stopped at the sight of Mrs Robertson, the depute head. *Cops and Robertson*, they called her—often shortened just to *Copsand*—for reasons nobody had ever quite been able to explain. It was assumed it had something to do with her police-state sense of discipline, but that was mostly just a guess. Only the original creator of the nickname knew for sure, and he or she had likely left school decades ago.

Copsand stood just inside the hall, dressed in a long grey skirt and an oddly puffy blouse, scanning Bennet's ball-bouncing classmates like she was selecting her next meal.

'Bennet. You're late. Why?' she asked, not bothering to turn and look at him.

He daren't say they'd arrived at school just after the bell had rung. His mum was supposed to be there from half-eight, and she stood to lose much more than he did if she fell under Copsand's scrutiny.

'Oh, eh, I got chatting in the corridor, Miss,' he offered, throwing himself in front of the bullet.

'Oh, eh, did you, indeed?' Copsand asked, mirroring his hesitation. 'Then how is it that I saw your mother's car pulling into the car park not five minutes ago?'

Damn it. Rumbled.

'We'll discuss this later,' the depute head said. She raised a wraith-like arm and pointed a skeletal finger at a plastic tub full of faded orange basketballs. 'Go. Get a ball. Bounce it.'

'Right, Miss. Sorry, Miss,' Bennet said, scurrying over to the tub.

He regarded the sad selection of remaining balls like they were the last pieces of fruit in the supermarket, plucked out the firmest and ripest, and gave it an experimental bounce. It gave a disappointing thup and bounced halfway back to his hand before flopping back to the floor.

Go on without me, it seemed to say, as it lay there unmoving on the well-scuffed wood. *I'll only slow you down.*

'Perhaps you misunderstood? The instruction was to bounce it, not stand there staring at it,' Copsand said.

Bennet picked up the ball, swapped it for another, and managed to dribble three times before it, too, sagged sadly to the floor.

'I can blow these up for you, Miss,' he suggested.

'That's quite all right, Bennet.'

'Fergus… Mr Forsyth, I mean. He sometimes gets me to blow—'

'Yes, well, maybe if Mr Forsyth had bothered to show up this morning, you'd be having a very different conversation right now,' Copsand spoke over him. 'But you've got me this morning. Lucky for all of us. Besides, the cupboard is locked, so you can't get the pump.'

'Is he sick?' Bennet asked. 'Mr Forsyth? Is he sick?'

'Fatima! Off the bloody wall bars!' the depute head shouted. 'They're not for climbing on.'

Actually, that was exactly what they were for, but six years of high school had taught the class not to talk back to Copsand, so everyone knew better than to point this out to her.

'Is Mr Forsyth sick, Miss?' Bennet asked again.

'God. Your guess is as good as mine,' Copsand replied. She pointed to the middle of the court like a demented queen sending a subject to the dungeons. 'Now shut up, Bennet, and go get bouncing.'

–

Logan squatted by the mouth of the passageway that ran under the monument, hands gloved, shoes covered, head ensheathed by something not unlike a shower cap. It would be an unflattering look on most men. On one of his size and stature, it looked positively ridiculous.

Geoff Palmer had insisted on him wearing it if he was going to follow the pathologist down to the body. Presumably, Palmer had imagined that the very thought of donning something so utterly unbecoming would be enough to put Logan off the idea, but the look of shock on his face when Logan had pinged it into place atop his head had been enough to make it all worthwhile.

Shona Maguire knelt a little further inside the tunnel, studying the remains that lay spread on the ground. Logan would've described the body's position as 'face-down', had it not been for the fact that the most important element in that phrase was conspicuous by its absence.

'Well, he's definitely dead,' Shona announced.

'Christ, all those years of medical training have certainly paid off,' Logan replied. 'You didn't have to check for a pulse or anything.'

'You get an eye for it after a while,' Shona said. 'You learn to spot the little tell-tale signs that the less-qualified observer doesn't notice.'

Logan chuckled. While Shona noted the time and scribbled down some initial impressions in a notepad, he looked around the mouth of the tunnel. It was a cramped, narrow, arch-shaped space, barely wide enough for Shona to squeeze in beside the body.

The smell of bodily fluids emanated strongly from within it. While much of that could be blamed on its current headless occupant, the sheer richness of the odour suggested it had reeked long before he got here.

The passageway narrowed at the far end into what looked like an even smaller arched doorway which presumably led through to some other chamber of the well. Logan shuddered at the very thought of it. He wasn't particularly claustrophobic, but there were few things he could think of that would be worse than being stuck down there, unable to stand up, or even turn around.

'Good job it's not Ricketts on duty,' Logan remarked. There was no way the older pathologist would be able to bend down far enough to get into the passageway, much less be able to do anything useful while he was there.

'He's asked not to attend scenes from now on,' Shona said, still writing in her pad. 'After Alness back at Christmas.'

Privately, Logan was delighted to hear that. The less time he had to spend in the company of Albert Rickett, the better. Still, everyone made bad calls from time to time. Logan knew that better than most.

'He's overreacting. He missed a few details, that was all.'

Shona nodded. 'Aye. He took it hard, though. Weirdly hard. That whole case seemed to knock him for six. Think it made a real dent in his confidence.' She looked back at him and smiled. 'Guess you'll just have to get used to seeing me at these things.'

Logan was about to bring up the wedding when he saw her eyes drift up to his crinkly bright blue plastic headgear and a smirk tugging at the corners of her mouth, and he decided that now probably wasn't the right time.

He'd ask her later. After the post-mortem, maybe.

Or he could go round tonight. They'd been dropping in on each other more frequently of late, ever since Logan had moved into his new place. It was a new-build, two-bedroom house, not far from where he'd been staying with Ben before—

'Right, I've got what I can,' Shona announced. She performed a deeply undignified backwards crouch-shuffle out of the passageway and accepted Logan's offered arm to help her back to her feet.

When she stood, she and the DCI were less than a foot apart. Although they weren't touching, Logan could *feel* her, like her body was altering the air pressure between them, pressing it more firmly against him.

He should ask her. He should just ask her to the bloody wedding. She was going to say yes. Of course, she was.

Wasn't she?

What if he was misreading the signals? What if, even after everything, she just thought of them as friends?

Jesus. He'd thought they'd just been taking things slowly, but was he wrong? Were they not 'taking things' at any speed? Were there even 'things' to be taken, at all?

He could read criminals like a book. He could spot a liar a mile off. Matters of the heart had always been more of a mystery to him, though, and right there and then, he had absolutely no idea if Shona thought of them as anything other than friends.

Still, friends could go to weddings with other friends.

Right?

But what if it made everything awkward?

It's already bloody awkward, he heard himself thinking. *You're standing staring at her in silence. Get it together, man!*

Fuck it. He wasn't twelve years old at a school disco. He was a bloody adult. A grown man. He was going to ask her, stupid shower cap or no stupid shower cap!

A voice rang out from the top of the ramp before he could open his mouth.

'You finished, then?' Palmer enquired. 'We want to get the body shifted so we can crack on.'

'Yeah, we're done,' Shona called back. And like that, the moment, and the opportunity, passed. Shona gave Logan a dunt with her shoulder, then motioned up the ramp. 'Lead the way, Detective Chief Inspector,' she instructed. 'And I might be nice to you and tell you what I found.'

Chapter 6

'Hey! Sinead! Fancy seeing you here!'

Sinead slowed momentarily on the way to her car, recognised the constable grinning at her, then picked up the pace again.

'Haha. Aye. Small world,' she said, carefully selecting a tone that made it very clear she didn't want the conversation to continue any further.

The uniformed constable didn't take the hint, however, and jogged up until he fell into step beside her. His name was Jason Hall. They'd crossed over briefly at induction and training. He'd seemed nice enough at the time, but since she'd made the move from PC to DC, he'd… well, he'd been something of an arsehole.

'Pretty crazy all this, eh?' Jason remarked.

'Aye. Pretty crazy,' Sinead agreed. In truth, it was no more crazy than usual, but anything to avoid further conversation.

'Aye. Pretty crazy,' Jason said again. 'I hear that your man's…' He drew a finger across his throat and made a sound meant to represent flesh and bone being split in two.

Sinead side-eyed him quizzically. 'What?'

'Your man. In the tunnel. The body. I hear he's been…' Jason repeated the mime. 'He's been decapitated. That right?'

'Oh. I don't really know,' Sinead said. 'I heard the same, but I don't really know any more than you do.'

Jason ejected a single mirthless 'Ha!' and stuck uncomfortably close to Sinead as she turned off the main road and into the car park. It was full of police vehicles now, and it took her a moment to identify her car in amongst them all.

'I doubt that very much,' the Uniform continued. 'You lot never tell us anything. Always keeping your wee secrets. Having

35

your little clandestine gatherings. Whispering away behind closed doors, while the rest of us are out here on the front line, cleaning up the mess.'

Sinead stopped dead. It took Jason three paces before he realised.

'What's your fucking problem?' she asked. To her annoyance, this just made his smile widen.

'Who says I've got a problem?'

'Clearly you do, Jason. Clearly, you're unhappy at the fact I've moved into the MIT,' Sinead insisted. 'It's not a slight on you. No one is saying that I'm better than you. It's not even a promotion, I'm just in a different role. We're all still on the same team, trying to do the same difficult job.'

The PC's smile remained painted across his face. That was all it was, though—a representation of a smile. An artist's impression.

'Aye, you just keep telling yourself that, Sinead. You just keep pretending you're still one of us, as we stand for hours in the pishing rain, directing traffic, while you swan around with the *big-I-ams*, kidding yourself on that your shit doesn't stink.'

Sinead crossed her arms. 'Fine. Is that how you want to play it, Jason? We can play it that way. Fuck off and man a cordon somewhere. Go and stand at a bit of tape and act like you're doing something important.'

The way his face changed made her regret the outburst almost immediately. She'd given him exactly the satisfaction he was after.

'There she is. Showing your true colours, at last!' he crowed, then his smile fell away and he closed the gap between them in two big steps. 'But don't ever talk to me like that again. Just because you're fucking your way up the ladder, don't think you're better than me. All right?'

'Everything all right here, DC Bell?'

Logan's voice came booming from halfway across the car park. Jason's body language changed in an instant, going from confrontational to subservient without actually making any discernible movements.

Sinead waited until Logan and Shona joined them before replying. 'Fine, sir. PC Hall was just leaving. Weren't you, *Const*able?' she said, putting heavy emphasis on the first syllable of that last word.

Jason smiled, and practically doffed his cap as he backed away. 'Aye. I should go stand by a cordon somewhere,' he said, his gaze lingering on Sinead as he retreated. 'Nice to catch up with you. You be sure to keep up the good work.'

He winked at her. Everything about it made Sinead's skin crawl.

'And maybe you and me can get together for a proper blether soon…'

The detectives and the pathologist stood in silence until Jason had rounded the entrance to the car park and was hiking back to his spot by the line of tape.

'Who's the arsehole?' Logan asked.

'He's just… some arsehole,' Sinead said. 'Harmless enough, I think.'

'Anything I can do?'

DC Bell shook her head. 'Nothing I can't handle, sir.'

'Aye. I quite believe that,' Logan said. He flicked his gaze across to where Jason was doing his best to look important. 'God help the bugger.'

Tyler appeared at the car park entrance, spent a moment looking for someone he recognised, then lit up with a goofy smile when Sinead gave him a wave. He broke into a happy little jog that both women found endearing, but drew a tut and a shake of the head from Logan.

'Christ, he's like bloody Lassie trotting along there.'

Sinead nudged him with an elbow. 'I think it's adorable,' she said. 'And besides, Lassie's a dog. Dogs don't trot. You're thinking of Black Beauty.'

DC Neish almost didn't slow his jog in time, and Sinead took a half-step back to avoid an embarrassing collision.

'Listen, son, if you've come to tell us that someone's down the well, we already know,' Logan remarked, which only made Tyler look confused. Even more so than usual.

'Eh, no, boss,' Tyler said. 'Just finished up the interviews with everyone in the coffee shop. Owners, tour driver, and the tour group.'

Logan's eyebrows raised, like they were impressed, even if the rest of his face wasn't. 'The whole tour group? Already? Good work.'

Tyler's smile didn't budge, but he shifted uncomfortably on the balls of his feet. 'Aye. Thanks, boss,' he said. 'I mean, there was just the three of them. But cheers.'

Logan's eyebrows fell like the strings pulling them up had been cut. 'Oh. Right. Well, what bloody kept you, in that case?'

'I'm guessing cake,' Sinead said.

'I resent that accusation, Detective Constable,' Tyler said, feigning hurt. 'You know me. I don't cake and drive, and I don't cake while on duty. That'd be highly unprofessional.'

'You've got icing on your top lip, son,' Logan pointed out.

'Shite. Still?' Tyler asked, wiping his mouth on the back of his hand, before realising he'd been tricked. His smile returned, a little less certain than before. 'Haha. I may have had one wee…' He cleared his throat. 'Wanted to check that it's OK to let the tour go.'

'If you think we've got everything we need,' Logan confirmed. 'Get contact details. If they're from elsewhere, get local details and home, too.'

Tyler replied to the instruction with a double thumbs-up. 'On it, boss,' he said, starting to back away.

'I'll come, too,' Sinead said. She shot Logan a very deliberate look. 'I'll leave you to get on, sir.'

'Eh? Oh. Aye,' Logan replied, just an *E* and a *U* away from completing the whole set. 'Right you are. There's not much more we can do here until Palmer's team is finished up, so head up the road when you're done. I'll see you both back at the station.'

The Detective Constables set off together, all springy-stepped and swinging arms.

'Oh, to be young and in love, eh?' Shona said, watching them go.

'Hm? Oh. Aye,' Logan agreed. 'Bastards.'

'Makes me sick,' Shona said. 'The wedding's soon, isn't it?'

Logan straightened, hardly believing his luck. The perfect way in had presented itself. The topic had been broached. All he had to do now was casually ask the question.

His lips remained pressed together. She looked up at him, the sunlight dappling the water behind her and casting a yellow-white aura around her head.

His stomach became a knot of densely-packed muscle that sat on his bladder like a lead weight.

Just ask. That was all he had to do.

Just ask her.

'Just under a fortnight,' he said, then his mouth welded itself shut again.

Shona blew out her cheeks. 'Wow. Not long, then. Not a lot of time to get organised. Are you all ready?'

'Um, aye. Think so.'

'Got your clothes all sorted? Because it would be short notice to get organised now,' Shona said. 'You know, if you were still waiting on your invitation, or whatever. Which you're not, obviously. But if you were, hypothetically, you'd want to know sooner rather than later, so you could get sorted. I mean, two weeks is cutting it fine, but if you only found out a week before, say, then it would be *much* harder to—'

'Would you like to come with me?' Logan asked. 'As my... accompaniment.'

Accompaniment? What the fuck had he said that for?

'Not "accompaniment". I didn't mean "accompaniment". I mean...' He took a deep breath. God, why was this so hard? 'Would you like to come with me as my date?'

Shona sagged like a balloon losing air, and Logan felt the first pangs of panic go pinging through him. But then he saw her smile, and stood bewildered as she raised her voice to a shout and wave to the retreating Detective Constables.

'Sinead!'

Over at the entrance to the car park, Sinead and Tyler both turned. Shona raised a thumb, which prompted Sinead to thrust both hands in the air, perform a brief round of applause, and then continue on her way.

'Wait. What?' Logan asked. 'What was that about?'

'Sinead told me weeks ago you were going to ask me,' Shona explained. 'She was worried you might do it the night before the wedding, and I wouldn't have enough time to buy a big hat.'

Logan snorted. 'I wouldn't have done it the night before.'

Shona regarded him impassively until he conceded with a nod that, OK, yes, he might have, before adding that he was going to have some very strong words with Miss Bell at a later date.

'So... is that a yes?' he asked, when he eventually realised she hadn't given him an answer.

'Yes,' Shona confirmed. 'I would love to attend the wedding with you. And I'm thinking sombrero. For the big hat, I mean. Or one of those Australian ones with the corks hanging off. But we can discuss that later.' She fished in her bag until she found her car keys. 'First, I have to go poke around in a dead guy's neck hole. You are, of course, more than welcome to join me.'

'You make it sound tempting, but I think I'll pass, and maybe join you later for the highlights,' Logan said.

'Well, don't say I didn't offer.'

Logan smiled, then a movement drew his eyes left, to where the sunlight danced on the water. There was something hypnotic about the way the light played across the surface. Something oddly moving. Logan wasn't a religious man, but he could imagine such sights would've inspired many a true-believer over the years.

'You heading back to the office when you're done here?' Shona asked.

'Aye. Eventually,' Logan said. He watched the rippling sunlight for a few seconds more, then sighed and turned his back on it. 'But before I do, it's high time I went and gave my regards to Ben.'

The headstone was a plain one. Nothing too grand or fancy. Expensive enough on a polis salary, mind you. It was black marble, maybe a foot and a half high, with gold lettering spelling the word 'FORDE' across the top in a simple, elegant script.

Logan had been to the grave just once since the funeral. He'd tried not to dwell too much on that. He'd given himself all the excuses of *not enough time* and *too much to do* and promised himself he'd go the next day, or the day after, or the one after that.

Days became weeks, became months. He knew he had to break the cycle before months became years. He owed his old friend that much, at least.

Because, the real reason he hadn't visited more often was nothing to do with a lack of time, and all to do with his sense of guilt.

He'd picked up the flowers almost as an afterthought on the drive back up from Loch Oich. The petrol station at Fort Augustus, to be precise. They had a surprisingly good selection of bouquets, all wrapped in plastic and sitting in buckets of water inside the door.

They'd had a two-for-one on sausage rolls, too. That had been a nice bonus, although he'd be hoovering flakes of pastry out of the Beamer for weeks.

Bending, he shoved the flowers, packaging and all, into the holder in the base of the headstone. 'There you go, you old bugger,' he said. 'Don't say I never bring you anything.'

'Are you no' supposed to take them out of the plastic first?'

Logan turned from the headstone to find Ben Forde hobbling across the grass, carefully weaving his way between the other graves, so as not to walk over anyone buried below. Realising he was standing directly over where Alice Forde herself would be resting, Logan took a judicious sideways step before Ben could give him any grief.

'Are you?' Logan asked. He looked down at the flowers. The holder wasn't a deep one, and they toppled sideways out of it before his eyes, landing on the grass with a crackling of the cellophane wrapping. 'You think she'll mind?'

Ben arrived at the graveside, kissed his fingers, then tapped the top of the headstone. 'Come on, it's Alice,' he said. 'Of course she'll bloody mind.'

Muttering, Logan picked up the flowers and set to work removing them from the plastic.

'You got daffodils,' Ben said, watching him at work.

'Aye.'

'She hated daffodils.'

Logan looked up from the tangle of tape, cellophane, and flower stems. Ben eyed him solemnly for a moment, then failed to hold back his grin.

'Just kidding. She'll love them.'

Logan resumed the unwrapping process. 'All this time off hasn't improved your sense of humour then, Benjamin.'

'No. Far from it. I've been bored out of my bloody mind,' Ben said. 'And it's only got worse since you moved out.'

Logan felt another twinge of guilt over that. It had been a mutual decision, though. They'd both agreed he needed his own place, and while Ben would never say as much, Logan knew he'd started to resent the DCI heading out to work every day, while he was stuck recuperating at home.

'You should make the most of it. I wish I had time to be bored,' Logan said. 'Body turned up this morning.'

'Homicide?'

'Headless and shoved down a hole.'

'Jammy bastard,' Ben said, positively green with envy. 'You, I mean. Not him. Or her. Is it a him?'

'Aye, it's a him. And how do you make me out as a jammy bastard?'

'Getting your teeth stuck into something like that. What I wouldn't have given for a headless corpse to pass the time these past few months,' Ben said. 'It got so bad, I even tried my hand at painting a few weeks back.'

'Landscapes?'

'By numbers. Downloaded a nice one of Elgin Cathedral off the internet,' Ben explained. 'But I didn't have half the colours, so it's mostly just brown.' He wrinkled his nose at the thought of the finished picture. 'Sort of looks like someone's made a dirty protest.'

Logan finished unwrapping the flowers and shoved them back in the holder. Both men watched as they fell out again.

'Fuck's sake,' Logan grumbled, bending to retrieve them once more.

'You need to trim the bottom of the stems off,' Ben told him. 'Did you bring scissors?'

'Of course I didn't bring scissors. Who in their right mind brings scissors to a graveyard?'

Ben produced a pair of scissors from his jacket pocket and handed them over. Logan took them without a word, and set about snipping three inches off the bottom of each stem.

He was really beginning to wish he hadn't bothered buying the things in the first place.

'Anyway, daubing the walls of Elgin Cathedral in shite was the final straw,' Ben said, getting back to the conversation. 'I'm ready to come back.'

Logan paused, mid-snip. 'You sure you're fit enough?'

'I'm fitter than I've been in ten years,' Ben said, then he saw the cynicism on Logan's face and begrudgingly amended it to five years. 'With the medication I'm on, the new diet, the exercise I've been getting, I'm fighting fit, Jack. I'm raring to go.'

Logan finished cutting the flowers. He knew better than to argue with Ben Forde when he'd set his mind to something, but it had been mid-January before he'd been released from hospital, and there had been a few scary moments before then when it had looked like his heart was ready to pack in completely.

'I mean, don't get me wrong, it would be great to have you back, but I just think maybe you should—'

'I've already spoken to Detective Superintendent Mitchell,' Ben said, rocking back on his heels. 'Technically, I start back tomorrow, but all this talk of headless fellas down holes has got me all pumped up and ready to go!'

Logan blinked. There was a snip as he cut the stem off the final flower. Ben coughed quietly.

'That sounded a wee bittie more sexual than it was meant to,' he mumbled. 'I just meant—'

'How about the two of us just agree never to speak of it again?' Logan suggested.

'Aye, that's maybe for the best,' Ben agreed.

Logan shoved the flowers in the holder for the third time. This time, to his considerable relief, they remained upright. Turning to Ben, he drew himself up to his full height.

'Right, then. Since it seems your mind's made up, are you ready to get back to work, Detective Inspector?'

Ben stood to attention and snapped off a crisp salute. 'Reporting for duty, sir,' he said, then his hand wavered and fell to his side. 'Assuming we've got time to pick up lunch on the way. I could eat a scabby horse...'

Chapter 7

Lana Lennon stood by the kettle in the staff room, waiting for it to come to the boil. The big tank thing on the wall that was supposed to give out instant hot water had been on the blink for months, and the ridiculous Highland Council procurement system meant someone had to come down from Inverness to supply and fit a new one.

The appointment had been arranged four times now, before being cancelled each time on the day. As a result, over forty members of staff now relied on one kettle at break-time. That didn't include all the teachers who'd snuck their own kettles into class.

Or, for that matter, those who'd found alternative ways of satisfying their between-class thirst. She was thinking particularly of Mr Newport from the Biology department, whose lessons were said to become increasingly incoherent as the day went on.

Lana had reached the staff room late and found the kettle empty. It was widely expected that anyone finding it empty should refill it to the top before clicking the switch, but if she had to wait for the full kettle to boil, the bell would have already rung for the next block of lessons. Better to take the dirty looks than a break-time without a brew.

She deposited a teabag in her mug, and got the English milk ready in anticipation of the kettle finally reaching the boil.

The milk was only English in that it had been marked with a sticker as being the property of the English department. Each department had its own supply, which they guarded with a level of ferocity that might someday start another world war.

Lana looked around the staff room while she waited. Most of the other teachers were sitting on the big square of sad-looking foam-cushioned chairs, cups of tea and biscuits in hand, legs crossed and eyes ablaze as they listened to the latest gossip about who'd said or done what to whom in their classes.

There was always some scandal or another going on. Such was the way when you spent your day surrounded by several hundred teenagers and the hot, heaving morass of hormones that comprised them.

Lana picked up on a couple of mildly juicy tidbits, but didn't tune into any one particular conversation. Instead, she cast her gaze from one end of the room to the other, searching for the one face she didn't find.

'Ah. Mrs Lennon. You finally made it in, then?'

Lana felt her face screwing up at the sound of Cops and Robertson's voice. The depute head's first name was Joan, but she'd been PT of Science when half the teaching staff were pupils at the school themselves, so nobody ever addressed her by it.

Likewise, she never called any of the other teachers by their first names, either, always crediting them with their full title. Rumour had it that, if the old bat ever addressed you by your first name, you were getting the boot. Lana had no idea how true that was, and she didn't ever want to end up in a position where she'd find out.

'Yes. Sorry, Mrs Robertson,' Lana said, raising her voice a touch to be heard over the sound of the kettle approaching the boil. 'I was just a few minutes late.'

'You were a few minutes after the bell, Mrs Lennon,' Copsand replied. She sounded almost helpful, like she was doing Lana a favour by clarifying the details of her tardiness. 'You were over twenty minutes late for your supposed start time. I say "supposed" because that's when you're "supposed" to turn up for duties. I thought that had been made clear?'

'It had. It has,' Lana said. She glanced around the staff room and saw half-a-dozen teachers watching the conversation from the corners of their eyes. 'Sorry. Won't happen again.'

'I trust you have a good explanation?' the depute head asked.

'Uh, yes. Had some… personal issues at home to deal with.'

Copsand's lips pursed. 'That's not an explanation, Mrs Lennon, it's an excuse.'

Lana frowned. 'What's the difference?'

This drew a long, drawn-out sigh from the depute head, like a slow puncture in a bike tyre. 'Is it any wonder English pass marks are down?' she asked, although Lana got the impression it was a rhetorical question, so she chose not to answer.

The kettle clicked off at her back. Lana mustered her best apologetic smile and reached for it. 'Sorry. Like I say, it won't happen again, Mrs Robertson.'

'Yes, well, see that it doesn't. I've already had to have words with your son about the situation at PE this morning.'

Lana looked up from where she was pouring water into her mug. 'You were taking PE? Is Fergus not in? Mr Forsyth, I mean.'

'He is not,' Copsand confirmed.

'Where is he? Is he all right?'

'I am neither his mother nor his nanny, Mrs Lennon,' Copsand replied. She gave Lana a fleeting up-and-down look, but managed to pack hours of carefully considered judgement and scorn into that brief half-second. 'Besides, I'm quite confident that you'd know more about his comings and goings than I would.'

She clicked her bony fingers and pointed to where water was now overflowing from Lana's mug.

'And clean that up,' she instructed. 'It's high time people treated this place less like a clubhouse, and more like a place of employment.'

Lana chose not to respond to that, and instead set to work mopping up the spilled water.

By the time she'd finished, Copsand had wandered off to moan at some other poor bugger, and all eyes were now on them.

Lana took the opportunity to take out her phone and opened up the most recently dialled numbers. The top entry read: Coleen (Work phone). Coleen was her sister, based just outside Liverpool.

She didn't have a work phone. She didn't currently have a job, for that matter, and it had been months since they'd so much as texted, let alone held an actual conversation.

Lana hated using her own sister as a cover story, but what choice did she have? Clyde was always so suspicious.

She tapped Coleen's name, listened to the phone ringing, then felt a little flutter of excitement at the voice of the man who answered.

The excitement curled up and died again when she heard the voicemail greeting. She hung up before getting to the part about leaving a message, then sent a text asking if everything was all right, agonised for a few seconds about whether to finish with one 'x' or two, then added both and hit send.

The bell rang just as she removed her teabag from the full-to-the-brim mug. She poured the tea down the sink, eyes fixed on her phone screen as she waited for the reply.

She was still waiting when the rest of the teachers started filing out of the staff room.

Julie, one of the other English teachers, caught her eye as she passed. 'Once more unto the breach,' she said. 'You coming? I'll walk you up?'

'Oh, uh, yes,' said Lana. She tore her eyes away from the blank screen of her phone, checked again, then returned the mobile to her bag. 'No rest for the wicked, I suppose.'

–

Sinead had already started on the Big Board when Logan threw open the doors to the Incident Room and announced that he'd picked up a stray on the way in.

The fuss was immediate, all thoughts of headless dead fellas forgotten as the younger detectives all rushed over to meet DI Forde at the door.

'All right, sir? You're looking well,' said DS Khaled, his Aberdonian accent more pronounced than usual, thanks to a five-day training course in the Granite City he'd just come back from.

'You're looking years younger, sir,' agreed Sinead, giving Ben a hug.

'She's right. You don't look a day over seventy, boss,' said Tyler, flashing a grin that earned him a roll of the eyes and a tut from the DI.

'He's still a pain in the arse, then?' Ben asked.

Logan confirmed this with a nod. 'Oh, aye. Worse than he used to be, if anything.'

'I find that very hard to believe,' Ben remarked, then he looked Tyler over and shrugged. 'No, actually I do believe it. You can tell by the look on his face.'

'Don't worry, you'll get used to ignoring him again, soon enough,' Logan said, clapping the older man on the back. 'And he's finally learned to make a good cup of tea.'

Tyler's chest puffed out a little at the compliment. 'Cheers, boss,' he said.

Logan and Ben stared back at him in silence, until the penny finally dropped.

'Oh. You want me to go make some now?'

Ben let out a low whistle, like he was genuinely impressed. 'God. He's catching on quick these days, right enough. Two sweeteners. Wee splash of milk. There's a good lad. You make yourself one, while you're at it.'

'Um… cheers. I'm all right for now, though, boss.'

Ben shrugged. 'Well, don't say I never offer,' he said. 'Now come on, chop-chop.'

Tyler replied with a grin and a raised thumb, and rushed for the door. He wasn't even halfway there when the other orders started coming through.

'Make us a coffee while you're there, will you?' Hamza asked.

'I'll have tea, if it's going,' Sinead added.

'Aye. A brew-up's in order all round, I think,' Logan agreed. 'Maybe nip across the road and get some of the good stuff. They'll probably have cakes on the go, too.'

'No cakes for me, Jack,' Ben said with a firm tone and a curt shake of the head. He lowered himself into his old chair, rocked

49

it back and forth, then looked over to where Tyler was dejectedly pulling on his jacket. 'Unless they've got a wee fruit scone, or an Empire Biscuit, in which case get me one of them. Nothing chocolatey, though. Unless it's a brownie. But otherwise, I'm fine.'

Tyler adjusted the collar of his jacket and nodded. 'Right you are, boss.'

'Unless there's something else nice that you see,' Ben added. 'If so, get me that. But don't go overboard. I'm going canny on what I eat.'

'Aye, sounds like it, right enough,' Logan remarked. 'Now, don't you go getting too comfortable, Benjamin.'

Ben looked up from his chair. He'd sunk into it like it was a favourite pair of old shoes, moulded to a perfect fit by the years and the mileage.

'No' kicking me out already, are you?' he asked.

'You'll maybe wish I was,' Logan said. 'Because you can bet your backside that Mitchell's going to want to see you before you get too settled in.'

Chapter 8

Detective Superintendent Mitchell made a very deliberate show of checking the date on her calendar when Logan led Ben into her office. Unlike her predecessor, who would've addressed the situation with a string of bellowed obscenities, Mitchell waited for Ben to take the lead.

'Aye. I thought, since I was at a loose end, and what with a new case popping up today, I might as well report in early,' he explained.

'So I see,' the DSup said, and the way she did so implied there was much more discussion to be had on the subject. Fortunately, she chose not to do it now. 'It's very good to see you, Ben. You're looking well.'

'So everyone keeps telling me. Thank you,' Ben replied. 'Just itching to get stuck in again, ma'am, if I'm honest. Been climbing the walls at home.'

'He took up painting by numbers,' Logan said.

Mitchell smiled grimly. 'I'm very sorry to hear that,' she said. 'Hopefully, we can find something for you to be getting on with.'

Logan frowned. There was something not right about that sentence. Some other meaning.

'Wait... what are you saying?' he asked. 'What do you mean we can find him something to be getting on with? There's plenty for him to be getting on with.'

Mitchell leaned back in her chair. 'In the MIT?'

'Of course! Where else would he be going?'

Ben looked from Logan to Mitchell and back again. 'Hang on, what's happening?'

'That's a high-stress position,' Mitchell said, her eyes still locked on the towering DCI. 'Stress poses a considerable risk to those with heart problems.'

'It's under control. I'm on medication for it. Loads of the stuff. If I jump up and down, I'll rattle. And I'm being very careful with my diet,' Ben said, electing not to mention the cake or cakes that may or may not be on their way over from across the road with his name on them.

Mitchell interlinked her fingers on the desk and offered up a smile that was as patronising as it was apologetic. 'I get that you've got your heart set on the MIT, Ben. I do. You've been in it in one form or another for… well, I'm sure none of us would care to count the years. So you know better than most just how relentless it can be. Demanding. I'm not sure that, given your condition—'

'He's got a heart complaint, he's no' pregnant,' said Logan, who'd heard enough. 'We've got a headless corpse in a place called the Well of the Seven Heads. If that isn't someone making a statement, then I don't know what is. We're going to need all hands on deck for this, and DI Forde is one of the longest-serving, most experienced officers on the force.'

'I'm no' sure I'd go that far,' DI Forde interjected.

'Ben, shut up,' Logan told him, glowering down at the Detective Superintendent. 'You want him sitting behind a desk, safely out of harm's way? Fine. But it'll be his desk, in my Incident Room. And if you don't like that, you'd better get someone else to deal with our headless friend, because I won't be doing it.'

Mitchell regarded him coolly for a long time, then shrugged. 'Fine.'

Logan hesitated, before replying. 'Fine? To which one?' he asked, his bluster fading. 'Him coming back to the team, or me quitting?'

'The former. Tempting as the latter is at times,' Mitchell said. 'But DI Forde runs the room. I'm not having him out gallivanting, putting himself at risk.'

'Wouldn't dream of it, ma'am,' Ben said. 'Cup of tea and a place to put my feet up'll suit me just grand. Just as long as I can be useful. Believe me, my days of chasing killers through the streets are well and truly over.'

–

Tyler was back with the teas, coffees, and a small but varied assortment of baked goods by the time Logan and Ben returned to the Incident Room.

'Now you're talking,' Ben remarked, his eyes practically bulging as he took in the range of goodies. There were no obvious scones or Empire Biscuits, which was fine. No brownies, either. Not a problem. There were plenty of other things to choose from, and despite his many obvious shortcomings, Tyler wouldn't have let him down.

'Found you this, boss,' the DC said, producing a vaguely mushroom-shaped item in a crinkly cellophane bag. Ben eyed it with suspicion, then accepted it warily, like it might explode in his hand.

He peered down his nose at it, then pulled on his reading glasses and examined it more closely.

'It's a wholemeal muffin,' Tyler explained. 'Sugar-free.'

Ben's eyes raised slowly from the item… no, not item—from the *abomination* in his hand.

'It's a what?'

'Wholemeal muffin. It's like a cake, but healthy. It's meant for diabetics, I think. That's why there's no sugar in it.'

There was silence in the Incident Room, broken only by a soft, whispered 'fuck' from Logan.

'Is this a joke, son?' Ben asked. He was holding the muffin by one corner of the plastic bag, as if he couldn't bring himself to touch the thing. 'Is this a wind-up for my first day back?' He grinned hopefully at the other detectives, but there was something a bit desperate and demented about it. 'Is that what's going on?

All having a bit of fun at my expense. Breaking me back in, sort of thing? Is that what's going on here?'

Tyler quietly dislodged something from the back of his throat. 'Eh, no, boss. I just thought... best of both worlds, innit?'

Ben held the bag aloft for all to see. 'If this is the best that *any* world has to offer, then I don't want to live in it.'

Around him, the others had all chosen their cakes, buns, and biscuits. Ben's stomach complained noisily as he watched them retreat to their desks with them.

'Anyone want to swap?' he ventured.

'You should give it a go. They're not actually that bad,' Logan said.

Ben turned in his chair. 'You swap, then.'

'Fuck off, I've got a chocolate eclair,' Logan replied, tilting the cream-filled pastry to better show it off. 'You'll have to prise this bastard from my cold, dead hands.'

'I'd swap, sir, only I've already had a bite,' Hamza said, his mouth so visibly full that the bite in question could only have taken place a fraction of a second before he started speaking.

Ben turned his gaze hopefully in Sinead's direction. 'Sorry,' she said, showing her empty hands. 'I'm off them until after the wedding. Then I'm going to eat like an absolute pig until I'm the size of a house.'

Tyler partly inhaled the frosting of his red velvet cupcake. 'Wait,' he coughed. 'What?'

'I can run over and get something else for you if you want, sir,' Sinead said.

Ben groaned. 'No. It's fine. He's right, I suppose. It's a compromise. It's like a cake, but healthy. That's good. It means I can still—' He pulled the seal of the wrapper apart and recoiled at the smell. 'Christ Almighty. That's honking. It's not meant to smell like that, is it?'

He thrust the open wrapper under Logan's nose. The DCI had a quick sniff, then nodded. 'Aye. That's about right.'

'Oh, no. No. I'm not eating that,' Ben said, folding the wrapper closed again. He leaned back, searched under his desk until he found his bin, then unceremoniously chucked the muffin into it.

That done, he picked up his briefcase, flipped open the top, and took out a pack of Tunnock's Teacakes.

The others watched as he opened the box, removed two of the teacakes, and set about demolishing the first one.

'Right, then,' he said, after washing down the first cake with a mouthful of tea. 'What have we got?'

Sinead, being the only one not currently stuffing her face, and—as luck would have it—the only one fully up to speed on all the developments in the case so far, took to the floor by the Big Board. There wasn't a lot pinned to it yet, beyond some cursory information about the body and where it was found, but a small stack of cards and paperwork sitting on the DC's desk suggested there would soon be more to come.

'OK, so the body's now up in Raigmore, but post-mortem hasn't started yet. We'll get the preliminary report on that in the next four or five hours.'

'Cause of death isn't going to come as a surprise, is it?' said Tyler.

'Why not?' asked Hamza.

Tyler rolled his eyes. 'Well, someone lopped his head off, didn't they? He's hardly going to live through that.'

Nobody replied. It was best, they'd found, to give him a moment to figure it out for himself. The weight of their expectant silence forced his brain to do a partial reboot.

'Oh. Unless he was dead before his head was cut off. Right. Aye,' Tyler said.

He shoved the rest of his cupcake in his mouth to stop himself saying anything more, then nodded for Sinead to continue.

'Scene of Crime didn't find any sign of the head, but divers are searching the loch. Nothing to indicate anyone had walked down to the shore recently, though, and I'm not sure it's possible to throw a head far enough from the monument that it would reach the water.'

'It is, if the hair's long enough,' Logan said, then he gave a shake of his head when the others all turned to look at him. 'Doesn't matter. Go on.'

Sinead appeared momentarily thrown by the comment, but then dismissed it with a half-smile and got back to her report.

'We did get a big break, though. Phone and wallet were both still on the victim. They were in his front pockets, so weren't found until he was moved. We got an ID.'

'Seriously?' said Logan. 'That's no' like us.'

'Aye, we got lucky this time, sir,' Sinead agreed.

She pinned a sheet of A4 paper slap bang in the middle of the board. A photo of a young man—presumably from a driver's licence or passport, given the dead-eyed stare and lack of smile— had been printed on the top two-thirds, with some identifying details directly below.

'Fergus Forsyth. Aged twenty-five. Home address is in Inver-garry, so not too far from where he was found,' Sinead said, clarifying the geography for Logan's benefit.

'He got a record?' Ben asked.

'Nothing's coming up, sir, no,' Sinead said. 'We're getting on to his GP for medical records so we can make sure it's him, since obviously the picture doesn't match-up with the body at the moment.'

It was only the cake that stopped Tyler suggesting that dental records might be worth checking. It was a fleeting thought that he spotted the massive flaw in just half a second later, but had his mouth not been full he'd have already voiced the suggestion by that point, and the damage would have been done.

He'd never been more grateful for anything in his life.

'What about the house? We checked that out?' Logan asked.

'No, sir. I thought it might be best if one of us does it, rather than Uniform. Council tax records and Electoral Roll show two adults living at the address, both male, but I don't know what the connection is. Might be friends. Could be partners. Could just be flatmates.'

'You fancy driving back down?' Logan asked her. 'You're good at talking to people. At times like this, I mean.'

Sinead nodded. 'No bother, sir. Be good to have someone with me, though, if I'm going in blind. Second set of eyes to watch for their reaction, sort of thing. You know, since they might be a brutal killer.'

'Say no more,' Tyler announced, swallowing the last of his cupcake. 'Happy to make myself available.'

Sinead smiled at him, not unkindly. 'I, uh, I actually thought maybe someone more senior.'

'I am more senior,' Tyler said.

'No, you're not,' Logan corrected.

'I am. I've been a DC for longer,' Tyler insisted.

'Sadly for you, it doesn't work that way,' Logan said. 'You're both the same rank, so you've both got the same level of seniority.'

'Which is none,' Ben pointed out.

Tyler looked positively outraged by this, and made a series of short, breathless noises that never quite became words.

'Anyway, I didn't mean someone more senior than me, I meant someone more senior in general,' Sinead said.

Her gaze flitted across to Hamza, much to the DS's obvious delight.

'Right. Aye. I get it. Why send a boy to do a man's job?' he asked, very much for Tyler's benefit. 'Of course I'll accompany you, DC Bell. It will be my absolute pleasure.'

Tyler held his hands up in a gesture of mock surrender. 'Right. Fine. I'll just mope around here on my own until you get back.'

'You wish,' Logan told him. 'I've got plenty for you to be getting on with.' He returned his attention to Sinead. 'You said they got his phone?'

'They did.'

'Locked?'

'Unfortunately, yes,' Sinead confirmed. 'PIN, which we don't have, or biometric security.'

Logan rubbed his hands together and fixed Tyler with a look that bordered on glee. 'Perfect. You can take it over to the mortuary, son, and get us a fingerprint to unlock it with.'

'Um, sadly not, sir,' Sinead interjected. 'It's an iPhone. Doesn't use a fingerprint scanner.'

Logan couldn't hide his disappointment. 'What? I thought you said it used biometric security?'

'It does.'

'Well, how do you unlock it, if it doesn't have a fingerprint scanner?' Logan asked, but the question descended into a low groan of realisation as it neared its conclusion.

'Aye, that's the problem, sir,' Sinead replied with an almost apologetic shrug. 'It uses facial recognition. And, well, we're currently a wee bit lacking on that front.'

Chapter 9

Fergus Forsyth's address turned out to be a small, semi-detached bungalow on a street called Garry Bank, which ran at a right angle to Garry Crescent, and which had led Hamza to remark on the lack of imagination by whoever had been on the naming committee that year.

The garden was well cared for, although given the size of it, it wouldn't have required much in the way of upkeep. Someone inside the house could practically have leaned out of the window to water the plants, but at least they'd made an effort.

There was a space between the bungalows and the start of a row of terraced two-storey houses that looked just about big enough to park a car in. It was empty at the moment, though, aside from four bins—two green, two blue— that stood facing each other across the gap, like soldiers on a battlefield.

Hamza was happy for Sinead to do the knocking and the talking, and stood a step behind her as they waited for the door to be answered. There was a bell, but it gave no indication that it was working when Sinead had pressed it, so she'd fallen back on the polis knock that she'd been cultivating since the day she'd first donned the uniform.

'No one in, do you think?' Hamza said, when the knock went unanswered.

'Not sure.' Sinead checked her watch. It was just after three. 'Could be out at work, maybe?'

She put her knuckles to use again, and this time followed up by calling out close to the door. 'Mr Lyndsay? Are you home? We'd like to talk to you.'

'He won't be in, love.'

Sinead and Hamza turned to find a woman with tightly-cropped silver hair and a haphazardly enthusiastic arrangement of makeup smiling at them from across the neighbouring fence.

'Do you know where he'll be?' Sinead asked.

The woman gave them a look over, deciding whether to share what she knew. 'Who's asking? Are you police? Has he done something?'

'Yes. I mean, no. He hasn't done anything, but we are with the police,' Sinead said.

The neighbour looked a little disappointed, like she'd been hoping for something scandalous. Her gaze returned to DS Khaled. 'Where are you from?' she asked.

Hamza blinked, taken aback by the bluntness of the question. 'Sorry?'

'I said *where are you from?*' the woman asked, slowing the question down and raising her voice, in the hope that this somehow made it clearer.

'Aberdeen,' Hamza replied.

'No, but originally, I mean. Where are you *from*? Where were you born?'

'Oh, sorry! Where was I *born*? I didn't quite understand what you were asking. Sorry. I was born in the Royal Infirmary,' Hamza said. 'In Aberdeen.'

The woman gave a tut like he was the one being difficult, but Sinead distracted her with a question before she could notch her casual racism up any further.

'Can you tell us where to find Mr Lyndsay? It's very important we speak to him. Urgently.'

'Well, I mean he'll be where he always is at this time of day, won't he?' the neighbour said in a tone that suggested Sinead was some sort of thicko for not already having figured this out for herself. 'He'll be hanging around outside the primary school, watching all the little kiddies coming out.'

Sinead and Hamza swapped looks, each as concerned as the other.

'Um,' Sinead began, already searching her pockets for her car keys. 'Where is this primary school, exactly?'

—

Sure enough, they found Ross Lyndsay standing talking to a group of primary school children, right by the school gates. He was roughly the same height as most of the Primary Sevens, and would have been difficult to spot were it not for his high-vis jacket, and the massive metal lollipop he wielded like some oversized wizard's staff.

'Well, this is a better outcome than I expected,' Sinead remarked, as they watched the children be led safely across the road. 'I thought "pervert" for sure.'

'Aye, I had "pervert" on my bingo card, too,' Hamza agreed. 'This job makes you too quick to imagine the worst, sometimes.'

They watched Mr Lyndsay laughing and high-fiving all the kids as he stopped traffic in the middle of the road.

'Might still be a pervert, of course,' Sinead said.

'Aye. Best not to rule it out.'

The lollipop man shot them a suspicious look as they watched from Sinead's car, then he returned to the school side of the road and waited for the next batch of youngsters to stop dicking around in the playground and set off for home.

'Sorry about the neighbour,' Sinead said after a while. 'I'm sure she didn't mean anything.'

'Nothing for you to apologise for,' Hamza said, staring straight ahead through the windscreen. 'And she meant plenty. You get used to it.'

They sat in silence for a while. Over by the school crossing, Ross Lyndsay dished out another batch of high-fives and sent eight more pupils on their way.

'So, I wanted to ask about the stag do,' Sinead said.

'Aha. So that's why you wanted me along, nothing to do with my experience and wisdom.'

Sinead smirked. 'It was both. Definitely the experience and wisdom, but also the stag do. I just… I was thinking. Does it *have* to be the night before the wedding? I'm just worried that something'll happen, and he'll end up in, God, I don't know… Cornwall, and won't make it back on time.'

'Why would he end up in Cornwall?' Hamza asked. His eyes widened in shock. 'Have you been reading my secret stag night schedule?'

'What? No! What?' Sinead started to babble, before Hamza laughed it off.

'I'm kidding. He won't end up in Cornwall. Or anywhere else. He'll be there on the day. I promise,' the DS assured her.

'Right. Right. Sorry. I'm just… I don't want it to go wrong on the day.'

'It won't. He'll be there,' Hamza said. He dropped his voice a decibel or two. 'No saying he'll be conscious, or have hair…'

Sinead chuckled. 'Oh, that's fine. Just as long as he's at the church on time and breathing. Anything else is a bonus.'

'Oh ho. Here we go,' Hamza said, unfastening his seatbelt.

Across the road, Ross Lyndsay had shed his jacket and sign, and was locking the door to his wooden hut.

He clocked them both getting out of the car, but tried very hard not to let on that he had, and set off quickly in the opposite direction, forcing Sinead to call out to him.

'Mr Lyndsay?'

He didn't stop. Not until she shouted a second time, this time with an air of authority that made it clear things would only escalate from here if he chose to keep ignoring her.

He waited for them to catch up, eyeing them warily as they approached.

'Yes?' he asked. 'I'm meant to be at work.'

Hamza glanced back in the direction of the school.

'My other work, I mean.' He looked from one detective to the other, then over to their parked car, trying to piece their identities together from what little evidence he had to hand. 'How can I help you?'

Hamza helped solve the mystery for the man by producing his warrant card. 'Detective Sergeant Khaled, Police Scotland Major Investigations,' he said, and the already diminutive Mr Lyndsay seemed to shrink an inch further. 'If you don't mind, we'd like to ask you a few questions.'

—

'How was your day?'

Bennet gave a shrug and watched the faces of his fellow pupils go sliding past the window as his mum pulled out of the car park and away from the school. They'd both had a free period last thing, and so had been ready to go the moment the last bell of the day had told everyone they were finally free to leave.

'That good?' Lana asked. Leaving so sharply meant they were at the head of the queue of traffic turning out onto the main road—the Blar, as it was known locally—and as there were no vehicles coming from the right, she was able to pull away quickly.

On a normal day, Bennet could detect her physically unwinding as they put distance between themselves and the school. Her breathing would change. Her posture would relax. She'd hum, or sing, or just witter any old rubbish about her day.

It would last until about Spean Bridge, then the thought of what was waiting at home would drag her mood down again, and they'd travel those final few miles to Roy Bridge in an apprehensive sort of silence.

Today, though, there was no lightening of her mood. Even the radio, which she was quick to sing along with at the end of the day, seemed to irritate her. She clicked it off with a jab, halfway through Steve Wright's *Factoids* segment, where Steve and his co-hosts gleefully spouted some poorly researched bullshit and tried to pass it off as fact.

'You all right, Mum?' Bennet forced himself to ask, despite the worry he currently had weighing heavily on himself.

'Fine,' Lana said, a little too quickly and high-pitched to be convincing. She clearly realised this herself and tried to compensate by shrugging and smiling, but this had the opposite effect to the one she'd been going for.

'Right,' Bennet said, turning back to the window. If she didn't want to tell him, that was fine. He'd asked. That was the main thing. It wasn't like he didn't have enough to worry about.

'Have you heard from Fergus?' Lana asked.

Bennet continued to look out of the side window. There wasn't much to see at the moment but trees, and poor examples at that.

'No,' he said, after a moment. 'Why do you ask?'

'Nothing,' Lana said.

'He was off today,' Bennet said, after a pause. 'We had Copsand for PE.'

'I know. I heard,' Lana said. 'He must be sick.'

Bennet nodded, and watched his reflection in the glass do the same. 'Yeah,' both versions of him said. 'Must be.'

Lana gave herself a shake, then plastered on a smile that was substantially more convincing than the previous attempt. 'I'm sure he'll be back tomorrow,' she decided. She gave the radio a prod, and music filled the car.

'Yeah,' Bennet agreed. He checked his phone screen, but found no notifications waiting. 'I'm sure he will be.'

Chapter 10

Once again, Logan was grateful to be standing down at the feet end of the gurney. Today, even more so than usual, in fact.

Shona stood at the head end—if you could call it that, given the victim's lack of one—her PP gear spattered in blood and bodily fluids, an assortment of tools neatly arranged on a trolley beside her.

When it came to the mechanics of her job—the part that involved cutting and weighing and measuring and sampling—Shona was meticulously organised. She was, without question, one of the best pathologists he'd ever worked with, and he'd been through a fair few over the years.

It was more than her organisational skills, of course. It was the way her brain worked. She could answer his questions before he'd even thought of them. She could 'see' a murder based on the injuries presented to her. On a pure logic and reasoning front, she was a better detective than he'd ever be.

Not that he'd ever tell her that, of course.

Not that he needed to.

This time though, thanks largely to the incompleteness of the victim, she was at something of a loss.

'So, you don't know?' Logan asked, his voice muffled by the protective mask he wore over his nose and mouth.

'I can make an educated guess,' Shona replied. 'But that's all it'll be at this stage. And I can tell you what *didn't* kill him, but that would be a very long list, and I'm not sure it would be very helpful.'

'Maybe give me the highlights,' Logan suggested. 'Then tell me your theory.'

'Sounds like a plan,' Shona said. 'And, as usual, a lot of this is preliminary, still waiting on results, blah, blah, you know the score. The big news, though, in case you hadn't spotted it, is that his head's missing.'

Logan pointed to the body. 'Who, this guy?'

The skin below Shona's eyes crinkled as she smiled behind her mask. 'Yes, him. It's meant to be here.' She gestured to where the neck abruptly ended in ragged flesh and gristle. 'But it isn't.'

'And that's your expert opinion, is it?'

'It is,' Shona confirmed. 'The good news for him is that it was done post-mortem. Decapitation wasn't the cause of death.'

'You sure?' Logan asked.

Shona shot him a look that said he was skating on thin ice. 'Are you casting aspersions on my judgement, Detective Chief Inspector?'

Logan held up his gloved hands. 'Sorry. Wouldn't dream of it,' he said. 'But, just out of interest, how can you tell?'

'A few reasons. Some sort of power saw was used to make the cut. Fine-toothed, probably a thin blade. It's not particularly neat, but a lot neater than it would be if he'd been alive, put it that way,' Shona said.

'Could've been unconscious.'

'That's why I said "a few reasons".'

She drew Logan's attention to the victim's back. It was flat against the slab, but there was a noticeable reddish-purple staining creeping up the side of his ribs.

'Livor Mortis,' Shona said. She didn't explain any further, and Logan got the impression he was being tested.

'Red blood cells sinking to the lowest part of the body,' he said, neatly summarising one of the many facts about human corpses he'd picked up over the years that he very much wished he hadn't. 'Takes a few hours, doesn't it?'

Shona nodded. 'Not bad. And yes, it starts about twenty minutes after death, but takes a couple of hours before it's notice-able from the outside. Based on his condition, I don't think there was much blood loss until hours after he died. Certainly not what we'd see with his throat cut, let alone his head removed.'

'Right. That makes sense,' Logan said.

'Oh, good. I'm glad you think so,' Shona teased, before turning her attention back to the body. 'There are no other obvious injuries, nothing to suggest drowning or asphyxiation. Poisoning or a drug overdose are both still on the table, but there's nothing in the initial tests, and no signs that he was a habitual drug user.'

'So, your theory is...?' Logan prompted.

'I'd put money on the head having a dirty great dent in it, when it eventually turns up,' Shona said. 'You know, if I was a betting woman.'

'You'd have to find one hell of a specialist bookie,' Logan remarked.

Shona smiled at that line, too. 'I think he was killed by a blow to the head, his body lay on its back for three or four hours, then the head was removed and he was relocated to the tunnel. That's my educated guess.'

'Aye, well, we might have to wait a while to find out if you're right,' Logan told her. 'Divers have done a sweep of the loch near where he was found. His head hasn't turned up yet. They're going to keep at it, but at this point, I'm not feeling very hopeful.'

'Well, much as I'd love to see your wee face light up if I pulled out his missing severed head now, I'm afraid I can't help you with that,' Shona said. 'I do have a couple of things that might be of interest, though.'

'Anything would be a help at this stage,' Logan told her. 'What've you got?'

She beckoned him up to the head end—or neck end, technically—and he reluctantly plodded around the table to join her. He wasn't sure if he was imagining it, but the smell of death was more pungent here, more insistent as it forced its way up his nostrils and flooded his lungs.

'What does that look like to you?' Shona asked, pointing to a purple splodge where the victim's shoulder met his neck.

'A bruise?'

'That's what I thought when I first saw it,' Shona admitted. 'But it's not. I mean, it is, but it's not.'

Logan blinked, not following. 'It is, but it's not?'

'It's a hickey,' Shona said. 'A love bite.'

Logan frowned. 'A nookie badge? Is that still a thing? People don't still do that, do they? Suck on each other's necks?' He seemed genuinely horrified by the idea, even with his face half-hidden by the mask. 'I mean, horny teenagers, maybe, but he's in his mid-twenties. You grow out of that shite by then, don't you?'

'Hey, I'm not here to judge, just to report the facts,' Shona said, skilfully avoiding the question. 'Someone gave him a love bite. Two, in fact. One on the neck, one on the inner thigh, about three inches south of his testicles.'

'Classy. He was sexually active, then,' Logan surmised.

'Either that, or he's got one hell of a slapdash hoovering technique,' Shona said. 'They're both recent, I'd say. A few days at most.'

Logan nodded. 'That's useful. Thanks. Are those the two things you said you'd found?'

'No. I counted them both as one. The other thing is *much* more interesting,' Shona said. 'Come and take a look at this.'

She led him over to a neighbouring table, where a sealed plastic tub contained something gelatinous and horrifying.

'Christ,' Logan muttered. 'Tell me that's not your lunch.'

'No. Actually, it's his. Stomach contents,' Shona told him. 'Nothing too unusual, really. He eats a lot of fibre, so he probably kept pretty regular. He'd likely have gone on to lead quite a long, healthy life, if it wasn't for the whole inconvenience of being murdered and having his head cut off.'

'Aye, that puts a cramp in your style, right enough,' Logan said. 'So, what am I looking at?'

'What I want to show you isn't actually in there anymore, I just wanted to gross you out a bit,' Shona said with a smirk. She produced a small plastic bag. Something metallic nestled down at one corner.

Logan studied the bag and its contents, the lines of his forehead furrowing into a series of parallel letter Vs. 'This was in his stomach?'

'Yep.'

Logan held her gaze for a moment, like she might be about to tell him why it had been there. But she couldn't tell him that, of course. How could she? Like him, she had absolutely no idea.

He looked over at the headless body on the table, then back to the metal item in the bag.

It was a key. A small silver key, like the sort of thing that would fit the lock of a window or a filing cabinet.

'Aye, you're right,' Logan muttered, holding the bag up to the light. 'This is *much* more interesting.'

Chapter 11

Ross Lyndsay sat at one end of an L-shaped couch, nursing the mug of tea that Sinead had made for him and staring blankly down at the patch of carpet between his feet.

'Dead?' he said, for about the fifth or sixth time now. 'Like... *dead* dead? Proper, actual *dead* dead?'

'I'm afraid so, Mr Lyndsay,' Sinead confirmed. Again.

She was sitting towards the middle of the couch, while Hamza perched at the far end, like they were scared the whole thing might tip over if they didn't evenly distribute their weight.

'Can you tell us when you last saw Fergus?' Hamza asked. It was the second time he'd asked the question. In hindsight, he probably should've waited for Ross to stop crying before he'd asked the first time.

'What? Oh. Aye. Yesterday. Morning. Before we left for school.'

'You both work at the school?' Sinead asked.

'Yes. No. He's a teacher.'

'At the local school?'

'Yes. I mean, no. At the secondary school down in Fort William. Lochaber High.'

Sinead's mouth formed a little circle of surprise at the mention of her old secondary. 'Oh. Right. What did he teach?'

'PE.'

'Was he quite new, then?' Sinead asked, having mentally run through all the PE staff who'd been teaching when she'd been there, and drawn a blank at anyone named Mr Forsyth.

Ross sniffed. His eyes were ringed with red from his initial reaction to the news, and the way his bottom lip was wobbling suggested they weren't past the crying phase yet.

'Yes. Two years. Or... I'm not sure. Longer, probably. Time goes so fast, doesn't it?'

Sinead just smiled sadly in reply to his question. 'We'll check with the school,' she said. 'So, you last saw him yesterday morning?'

A nod in response. A brief raising of the eyes to meet hers.

'How did he seem?'

'Fine. No different to usual, really.'

'Not stressed, or worried about anything?'

'Not that he let on to me, no,' Ross said. 'We just sort of passed each other by, really. Quick "hello" when he was coming out of the bathroom and I was going in, then he said he'd see me later as he was heading out the door. He leaves much earlier than me. Got further to go.'

'Aye. Quite a trek from here to LHS and back every day,' Sinead said. 'Couldn't he find somewhere closer?'

'Not when he first started. Rental market down there is in a right state,' Ross explained. 'And he landed a part-time job up here at the hotel in the evenings, so when he saw I had a room for rent, he jumped at it. Been here ever since. He has a motorbike, so he can make the trip pretty quickly.'

'What does he do at the hotel?' Hamza asked.

'Bar, mostly. Sometimes through in the kitchen with me, if we're stretched. Two or three nights a week, just. Bit of pocket money, he always said.' Ross sagged back into the couch. The cushions almost devoured his diminutive frame. 'What happened to him? Can I ask that? Are you allowed to say?'

'I'm afraid we can't say too much at this stage, Mr Lyndsay, no,' Sinead told him. 'Does he have any family you know of? Next of kin?'

Ross shook his head. 'He never mentioned anyone. No one alive, anyway. I think his parents are dead. I know his mum is.

She died shortly before he moved up. I think his dad died when he was much younger.'

'Do you have an old address for him?' Hamza asked.

Another shake of the head. 'No, I—oh. Wait. I got him to fill in an application form thing before he moved in.' He held his mug in one raised hand and used the other to shuffle himself forward until his feet reached the floor. 'You've got to keep it official, haven't you? Got to do the paperwork. Judge Rinder says that on the telly. And he's a judge, so I suppose he should know.'

Ross took a drink of his tea, then set the mug down on a coaster on the coffee table. 'Hang on, it's all in a box file in my bedroom. Won't be a minute.'

The detectives shifted their legs to let him pass, then listened to the pitter-patter of his little feet as he walked along the hall and into a room at the far end.

Hamza turned to Sinead, and she could guess what he was going to ask before he opened his mouth. 'Is he a dwarf?' the DS whispered. 'I mean, he doesn't look like a dwarf—he's in proportion, and everything—but... what height do you have to be under to be considered a dwarf?'

'I don't know. Five feet?' Sinead guessed.

There was a faint thump from along the hall. Like a cupboard door was being closed.

'Is he less than five feet?' Hamza wondered. He brought out his phone and tapped the screen. 'I'm going to Google it.'

'How will Google know how tall he is? It's clever, but I don't think it's *that* clever.'

'I'm Googling how short you need to be before you're considered... four foot ten,' he said, turning the screen to show Sinead, in case she was thinking of doubting him. 'You're a dwarf if you're under four foot ten. He's under four foot ten, isn't he?'

'I don't know,' Sinead replied. She looked out into the hallway and along the corridor.

'I bet he is. How can we measure him?' Hamza asked.

'You're a Detective Sergeant in the police,' Sinead reminded him. 'You can't go around measuring dwarfs.'

'No, but you could.'

Sinead tried to subdue a half-laugh. 'Sorry, you've got the wrong DC with you. I'm sure Tyler would be right up for it, but you're shit out of luck with me, Sarge.'

'Dammit. You're no fun,' Hamza tutted. 'And don't call me "Sarge".'

'Is that an order?' Sinead asked. She knew how much Hamza's promotion still bothered him, and how uncomfortable it made him when his higher rank was pointed out. Tyler had turned it into an art form, and the rest of the team contributed as and when they could.

'No! It's not an order, it's just—' Hamza began to protest, before he realised what was happening. 'Oh, shut up,' he muttered. 'And *that*'s a bloody order.'

Sinead smiled, then leaned over and took another look out into the hall. 'He's taking a while, isn't he?'

Hamza joined her in looking out through the open living room door. 'Aye, he is a bit.'

'You all right, Mr Lyndsay?' Sinead asked.

Silence.

Both detectives rose to their feet.

'Mr Lyndsay?' Hamza called. 'Everything OK?'

A few moments later, they discovered that Mr Lyndsay was absolutely fine. At least, they assumed so, but as the slippery little bugger was nowhere to be seen, they couldn't say for sure.

'Ah,' Sinead groaned, as a breeze blew in through the open window and billowed the curtains. 'Bollocks.'

—

Logan blew air out through his nose until there was nothing left in his lungs, took a couple of paces to get clear of his own exhalation, then breathed in again. It was his own private little custom whenever he left the mortuary. A cleansing ritual, to clear the smell of death from the pipes.

It never fully worked, of course. The smell lingered in his hair and in his clothes. It clung to his skin in microscopic beads. It would follow him home tonight, like it had followed him for the best part of twenty years.

Shona followed him into the outer area of the mortuary, where she kept the office equipment and Pot Noodles. If she deployed the same lung-cleansing exhalation technique as Logan, it was too subtle for him to pick up on. Mind you, she never seemed bothered by the sights and smells she had to deal with. He supposed you couldn't be, in her line of work. You'd certainly want a few choice words with your school careers advisor, if you were.

They removed all their PPE, deposited it in the medical waste bin, and then Logan set the two plastic bags he'd been handed down on one of the worktops. One of the bags contained the key that had been in the victim's stomach. The other held an assortment of personal effects that had been found on him. A watch. A handful of loose change. A pack of Lambert & Butler cigarettes, still sealed in its thin plastic wrapper.

'I'll finish typing up the preliminary report and email it over,' Shona told him. 'It'll be a while before we get the full spectrum of toxicology results, but whenever anything comes in I'll ping it over.'

Logan nodded, then a thought struck him. 'I forgot to ask about—'

'I'd put time of death as yesterday afternoon, or early evening,' Shona said, correctly predicting his question. 'Decapitation a few hours later.'

'Body was probably moved under the cover of darkness, then,' Logan concluded.

'Well, I doubt you'd want to go hauling it around with you in broad daylight. People tend to notice that sort of thing.'

Logan grunted. 'You'd be surprised what people fail to notice.'

Shona's eyes twinkled. 'Aye,' she said cryptically. 'Tell me about it.' She checked her watch, then gestured to the door. 'Well, much as I always enjoy the pleasure of your company, I need to get this report finished up so I can get home. I've got a date tonight.'

Logan made a sound that was like the start of several failed sentences all crashing together at once. 'A date?' he asked, once he'd untangled himself from the verbal wreckage.

'Olivia. It's a movie night.'

Logan's blood started to move through his veins again.

'Oh. Right. Christ, is that still happening?'

'Down to once every couple of weeks, but yeah,' Shona confirmed. 'She's still coming over.'

Logan bit his bottom lip. 'God. I feel partly responsible.'

'You're fully bloody responsible!' Shona reminded him. She gave a one-shouldered shrug. 'But it's fine. Don't tell anyone, but I actually kind of enjoy it. She's grown up a lot recently. She's actually becoming pretty good company. And, well, I don't think her mother has a lot of time for her. She's a pretty lonely kid.'

'You're a soft touch.'

'You're welcome to join us,' Shona said. 'We're doing an 80s movie night.' Her voice became a Schwarzenegger-esqe monotone shout. 'Do it! Come on! Kill me!'

Logan regarded her blankly.

'*Predator*,' she explained.

'Oh, right,' said Logan. 'Who's in that?'

Shona tutted. 'Arnie, obviously. *Get to the choppa!*'

'Is that who that's meant to be?' Logan asked. 'I thought it was Michael Caine.'

'No. This is Michael Caine. "Hello, my name is Michael Caine",' Shona said, in what surely qualified as the single worst impersonation of all time.

'Jesus Christ. Has he had a stroke?'

'You were only supposed to blow the bloody doors off!'

'You're all right, Michael. I've called an ambulance. Help's on the way,' Logan said, speaking slowly and calmly, as if to a pensioner who'd just taken a nasty fall.

Shona laughed, and then punched him playfully on the arm. 'So, you joining us for *Predator*?'

Logan would've loved to. Even with the offspring of a former nemesis hanging around and hoovering up all the popcorn.

Unfortunately, duty called.

'Next time, maybe,' he told her. 'Was there a *Predator 2*? I'll come for that.'

'There was, but it was shite,' Shona said.

'Maybe not, then,' Logan said. 'What about the other one? The one with the aliens? What's that called?'

'*Aliens.*'

'Is it? God, they must've been up all night coming up with that one,' Logan said. He picked up the plastic bags. 'Anyway, good luck with Olivia.'

'Good luck with the head-stealing murderer,' Shona replied.

Logan contemplated this for a moment. 'Do you know,' he said, after some thought, 'I'm not actually sure which one I'd prefer to be dealing with...'

Chapter 12

Tyler sat at his desk, scowling at the iPhone that was currently sitting on it, like he might be able to unlock it using willpower alone.

So far, this approach had not proved fruitful.

Forensics had given it a going over, but had found no prints anywhere on it. Given that people generally touched their phone screen several hundred times a day, the lack of fingerprints was a bit of a mystery.

Or, rather, the lack of fingerprints had an obvious answer, but one that didn't make a whole lot of sense. Someone had wiped the phone completely clean of prints, but then returned it to the dead man's pocket.

Why? Why not just take the phone and get rid of it somewhere? Why leave it with the body?

'How you getting on, son?' Ben asked, rolling over to the DC's desk on his chair. 'Getting anywhere?'

Tyler shook his head. 'Not yet, boss, no. I should probably turn it over to the tech bods. You've only got a certain amount of tries before it wipes all the data, or bricks the phone on you for good. Ten, I think.'

'And how many have you done?'

'Nine.'

'Fuck!' Ben ejected.

The corners of Tyler's mouth twitched upwards. 'Nah, just kidding, boss. None. Going to wait and see if Sinead and Ham get anything from the fella the victim lived with. He might know what it is. Save us trying to crack it.'

'Worth a try,' Ben conceded. 'But unless this department's luck has changed significantly in the time I've been off, I won't be holding my breath.'

Tyler agreed that this was probably wise, then both men turned as the double doors of the Incident Room were battered wide open.

At first, nobody seemed to be responsible for the doors opening. It was only when both men stood up and looked over the top of Tyler's monitor that they saw Dave Davidson rolling into the room in his wheelchair.

'All right, gents?' he said, a good fifty percent of his face taken up by a grin. 'I hear you lot are in need of my unique set of skills. By which I mean my ability to put things in bags and write on them.'

'Dave! Good to see you, son,' said Ben.

'You too, sir,' the uniformed constable replied. It was rare that he referred to a superior officer by any sort of rank or title, and those three letters of that one word spoke volumes about his respect for the Detective Inspector.

This did not, however, extend to the other detective standing beside him.

'Right then, Tyler,' Dave said, rubbing his hands together in anticipation. 'Is it my imagination, or do I hear the kettle boiling?'

–

Lana was tapping at the keyboard on her phone when Bennet appeared around the kitchen doorframe. She jumped and instinctively tucked the phone down at her side, then let out a shaky breath of relief.

'God. You gave me a fright,' she said. 'I'm just doing dinner.'

'Is it all right if Lachlan comes in?' Bennet asked. 'We'll go upstairs.'

Lana shot a glance out through the kitchen window. The two-car driveway curved around the back of the house. Currently, hers was the only car in it.

'Right, fine, but don't make too much noise. And if your father comes home and says he has to leave, he has to leave, all right? I'm not having him having a face like thunder on him all night. It's me who doesn't hear the end of it.'

'Yeah. OK,' Bennet said. It didn't seem fair, but then nothing ever did where his dad was concerned.

He gestured along the hall, and Lana heard the front door close.

'Hello, Lachlan!' she said.

A few moments later, Lachlan joined Bennet in the doorway, all sticky-up hair and braces on his teeth.

He was a couple of years older than Bennet, but they stood around the same height. Lachlan hadn't got his braces fitted until a few months after Bennet had, and was due to get them off any time now. At first glance, Bennet looked the older of the two, although their similar builds and hair colours meant there was very little in it.

They'd met at a part-time job at the same local hotel, had hit it off quickly, and had been friends now for a couple of years. Prior to that, Bennet hadn't had many friends. Not the sort that would call round to visit.

Not once they'd seen his dad in action, at least.

Perhaps it was on account of being that bit older, but Lachlan seemed more able to tolerate Clyde's outbursts. He let them wash over him. He almost seemed amused by them, sometimes, like he was watching a monkey losing the plot over something at a zoo. This only infuriated Clyde more, and Lana feared that it was only a matter of time before he banned the boy from the house altogether.

'Hiya, Mrs Lennon,' Lachlan said, giving her a little wave.

'We're heading upstairs,' Bennet said, cutting short any awkward small talk before it could start. 'Shout me when dinner's ready, will you?'

'I will do,' Lana said.

'Right, cool.' Bennet glanced at the phone in her hand. 'You texting Dad?'

'Hmm?' Lana looked at the phone and seemed surprised by it. 'Oh. No one. Just looking for a recipe,' she said. 'That's all.'

'Oh. Right. OK. Good luck with that.'

'Nice to see you, Mrs Lennon,' said Lachlan, then he was bundled off along the corridor, and they both went thumping up the stairs.

Lana waited until she'd heard the bedroom door close, and listened for the telltale bleep of the PlayStation switching on, then turned her attention back to her phone, finished typing her message, and hit send.

–

Sinead stood in the doorway of Fergus Forsyth's bedroom, listening to Hamza dishing out orders to the handful of uniformed constables who had been sent up from Fort William to help with the search for the missing Ross Lyndsay.

You could tell a lot about someone by their bedroom. That was one of the first bits of advice DI Forde had shared with her after she'd made the move out of uniform and into the ranks of the MIT.

It joined such pearls of wisdom as 'never stand when you can sit', 'there's no point rushing if you don't have to', and 'ultimately, at the end of the day, no bugger knows anything, anyway'.

She wasn't sure about the others, but the bedroom one was spot-on. Looking into someone's bedroom was a bit like peeking into their head. A messy room, for example, could speak volumes, although the type of mess was just as important as the mess itself.

Masses of nearly-empty makeup containers scattered across multiple surfaces suggested a level of insecurity. A scrupulously tidy room with a well-made bed and perfectly balanced curtains hinted at OCD levels of neatness.

Piles of clean clothes waiting to be put away might signal that someone was disorganised, or consistently pressed for time.

Piles of dirty clothes might imply a lazy bastard.

The size and placement of mirrors could say a lot about the person who slept in the room, too, just as the decor could reveal plenty about their tastes and styles. Of course, both depended on if they owned the house or rented, how long they'd been there, and a hundred other factors that made the whole thing more of an art than a science.

Fergus's room didn't make it easy to start building a picture of its former occupant, largely because there was very little noteworthy about it.

The bed was a double divan, with a plain red duvet cover and matching pillows. Someone had made the bed, although this seemed to have involved just chucking the bedclothes into roughly the right position, and then calling it a day.

Not too fussy, then, but not untidy, either.

This was a theme that continued through the rest of the room. The curtains had been opened, but they were a little off-balance. There was some clutter on the dressing table—an electric razor, some moisturiser, and hair wax—but it was all gathered together at one end, leaving most of the top clear.

Donning a pair of gloves, Sinead entered the room and started with a check of the back of the door. A dressing gown was hanging there. It was black with yellow trim, and the name 'Balboa' emblazoned across the back. She searched the pockets, but found only a slightly crusty tissue that she chose not to spend any time dwelling on.

There was a large wardrobe to the left of the door. It was tall, wide, and ancient-looking—the sort of wardrobe that made her think back to all those Narnia books she'd had read to her as a child. Unlike that one, though, someone had tried to paint this one a bright shade of red at some point. The colour hadn't stuck to the varnished wood, and less than half the paint now remained, so it looked like the wardrobe was on the mend from a nasty rash.

Opening the doors, Sinead found nothing out of the ordinary. A few shirts. A few pairs of trousers. A selection of shoes at the bottom, from polished black brogues to an assortment of well-worn trainers. Nothing unexpected.

Next, she crossed to the bed and carefully lifted the duvet cover. The sheet was smooth on one side of the bed, but well-crinkled on the other. Fergus had been sleeping alone, at least in recent days.

She checked the bedside cabinet closest to the crinkled side. Phone charger. Kindle. Nothing exciting.

The second drawer was all socks. They had been paired together, but even at first glance, Sinead could see they hadn't necessarily been matched up first. She had a quick prod around, then closed the drawer.

The rattle of something rolling around inside made her open it again. There, right down at the front, half-hidden beneath a pair of white sports socks, was a ballpoint pen.

Sinead plunged her hand all the way into the sock pile and rummaged around, like the drawer was a lucky dip. Propped up against the back wall of the drawer, she found a small spiral-bound notebook.

She had barely begun flicking through the pages when a voice spoke behind her.

'Find something interesting?'

At first, Sinead expected to find Hamza in the doorway, but recognition began to filter through as she turned to look, and by the time she saw the Uniform standing just inside the bedroom, his presence came as no real surprise.

'Jason? What are you doing?' she demanded, straightening up. 'You're not supposed to be in here.'

Constable Hall took his time looking around at the room before answering. 'Oh, and you are, I suppose?'

'Yes. I am,' Sinead said. 'Now, get out.'

'Are you going to make me?' Jason asked. The smile on his face was an invitation. A challenge. A dare. 'You're not my boss. You might tell yourself you are—that you're better—but you don't get to tell me what to do. I hate to break it to you, Sinead, but you're just a lowly constable, just like me.'

She placed the notebook on the bedside table, walked around the bed, then stood facing Jason. He was a few inches taller than her, and he had a sizeable weight advantage. He'd have the advantage in a straight fight. Luckily, they weren't in a boxing ring or on the playground.

'Fuck off, Jason,' she said. 'Stop acting like such a twat.'

'Oh, *I'm* the twat?' the constable said with a snort.

'Yes. Absolutely. No question about it,' Sinead replied, holding his gaze. 'And I think you know that. I think you know you're coming across as a sad, bitter little wanker who can't stand the thought of someone—especially not a woman—being recognised above himself.'

Jason made another snorting sound, but there were no words to accompany it this time.

'So, grow up. Stop behaving like an arsehole, and step back out of this room,' Sinead told him. 'Same rank or not, that's a fucking order.'

The constable's fixed smile had faded further and further with each word out of Sinead's mouth, until he was just standing there eyeballing her, seething with impotent rage.

'You think you're so much better than me, don't you?' he asked her.

Sinead thought this over for a moment, shrugged, then said, 'Yeah. Actually, yes. I do.'

The front door of the house opened and Hamza called out as he wiped his feet on the mat. 'You there, Sinead?'

'In here,' Sinead said, not taking her eyes off Jason.

The PC leaned in a little closer and dropped his voice so only she would hear. 'Saved again,' he muttered, then he stepped out of the room and passed Hamza with a nod as he headed along the hallway and made his way outside.

'Everything all right?' Hamza asked when he reached Fergus's bedroom. 'What was Uniform doing in here?'

'Nothing important,' Sinead said.

She glanced out of the bedroom window and watched Jason get into his car. Their eyes met for a moment, then he fired up the engine, switched on the blue lights, and pulled away.

Hamza pulled on a pair of disposable gloves that perfectly complemented Sinead's, flexed the fingers, then checked the back of the door just like the DC had done.

'Find anything interesting?' he asked.

'Actually,' Sinead said, lifting the notebook from where she'd placed it on the bedside cabinet. She opened it to reveal a list of dates and a couple of longer numbers. 'I think maybe I did.'

Chapter 13

It was getting on for six o'clock when Logan made it back to Burnett Road. To his utter dismay, he found two seedy-looking bastards in cheap suits hovering around the front door of the station. To the untrained eye, they looked like the type that might try and pressure him into buying either a set of encyclopaedias or a new belief system.

Logan knew better, though. He knew *precisely* what they were.

'No comment,' he told them as he went sweeping past. He was inside the building before they could get their questions out.

It would've been sensible to leave it there, but some deep-rooted compulsion drove him to open the door again, poke his head out, and bark, 'now fuck off' at them in the most commanding of his many authoritative tones.

He caught a couple of garbled queries about dead bodies and missing heads, but his brief outburst had been cathartic enough that he could comfortably walk away without feeling the need to engage any further.

By the time he'd plodded up the stairs and along the corridor to the Incident Room, though, his mood had shifted once again.

'Bastards,' he announced, as he shoved open the doors.

Ben, Tyler, and Dave Davidson briefly exchanged glances, all wondering which of them was in line for the high jump.

'Well, it can't be me,' Ben said. 'I'm not technically even back yet.'

Logan crossed to the window, brought his head close to the glass, and checked if he could see the men down at the front door. Fortunately for them, he couldn't, otherwise he might have been tempted to drop something heavy on them, like a chair, or a monitor, or DC Neish.

'Not the press?' Ben guessed, recognising the way Logan's nostrils flared and his fists clenched.

'Aye. Two of them so far, but that'll only grow,' Logan sighed, turning away from the window.

'Headless body found in a place called the Well of the Seven Heads, boss,' Tyler said. 'It was bound to get a sniff from the tabloids.'

'Aye. Aye, I suppose,' Logan conceded. 'I was just hoping... we did well keeping the Iceman stuff quiet until it was mostly all over. I just hoped we'd make a bit of headway on this one before they got wind of it.'

'We have a bit,' Ben said. 'Hamza phoned in some info he and Sinead got from the victim's flatmate. Fergus Forsyth was a PE teacher at Lochaber High School. Also worked part-time at the hotel in Invergarry. Front of house.'

Logan slumped into his chair. 'Right. What else?'

'Nothing.'

Logan rubbed his temples with the thumb and middle finger of one hand, then ran his hand down his face before responding. 'Nothing? That's all we've got?'

'The flatmate ran off before they could get anything else out of him,' the DI explained.

Logan frowned. 'Ran off? What do you mean?'

'I mean, he told them he was going to get them the paperwork Fergus had signed when he first moved in, then he climbed out the window and did a runner.'

'Uniform's searching for him now, boss,' Tyler added. 'Doesn't have a car, so they don't think he'll have made it very far. Ham's pretty confident they'll get hold of him in the next couple of hours. They're going through the house in the meantime to see what they can find.'

'And who is he? The flatmate, I mean. What do we know about him?'

Tyler consulted the notepad on his desk. 'Ross Lyndsay. Mild-mannered school lollipop man by day, kitchen porter by night.'

'And he owns the house?'

'Yeah, boss. Dave poked around in the Land Registry stuff. Looks like he used to live there with his mum until she died, then he inherited the place.'

'Has he got a record?' Logan asked.

'Nothing showing up, boss, no. Squeaky clean, by the looks of things.'

'Clearly got something to hide, though,' Logan remarked. 'You don't tend to leg it through a window for no good reason.'

'Aye, well, we should have him soon enough,' Ben said. 'We can haul him in for questioning and see what he has to say for himself.'

Logan nodded slowly, then looked over to where the DI sat behind his desk. It was probably the DCI's imagination, but Ben seemed a little smaller in his chair now. A little more shrunken. Age had been creeping up on him for a while, but it had picked up its pace in recent months.

'You up for sitting in on the interview?' Logan asked.

'Try and bloody stop me!'

'Heart's not going to explode out of your chest?'

Ben shook his head. 'I've got my tight vest on. I'll be fine.'

After her speech earlier, Logan didn't think that Detective Superintendent Mitchell would approve of Ben being involved in the interview of a potential murder suspect, but there was a very elegant solution to that.

They wouldn't tell her.

'Anything interesting turn up in the post-mortem?' Ben asked.

'Bits and bobs,' Logan replied. 'Nothing definitive. You'll be sorry to hear, though, Tyler, that decapitation wasn't the cause of death. Killed first, beheaded a few hours later.'

'Probably best, all-round,' Tyler remarked.

'Aye. Certainly from his perspective, I'd have thought. He had a couple of love bites on him.'

'Love bites? Do people still do that?' asked Ben.

'That's what I wondered. I didn't think it was still a thing,' Logan said. He and Ben both turned to Tyler.

'What?' the DC asked, when the weight of their eyes on him became too much.

'Do young folk still give each other nookie badges?' Logan asked.

'I mean… I don't know. Maybe,' Tyler said. 'I think I had one once when I was, like, fifteen.'

'Fifteen?' Ben exclaimed. 'What the hell were you doing getting nookie badges when you were fifteen? At fifteen, I was still playing with toy cars.'

Logan shot the DI a sideways look. 'I think that says more about you than it does him, Benjamin.'

'It still goes on,' Dave chipped in from the sidelines. 'There's a lassie I know who's right into giving them. Like, obsessed.' He tried to pull down the collar of his shirt to show his neck, but couldn't quite manage the big reveal. 'There's one there, anyway. Big bastard of a thing.'

Logan stared at him for several seconds, unblinking. 'I see,' he eventually said. 'And how old is she?'

Dave puffed out his cheeks and raised his eyes to the ceiling, possibly doing some sort of mental calculation. 'I don't know. Like… sixty?'

'Right,' Logan said. He scrabbled around for more to say, but came back empty-handed.

Tyler, unfortunately, had no such problem.

'Sixty? Fucking hell. You're only, what, mid-thirties?'

'What can I say? I enjoy the company of an older woman.'

'Aye, but…' They all watched Tyler tapping the tip of his thumb against his fingers as he silently did the maths. 'She could be your granny!'

'I bloody hope not,' Dave said. 'The things that woman's had me do.' His face took on a wistful look for a few moments, then he dismissed the thoughts with a shake of his head. 'Anyway, like I say, she's right into giving love bites.'

'Interesting. Thanks,' said Logan.

'Having no teeth helps a lot,' Dave added, turning back to his desk. 'A *lot*.'

The others all tried very hard to keep that image out of their head, with only moderate success. Logan and Ben managed to shrug off the effects quite quickly, but Tyler spent the next fifteen seconds staring into the middle distance, like a veteran who had seen one too many of the horrors of war.

'There was something else unusual at the PM,' Logan said.

'Oh, Jesus, what now?' Tyler muttered.

'Nothing that'll haunt you like that last conversation, don't worry,' Logan assured him. He set the plastic-bagged key down on his desk with a click that rang out in the momentary silence. 'This was in his stomach.'

Ben and Tyler both rose from their seats so they could look more closely at the evidence Logan had presented.

'How? Stabbed in, or swallowed?' Ben asked.

'Swallowed.'

'What does it open?' Tyler asked.

'That's the big question. Or one of them,' Logan said. He leaned forward and slid the key closer to Tyler. 'I want you and Dave working on it. Find out what it's for. If we can figure that out, it might tell us why he felt compelled to eat the bloody thing.'

'He must've been hiding something,' Ben commented.

'Aye. Can only assume so,' Logan agreed. 'If we find out what and why, I've a feeling we'll know who our killer is.'

Tyler picked up the bag and turned the key over. In an ideal world, it would've had something etched onto it. A serial number, maybe. Or, if the universe was feeling particularly generous, a manufacturer's name and a small but intricate diagram of what the key unlocked.

As the world kept reminding him, though, it was far from an ideal place.

'It's blank,' Tyler groaned, studying both perfectly smooth sides of the metal. 'It's completely blank.'

'Aye,' said Logan. 'I never said it was going to be easy.'

–

Clyde Lennon was in a foul mood when he returned home. Lana could tell from the way his van pulled into the driveway a little too quickly and braked a little too hard, that her husband's form would not be good.

The way he jumped out of the van, shot daggers at the kitchen window, then slammed the door behind him, let her know that she should probably brace herself.

God. What had set him off now?

She clicked the kettle on and took a can of lager from the fridge, and was ready to present him with both options just as he came thundering through the front door.

She heard him hang up his jacket with exaggerated force, listened to him muttering as he thumped his way along the hall, then plastered on a smile as he arrived in the kitchen.

'Hi,' she chirped, presenting the chilled lager as a pre-emptive peace offering. 'How was your—'

'The fuck's this order from *Very* on the bank account?' he demanded, snatching the can from her hand.

Lana came very close to laughing with relief.

'Oh. That. Well, we needed that new coffee table we've been talking about, and—'

'I told you, I'll make the fucking coffee table,' Clyde snapped, cutting her off again. He cracked open the ring-pull of his can with a sudden violent jerk. 'Didn't I tell you that? We don't need to buy one, I'll make one. Didn't I say that to you a dozen bloody times already?'

Part of Lana wanted to point out that the fact he'd said it a dozen times already, but had not actually done it yet, was the reason she'd had to order one.

Another more sensible part of her knew better, though.

'You've got so much on, I didn't want to keep bothering you,' she said. 'And it's the catalogue, so we can pay it in instalments.'

Clyde almost choked on his Tennent's. 'What? That's just an instalment? Fucking hell, Lana. Do you think we're made of money? How much is it?'

Lana tried to laugh the question off.

Big mistake.

'Don't fucking roll your eyes at me,' he warned, stepping in closer so the musky scent of sweat and sawdust filled the air around her. 'How much of our money did you piss away on a stupid bloody coffee table that we don't even need, Lana?'

She didn't want to tell him. Didn't want to say. Even if she downplayed it—halved it—he'd be fuming.

But she'd been waiting over a year now. In a moment of reckless abandon, she'd had enough.

'Three-hundred,' she said.

She felt the sting of the slap out of nowhere. It made the whole world flash white for one brief, blinding moment, then the stinging heat began to bite, burning quickly across her cheek and down her jaw.

'Three-hundred quid? For a cheap shite catalogue coffee table?' Clyde spat. 'No fucking way. No fucking way! Get on the phone and cancel it.'

'It'll come out of my money,' Lana promised, a hand laid gingerly across the side of her face where he'd hit her. 'I've been putting money aside for it.'

His movement was sudden. Erratic. Violent. He thrust a hand into the pocket of her jeans, pulled out her phone, then practically punched her in the chest with it.

'I told you to fucking cancel it. Now!'

She took the phone right away. She couldn't risk him looking at the screen, just in case there were any messages there. He was this furious over a coffee table.

She didn't want to think about how he'd react to her affair.

'Right. OK, Clyde. I'll cancel it. You're right,' she said.

'Aye. Hindsight's a wonderful fucking thing, eh?' he seethed. 'Three-hundred quid for a coffee table. I said I'd make one, didn't I?'

'When?'

The question came from the kitchen door. Lana gave a frantic shake of her head, warning Bennet not to do this. Pleading with him.

Clyde turned slowly. Deliberately. Gave his son time to dwell on what may or may not be about to happen. A classic bully's tactic.

'What was that?'

Bennet stood framed in the doorway. The empty space around him made him look smaller than he actually was.

'Go to your room, Bennet,' Lana began, but Clyde silenced her with a look.

'The boy said something. I want to know what it was.'

Bennet swallowed. There was a shake to his voice when he spoke. 'I asked when you were going to do it. Build the table, I mean. Mum's been asking for ages.'

'Oh, has she? Been asking for ages, has she?' Clyde mimicked. He took a swig of his lager, set the half-empty can on the table, then swaggered closer to where his son was trying hard to stand his ground. 'Well, maybe if I didn't have to work morning, noon, and night to take care of an ungrateful wee bastard like you, I'd have more time to do everything that's asked of me.'

'You were out at the pub all last night,' Bennet said, the words slipping out before he could stop them.

Clyde took two big steps, his hand already drawing back.

'Evening, Mr Lennon.'

Clyde quickly aborted the attack when Lachlan appeared out of nowhere and stood shoulder-to-shoulder with Bennet in the hall. He was the only person in the house who was currently smiling—a big, friendly grin that didn't fit with the atmosphere in the kitchen at all.

The sight of the young man threw Clyde off his stride. There were things he could say to Lana and Bennet—things he could do—that he knew they'd never speak about to anyone else. They were too scared, too ashamed, too worn down by their own inaction to speak up outside.

But Lachlan was an unknown quantity. A fox in the henhouse. It was a small village, and if he started blabbing his mouth, it could complicate matters.

'How was work today?' Lachlan asked, still all smiles. 'Must be hard, running your own business. Bennet was telling me all about what you do. Everything.'

Clyde's eyes narrowed, trying to work out the meaning behind the words. 'Aye,' he said with a grunt, then he turned to his wife, told her they'd continue the conversation later, and announced that he was going for a drive.

Bennet and Lachlan both shuffled aside as he came storming past. They joined Lana in the kitchen, and then all flinched at the force with which the front door was slammed.

'Right, then,' Lana chirped, in the uncomfortable silence that followed. 'Who's on for pizza and chips?'

Chapter 14

Tyler jammed the heels of his hands into his eye sockets, rubbed vigorously, then let out his frustration as a long, protracted sigh.

'How long is that we've been looking at pictures of keys now?' he asked.

At the desk beside him, Constable Dave Davidson checked his watch. 'Eleven minutes.'

'Fuck! Seriously? It can't be!' Tyler groaned and gestured to the page of pictures on his screen. 'There must be a better way to do this than just typing "key" into Google Images.'

Dave clicked his tongue against the roof of his mouth, then shrugged. 'We could try "small key", maybe?'

Tyler sat up a little straighter, nodded, then typed 'small key' into the search box, and clicked the button to go.

They waited for the pictures to load. Thirty or more of them popped up after just a moment or two. Judging by the scroll bar at the side of the page, there were an infinite number of results lurking below those already visible.

Tyler glanced down at the key in the plastic bag, then checked it against each of the images on-screen in turn.

'No, no, no, no. No, no, nope, no, that one's not even a key, no, no, no...'

He rolled the mouse wheel, scrolling down the page. There were more keys—so very many keys—but none of them matched the one that had been in Fergus Forsyth's stomach.

None of the first couple of hundred, at least. That left only *infinity small keys* left to check.

'There's got to be a better way,' he said again. 'I mean, seriously, I could probably just go around the world checking every lock, and I'd find it quicker than searching like this.'

Dave picked up the bag, turned it over a few times, then set it back down again. 'What if we try "very small key"?' he suggested. 'Because I'd say that's very small. Wouldn't you?'

'I'm not sure I'd say it's very small,' Tyler argued. 'I'd say very small was like a suitcase padlock size. You know, them cheap ones you get? This is bigger than one of those.'

'Aye, but those would be tiny keys,' Dave countered. 'This one's bigger than that, but it's still smaller than a small key, I reckon.'

Tyler didn't see any real point in debating the semantics of it, and typed 'very small key' into the search box.

More keys came up. Many of them the same ones he'd just looked at.

None of them matched.

'Bollocks,' he ejected. Leaning back, he interlaced his fingers, placed them behind his head, and glowered at the screen.

His detective instincts told him that there had to be a better way of approaching the problem than this. There *had* to be.

Unfortunately, that was as far as his instincts currently went. The finer details of that 'better way' remained a mystery to him.

'You know what I think the problem is?' said Dave.

Tyler shifted his gaze to the man in the wheelchair. 'What?'

'We don't have a fucking clue what we're doing.'

Tyler half-smiled. 'Aye. That could be a contributing factor, right enough.'

They both stared at the screen for a while, then Tyler unhooked his fingers from behind his head, changed the 'small' to 'little' and the 'very' to 'quite', and prepared for another long list of disappointments.

Over near the centre of the Incident Room, Logan sat across the desk from Ben, both men nursing the final dying dregs of what had been two very good cups of tea, if Logan said so himself. Ben had attempted to further enhance their enjoyment by producing a pack of biscuits from the bottom drawer of his desk, only to find that some bugger had discovered them weeks ago, and they'd long-since been devoured.

They'd been Tunnock's Caramel Logs, too. Was nothing sacred?

'It's a message, isn't it? Got to be,' Ben said, after a sip of tepid tea that was so microscopic it barely so much as wet his lips. 'Someone's making a point.'

'By lopping the fella's head off?'

'Not even so much that,' Ben replied. 'I meant by leaving him there. At the well.'

Logan gave a nod, but it was an unconvincing thing. He hadn't yet had a chance to jump on Wikipedia and read up.

'Don't tell me you don't know the history. The Keppoch Murders?' Ben tutted. 'Call yourself a Scotsman?'

Logan frowned. 'Keppoch Murders? Case doesn't ring a bell.'

Ben snorted. 'No bloody wonder. It's from the seventeenth century. I don't think even cold cases stretch back that far.'

Logan resisted the temptation to make a joke about Ben being the SIO on the case. He'd always been quick to tease the DI about his age, but it seemed less funny now that he was looking older than he'd ever looked. There was no need to kick a man when he was down, after all.

It was more than that, though. Joking about Ben's advancing years forced Logan to face the fact that, while he might be back on the job now, he wasn't going to be around forever.

None of them were.

His mind wandered to his daughter, and then to her number in his phone, but Ben was blethering again, and he forced himself to pay attention.

'Alexander MacDonald. Chieftain of the Keppoch MacDonalds. Him and his brother—I forget his name—were murdered back in sixteen-something or other by a bunch of fellas. Some argy-bargy about who should be chief, or something along those lines.'

'God, this is just like a documentary on the History Channel,' Logan remarked. 'The level of historical detail is astonishing.'

'Aye, aye. Funny bastard. At least I'd heard of it,' Ben countered. 'So, anyway, these fellas murdered them both. No one knew who'd done it. Didn't have Forensics or CCTV, or what have you, to go on in them days. But, after a couple of years, some other fella—aye, a friend of the two dead boys—he tracks them down, doesn't he?'

'Tracks who down? The dead boys?'

'The murderers! Why would he be tracking down the…? They know where the dead boys are. They're dead. They're not going anywhere,' Ben said. 'He tracks down the killers. Seven of them, there were. So, they round them up, then this other fella—Iain Lom, who was a poet—cuts off their heads, using the very murder weapon used to kill Alexander and his brother.'

Logan frowned and opened his mouth to speak. Ben acted quickly to shut him up.

'I don't know why they got a poet to do it,' he said. 'I'm sure they had their reasons. Maybe he was going to write a funny limerick about it, afterwards. I don't know.'

'This is all fascinating stuff, Benjamin. But, what's the well got to do with it?' Logan asked, rapidly losing interest.

'That's where he washed the heads before presenting them to Lord Something or Other in Glengarry.'

'Who, the poet?'

'Aye.'

'What's he washing them for?' Logan asked.

'Well, I don't know, do I? To make them look nice.'

'It's seven recently decapitated human heads. I don't think running them under a bloody tap is going to improve the look of them,' Logan argued. 'And what's he doing presenting them to anyone? What sort of present's that?'

Having exhausted his limited knowledge of the subject now, DI Forde's only reply was a shrug.

Logan screwed his face up in revulsion and mimed accepting the grisly offering. 'Oh, cheers. You really shouldn't have. A card would've been fine,' he said, then he arched his eyebrows as another thought hit him. 'And there's a big river right next to it. Why's he washing them in a well in the first place? Is that no' where people get their drinking water from? Some poor bugger would've been making the tea that morning and going, "here, does that taste funny to you?"'

'Aye, it's a clarty bastard move, right enough. No denying that,' Ben agreed. 'But my point is, there might be something in the history that helps with our case.'

'You think we're looking for a manky poet?' Logan asked.

Ben tutted. 'I mean, those seven fellas were killed and beheaded as an act of vengeance. That's well known. By most people, anyway, present company no' included. The fact that our victim met the same fate, and was left in that spot for someone to find, could mean that the motive's the same.'

Logan drained the last of his tea, then glanced forlornly into the empty cup. 'You think someone was taking revenge for something? Or... shite. You don't think we might be dealing with another vigilante, do you?'

'It's a possibility,' Ben said.

It was definitely a possibility, Logan thought. Unfortunately, they had a near-limitless number of possibilities at the moment, and currently no way of excluding any.

'Aye. Well, we'll see,' he said, not committing to anything yet. 'The flatmate might be able to point us in the right direction.'

Ben nodded and looked out of the window. The days were stretching, and there was still plenty of light left. The sun was on a definite downwards dip towards the horizon, though, and darkness was already creeping up from the opposite horizon.

'The question is, will we be able to find him?'

—

What in the name of all that was good and holy was he thinking? Where was he going? Why had he run? How was this possibly going to end well for him?

He'd panicked, that was all. He'd never been good with authority figures. And he was still reeling from what had happened. Yes. That was it. He was still upset. He didn't like drama. Couldn't deal with confrontation.

It was a stress reaction. An anxiety response. That was all there was to it.

That was why he'd legged it. That was why he'd climbed out of the window and run as fast as his legs would carry him away from his house, and from the two police officers sitting in his living room.

That, and the fact that they might discover the truth.

He walked quickly, head down, along the back road that ran mostly parallel with the River Garry, on the opposite side to the A87. It was a route he had wandered along on many an afternoon walk, traipsing three or four miles along the single-file, woodland-lined road before turning back when it became a maze of narrow tracks he was worried he might get lost in.

The route was mostly private, aside from a hostel and a scattering of houses dotted along it at irregular intervals. It was rare he'd meet anyone along the way, and as he walked he prayed that today would not turn out to be one of those exceptional occurrences.

The back road was the first place he'd headed to when he'd left the house. Ultimately, though, he had no idea where he was going, only where he didn't want to be. There had been no plan in his head when he'd made his break for freedom. He hadn't thought to grab anything before his great escape. No jacket. No keys. Not even his wallet.

He could still pay for things with his phone, thankfully. He'd need that, if he was to survive out here for... well, forever, if it came to it. He was already starving, and he'd only been on the run for twenty minutes.

Wait. His phone! They could track phones, couldn't they? He'd seen them do it on *CSI*. Oh, God. Oh Jesus! Oh no! They were probably running a trace on him even now. There'd be a helicopter swooping overhead any minute!

Whipping the phone out of his pocket, he tossed it from hand to hand, like it was a hot coal.

He had to get rid of it. But how?

He tried snapping it in half like they did on the telly. The problem was, those phones were generally the kind that flipped open in the middle. His was a solid slab of metal and glass that would give Hercules himself a hernia, and no amount of force was putting so much as a bend in it.

In a panic, he tried biting it.

No, that wasn't going to work, either.

Turning on the spot, he chucked the mobile into the woods on his right, putting as much strength into the throw as he could. Then he watched in dismay as it bounced off a tree and landed on the ground at his feet.

'Fuck off!' he told it, like it was some unwanted dog that insisted on following him home. He stamped on it. Once. Twice. Nothing happened. *Jesus, what was the fucking thing made of?* 'Just piss off, will you?!'

There was a stone around the size of a bowling ball by the side of the track, a little way further along. It was heavy for a little fella, but he managed to get it off the ground and then started the long waddle back to where the phone lay.

It was only when he had struggled all the way back with the boulder that it occurred to him he could've moved the phone closer. This prompted a short outburst of swearing, and his anger granted him the strength he needed to hoist the stone aloft and drop it onto the mobile.

Clunk.

Missed.

'Fuck!'

He tried again, but didn't raise the rock too high this time. He let it fall from a couple of feet up, and heard the satisfying crunch of components breaking.

'Yes!' he cheered. 'Take that, you bastard!'

There was a brief moment of elation, before it occurred to him that he'd just smashed a device worth several hundred pounds that was his only means of paying for anything.

He heaved the rock off the ground, half-hoping that he'd find the phone still in one—

Nope. Totally fucking destroyed.

He swept the debris of it into the grass beside the track and tried to console himself with the fact that he'd done the right thing. It was a bold choice, but the correct one. He may have lost his phone, but he'd gained a greater chance at freedom. He was a survivalist now. Difficult decisions had to be made. It was him against the wilderness. His past life and all its trappings were gone. He was a lone wolf now. A mystery man of the mountains.

That said, he wished it had occurred to him to go to the toilet before fleeing his house. He didn't mind doing number ones out in the open, but number twos? Outside? Without access to running water or toilet paper?

The very thought of it made his stomach churn. Which, ironically, only increased the likelihood of it happening.

Oh, God. What if he had to poo in a bush? And what if something crawled up there while he was doing it? A worm. Or a spider. Or a mouse.

A *squirrel*? Would a squirrel fit up his arse?

Maybe. If it was determined enough.

How would he stop it? And, if he couldn't, how would he get it back out?

Coax it with biscuits? Possible, aside from the fact that he didn't have any. He daren't go back to the shop, either, even if he'd had a means of buying anything. They would be looking for him. Searching. Hunting him down. Probably with big, angry dogs.

The dogs would get the squirrel out, he imagined, but he very much doubted their method would involve the use of biscuits.

Ross felt the familiar panicky prickling start on his chest and spread like a rash to encase his whole torso, squeezing his chest and compressing his lungs until his breathing became short, and his air supply thin.

Pinpricks of starlight sparkled at the edges of his vision as his head filled with some lighter than air gas that threatened to float it right off his shoulders.

He had a dozen techniques ready for just this sort of attack. Nine of them didn't work. He went straight to the tenth, and began quietly reciting the names of the children he'd escorted across the road on the way to and from school, putting emphasis on the names of those who had high-fived him.

'Charlotte. Aubrey. *Rowan. Jake,*' he whispered, the names falling into a sort of rhythm that played like music through his head. 'Yoka, *Thomas*, Elsie, *Paul.*'

It was working. He could feel it. His breathing was coming more easily, and he no longer felt like he was at risk of fainting.

He was about to start on the next batch of names when he heard the sound of a car engine approaching from behind. It was a good way off, hidden by the series of twists and bends in the track, but it was quickly getting closer.

His anxiety rallied, panic attacking him once again. Rather than hyperventilate himself into unconsciousness, though, he scrambled up the slope on his right, grabbed a low-hanging branch, and dragged himself into the trees that stood between the river and the road.

Ross dropped into the scrub, burying himself in bracken and jaggy bushes. He watched through the foliage, breath held, as a police car went trundling west along the track, a single uniformed officer squinting out from behind the wheel.

He saw the policeman's head start to turn towards him, and pressed his face down into the dirt. He didn't hold his breath. He didn't need to. It was refusing to come, anyway, even if he'd wanted it to.

How long did he lie there? One minute? Five? Time lost all meaning. His head held no thought but the worry of whether the policeman had seen him, and the fear that he might feel a hand on his back at any moment, hauling him to his feet.

At one point, as he lay there face down in the bracken, he grew concerned that a squirrel or similar like-minded creature might seize the opportunity to violate his most private of orifices, but the fear of being dragged off to jail soon superseded it again.

Eventually, when no feet came trudging through the undergrowth, and no hands hauled him upright by the scruff of the neck, Ross risked raising his head.

The road beyond the tree line was clear. The police car had moved on.

He bounced to his feet, danced on the spot as he brushed away the twigs, dirt, and bugs that clung to the front of his sweatshirt, and then clambered unsteadily down out of the woods and onto the road, his chest swelling with pride that he had successfully evaded capture.

The police car hit him coming the other way. Ross felt the impact, then a fleetingly enjoyable sense of weightlessness, then the pain as the back of his head hit the pockmarked tarmac track, and his leg made a sound like an axe splitting wood.

'Jesus Christ, where did you come from?' yelped the policeman, jumping out of his car. He stopped almost immediately, his hand going to his mouth, his gaze going to a spot just below Ross's right knee. 'Oh. Fuck.'

Ross didn't like the sound of that. He sat up. For the first time in as long as he could remember, he saw the sole of his foot.

He lay down again.

He rubbed his head.

And then he screamed.

Chapter 15

DI Forde hung up the phone, pumped a fist in the air, and let out a triumphant, 'Yes!'

Across the room, Tyler's head snapped up from his computer, his eyes ringed with red and his hair uncharacteristically dishevelled. 'Did you find a match for the key?' he practically sobbed.

'What? No. But we got Ross Lyndsay. Fergus Forsyth's flat-mate!'

Logan spun in his chair. 'Seriously? Where? When? Are they bringing him in?'

Ben shook his head. 'Not yet. A constable hit him with his car on the back road just outside Invergarry. His leg's badly broken, and he's taken a bit of a dunt to the head. Ambulance has taken him to the Belford in Fort William. They're keeping him in tonight, at least, but probably for a few days. The leg's in a bad way, by the sounds of things.'

Logan jumped to his feet and grabbed for the coat that was draped across the back of his chair. 'Right, then I guess I'm heading down the road for a chat with Mr Lyndsay.'

'They're not letting us talk to him tonight. Doctor's orders,' Ben said. 'Uniform's standing guard, but there's very little danger of the bugger making another run for it with his foot pointing the wrong way.'

'I'm sure I can persuade them to let me in to ask a few questions,' Logan reasoned.

'I'm sure you could, but do you no' think their jobs are hard enough without a big-mouthed surly bastard like you coming in and shouting the odds?' Ben countered.

It was the sort of sentence that only Ben Forde would dare say to him, because only Ben Forde had earned the right to.

'My advice?' the DI continued. 'We get organised here, get on the road sharp in the morning, and set up in the station down in the Fort.'

'Mitchell doesn't want you gallivanting around,' Logan reminded him.

'I won't be gallivanting anywhere. I can sit on my backside behind a desk just as easily down there as I can up here. Invergarry's closer to the Fort than it is to here, and one of the few things Sinead and Hamza got from the flatmate before he made a run for it was that the victim was a teacher at Lochaber High School. That's three hundred yards from the polis station.'

Logan held up his hands. 'Fine. Right, aye, you've convinced me. We'll relocate,' he said. 'Get on the phone to Sinead and Hamza. Tell them it's their call if they stop down there for the night, or come back up then travel down again tomorrow.'

'Sinead's not going to like being down there, boss,' Tyler warned.

'Why not?' Logan asked. Sinead had grown-up in Fort William and generally seemed pleased when they returned to her old stomping grounds.

'We've still got stuff to sort out for the wedding. She's stressing out about it. You wouldn't know it in here, but at home, she's a nightmare,' Tyler said. His eyes darted to the other men in the room. 'Please don't tell her I said that.'

'Your secret's safe with us, son,' Logan said. 'Shite. Aye. I hadn't thought of that. We'll make allowances. Try to get you both back up here as soon as possible. You've got Harris to think about, too, of course.'

'Yeah. He's generally happy at their auntie's, but it's not ideal,' Tyler said. 'But, eh, speaking of the wedding, boss, how's your speech coming along?'

Logan tapped the side of his head. 'All percolating away. Brewing up nicely,' he said, hiding the fact that he'd barely given it any thought whatsoever. 'Yours?'

Tyler crinkled his nose. 'Done a few drafts now. All shite, though.'

'Most wedding speeches are, to be fair,' DI Forde pointed out. 'Always the low point of an otherwise nice day out for me. Either they do them before dinner, so you're left sitting there starving, listening to some bugger droning on and on, or they do them after dinner, so you struggle to stay awake. Waste of bloody time, in my opinion. I'd do away with them completely, if it were up to me.'

'Shame it's not up to you,' Tyler said. 'I'd happily not bother, but Sinead's right into the idea.'

'What, of you standing up in front of everyone you know and making a tit of yourself?' asked Logan. 'Can't imagine why the thought of that might appeal to her...'

Tyler's face froze into a dead-eyed rictus. 'Cheers for that, boss.'

'Right, well, talk to her and Hamza,' Logan said. 'Makes no difference to me what they do tonight, but someone make sure we can get into one of the hotels this time. Get admin to sort it with the team down the road, so we're not scrabbling around trying to find somewhere to kip.'

He dropped his coat onto the chair again, rolled his head around on top of his shoulders, and let out a long, quiet groan.

'Something the matter, Jack?' asked Ben, noting the DCI's discomfort.

'Not yet,' Logan replied. He sighed and shot a look at the Incident Room door. 'But I'm about to go and tell Mitchell that we're taking you out of the office, so no doubt it's only a matter of a time...'

–

Shona Maguire had rushed home, got showered, got dressed, zapped a selection of popcorns in the microwave, put crisps in a big bowl, and brought two cans of Cherry Coke through to the living room when she got the call telling her it was all for nothing.

'Oh. You're not coming?' Shona asked, doing an admirable job of masking her disappointment. 'Right. Homework is it, or...?'

'I'm just busy tonight,' said the voice on the other end of the line.

Olivia Maximuke was not a friend. She was far too young to be that, and Shona's relationship with the girl was infinitely more complicated—to the point where Shona herself had absolutely no idea how to define it. Stockholm Syndrome was almost certainly a factor, although Shona could never quite decide which of them was the one affected by it.

'Sorry, you didn't go to any special effort, did you?' Olivia asked.

Shona didn't look directly at the table of goodies, but managed to see it from the corner of her eye, regardless.

'What? No,' she scoffed. 'No. Nothing like that. I'm just... you're OK, aren't you?'

'I'm fine. Why?'

'Just... for the last few months, you've been...' The rest of the sentence trailed off into a sigh. 'Just remember I'm here if you need to talk to me. About anything.'

'Thanks. I know. But there's nothing,' Olivia insisted. 'I'm just busy tonight. I can do tomorrow night, though, if you're free?'

'Tomorrow should be fine,' Shona said. 'As long as nobody dies in mysterious circumstances, my diary should be clear.'

'Great!' Olivia said, and she sounded genuinely pleased. 'Same time?'

'Same time,' Shona agreed. 'Take care.'

She hung up the phone, stared at it in concern for a few seconds, then set it back onto the base. Only then did she turn and regard the table of food spread out before her.

'Ah, bugger it,' she whispered, then she picked up a bowl of popcorn, flopped onto the couch, and reached for the remote.

—

Detective Superintendent Mitchell was packing up for the day when Logan entered her office. She made a show of checking her watch, instructed him in no uncertain terms not to bother sitting down, then asked him what he wanted and suggested that he 'be succinct'.

'We're going to relocate down to Fort William in the morning,' he told her.

'Again? Do you own shares in the hospitality trade down there or something?' Mitchell asked. 'Excuse me.'

She motioned for him to move, and Logan stepped aside, allowing her access to the peg where she'd hung her coat. It was a puffy purple number with a faux fur hood and a suggestion of silver sparkles in the fabric. It didn't fit the professional image the DSup had worked hard to cultivate at all.

'Present from my partner,' Mitchell said, clocking Logan's expression. 'She thinks it suits me. Personally, I think it's an abomination, but we pick our battles, don't we?'

She pulled the jacket on, then made a hand motion that told Logan to get a move on.

'Right. Aye. We've got a key witness in hospital down there. Broken leg.'

'Is this the one the constable hit?' Mitchell asked. 'That's going to be a right headache, let me tell you.'

'That's him,' Logan confirmed. 'Victim was a teacher at Lochaber High School, too, so we also thought—'

'Fine. Yes. All makes sense,' Mitchell said, patting her pockets for her keys.

'Dave's got a couple of physio appointments in the next couple of days, so he'll join us when he's done. We'll get someone local to log evidence until then.'

'Fine, yes, fine. And DI Forde will be staying here, of course.'

'What? Actually, I thought—'

'There's a stack of "welcome back" paperwork with his name on it that he'll be starting first thing tomorrow,' Mitchell said. 'As time permits, he can assist from up here. Until such times as I'm confident he's fully fit, he won't be working from anywhere but this building. Is that clear?'

'Well—'

'Is it clear or isn't it, Jack?'

'I mean, aye, but—'

Mitchell's nod was so curt it served as a full-stop on the entire conversation.

'Good. Then, I'll bid you goodnight, Jack. Good luck down the road. Keep me informed. I'm sure you've noticed, but the press is already sniffing around this one, so try not to make too much mess.'

Before Logan could reply, she made a shooing motion, ushered him out of the office, then locked the door behind them.

'Goodnight again, Jack,' she said, setting off along the corridor.

'Night, ma'am,' Logan replied. 'Oh, and for what it's worth, I think you're right, by the way.'

The Detective Superintendent stopped and turned. 'About?'

'The jacket,' Logan said. He shook his head and flinched, just enough for her to notice. 'It doesn't suit you at all.'

–

'How did it go?' asked Ben, when Logan returned to the Incident Room. 'She all right with me joining you on your road trip?' His smile faded, just a fraction. 'Or am I a liability?'

'You're a liability all right, but then you always bloody have been,' Logan told him. 'Aye, she's fine with it. Took a bit of convincing, but she saw sense in the end.'

'Magic, Jack. Well done!'

Ben seemed to grow an inch or two before Logan's eyes, and maybe shed a few years, too. Logan took a moment to memorise the look of relief on the DI's face, and the way the happy lines crinkled around his eyes.

It would be something to hold onto during the weapons-grade bollocking he'd just set himself up for.

Chapter 16

Logan's house was a two-bedroom semi-detached on one of the new estates, with a brick driveway, an environmentally-friendly heating system, and a sense of smug superiority that had, so far, prevented it from feeling like home.

It was early days, of course. The walls were all still the same uniform magnolia that the developers had applied. The carpets in the main rooms were all matching shades of dark brown, and the wood-effect vinyl flooring that covered the floor in the hall, kitchen, and downstairs bathroom remained boringly blemish-free.

It was a nice house. And therein lay the problem.

It felt too nice for him to live in. It was a family home, meant for a couple and a young child or two. A dog, maybe, or a rabbit in a hutch in the garden out the back. It was a house that longed for fun and chaos, bedtime stories and stolen kisses. It was a blank canvas, waiting for life and love and laughter to be imprinted on it.

What it had ended up with was a bitter, middle-aged man with a list of regrets and an insomnia problem. That was why he was sitting in the dining room drinking a glass of milk in the middle of the night, and munching his way through a packet of wafer-thin ham that had technically gone out of date three hours earlier.

And yes, he had a dining room now. Only a small one, but still. He hadn't had a dining room in a very long time. Not since he'd shared a house with Vanessa and Maddie.

Because that's all he'd been doing in the end. Sharing a house.

He folded a piece of ham into a triangle, shoved it in his mouth, then went into the messages on his phone. There had been no notifications, but sometimes he missed them. Sometimes, he'd discover an unopened message from days before that he'd somehow managed to overlook, and there was a chance that…

No. Nothing.

He checked for missed calls.

None of those, either.

Maddie had taken herself off Facebook after… everything that had happened. Logan went to the site and searched her name, in case she was back on.

She wasn't.

Or if she was, she was doing a solid job of hiding from him.

'Married, eh?' he said out loud.

The house didn't answer. It just sat there, quietly judging him and no doubt resenting its lot in life. It could have been coorying in a couple of sleeping kiddies right now. Or maybe spying on a hushed under-the-covers fumble by two tired parents stealing a moment together.

'Aye, well, life doesn't always work out the way we might hope,' he announced, then he raised his glass of milk in toast, knocked it back, and sighed. 'I'm talking to a fucking house,' he muttered.

He ate another piece of ham, chewed it slowly and thought-fully, then searched Maddie's name in Google. He was about to hit send, then added 'wedding photographs' to the search, before thumbing the button marked 'Go'.

Her name was the third result down, below two adverts for wedding photography services. Her new husband's name was there, too.

Anderson Crawford.

Logan tutted. 'Was there a first name shortage the day he was born?' he muttered. He hovered his finger above the link, but didn't press it. Not yet. Not right away. 'Parents probably a right pair of arseholes. Tweed-wearing, Burberry-wellied bastards.' He lifted his gaze to address the house. 'You mark my bloody words.'

The house, for its part, said nothing.

Logan could almost see him now, this 'Anderson Crawford'. This so-called son-in-law. He'd have one of those faces, wouldn't he? Smug. Self-satisfied. Big teeth, probably. The parents would be from the fox-hunting set, and that lot tended to have that look about them.

Blue-blood, dyed-in-the-wool Tories, they'd be, too. Which was fine. Each to their own. Who was he to judge?

But they'd be the type that was right up in your face with it, complaining about people on benefits having big tellies, or about them wasting their money on such lavish luxuries as internet access and McDonald's, while they kicked back in their private yacht eating bloody caviar and smoked salmon.

'We don't mind helping those down on their luck,' they'd say, in their grating, braying voices. 'But they've got to help themselves, too. We can't bail out everyone, now, can we!'

'No, maybe not,' Logan would reply. 'But we bailed out the fucking banks you work in, quick smart. Didn't hear you complaining when you got your big bonus, did we?'

Because they worked in banking. The whole bloody family.

He assumed.

There was a force field over his phone screen, holding his finger at bay. He poked at it a couple of times, and came close to making contact with the blue-highlighted search result link, but didn't quite connect all the way.

He looked up. The house was judging him. He could feel it.

'Fine. Right. Fine,' he announced, then he punctured the force field, tapped the link, and steeled himself against the inevitable burning rage the very sight of Mr Anderson Crawford would ignite deep within him.

He was younger than Logan had been expecting. About Maddie's age. He'd pictured him older.

There were no big teeth or horsey smiles in the pictures. No air of superiority. In every picture, he just looked... smitten. Like he couldn't believe his bloody luck to be standing next to his new bride.

Logan hadn't looked at Maddie yet. No more than a fleeting glance, anyway. There'd be time for that, but it needed a build-up.

The wedding wasn't big, going by the pictures. Nothing extravagant. A dozen guests, none of them in tweed, none of them carting around big bags of money and looking pleased with themselves.

Just a relatively small group of people, all looking happy. Together.

If anyone looked smug, it was Vanessa. Of course, he was probably imprinting that on her. In truth, she just looked pleased, and—in some of the later pictures—ever so slightly drunk.

Logan put the phone down, stood up, and paced a full circuit of the table before returning to his seat. He ate a piece of ham, wiped his hands on his bare legs, then picked up his phone again.

He couldn't put it off any longer.

When he looked at her—when he finally saw her—wrapped in an unfussy white dress, hair and makeup done fancy without being over the top, his heart ached. Not in a metaphorical sense. This was physical. A rabbit-punch of pain, square in the chest, that drew a grunt and a grimace, and a sharp intake of breath.

'Jesus Christ,' he said, although if pressed he wouldn't have been quite able to explain why. He drummed his fingers on the side of his milk glass and scrolled to the next photo.

Vanessa was right. She looked happy. Truly, madly, blissfully happy. There wasn't a photo where she wasn't smiling, where her eyes weren't sparkling, where her whole face wasn't lit-up. Alive.

She radiated joy in every picture. Everyone did, but her more so than the rest. She looked so happy, in fact, so utterly carefree, that he barely recognised the woman in the photos as the girl he'd once known.

Logan fished in the packet for more ham, but found it empty.

He looked around at a house meant for the love and laughter of a family.

'Ah, fuck it,' he said, clicking off his phone.

And on that note, he went to bed.

Chapter 17

Ben practically skipped up the path from his front door, a holdall in one hand, a coat draped over his other arm. He dumped both in the back, then clambered into the front seat of Logan's BMW, closed the door, clicked on his seatbelt, then slapped both hands on his thighs.

'Right, we're all set!' he chirped, all smiles and shiny teeth. There was a wee daud of toilet paper fixed to his chin with a spot of red, but otherwise, he looked in good shape.

Which was more than could be said for Logan.

'Christ, what's wrong with you? Are you ill?' Ben asked, his smile falling away somewhat.

'Just tired,' Logan explained. He yawned, as if to help his case. 'Didn't get much sleep.'

'Are you sure that's all it is?'

'I'm sure.'

'Because you look like Patient Zero in some sort of zombie virus pandemic,' Ben continued. 'No offence.'

'How am I meant to no' take offence to that?' Logan asked. He folded down his sun visor, checked himself in the mirror, then grunted and closed it over again. 'No, fair enough. You're bang-on.'

Ben studied him closely. Not that he really needed to. They'd known each other long enough to recognise the signs in each other with little more than a glance.

'Something's bothering you, Jack.'

Logan flexed his fingers on the steering wheel, sighed so hard the windscreen directly in front of him fogged up, then shook his head.

'It's nothing. Let's just focus on getting this case squared away so we don't mess around too much with the planning for the kids' big day.'

Ben nodded slowly, then hoisted his smile back up his face. 'Right. Aye. Let's do that. But if you ever need—'

'I know,' Logan replied. 'But I'm fine. Honestly.'

'I'll believe you. Thousands wouldn't,' Ben said. 'Oh! Before we head down the road, we should probably swing by the office. I think I've got some stuff I need to sign.'

Logan hesitated. 'I'm sure it can wait until we're back,' he said, then he started the engine, pulled away from Ben's house, and set off on the journey south.

–

Ross Lyndsay woke from a mid-morning, morphine-induced snooze to find a large man in a heavy coat standing at the foot of his bed.

At first, he thought he might be a doctor, but this notion quickly faded when he saw the expression on the man's face. Doctors didn't tend to look at their patients like that.

Then he thought the man might be some sort of ogre or troll, but decided that this might have been the painkillers talking.

He was about to have another guess when the man introduced himself. Again, it might have been the effects of the drugs, but his voice rumbled like thunder around Ross's private hospital room.

'Mr Lyndsay?' he boomed. 'My name's Detective Chief Inspector Jack Logan. I'm here to ask you some questions about your late flatmate. Is now a good time?'

Ross used his elbows to ease himself a little higher up the bed. His leg hadn't been cast in a stookie, but was instead encased in a series of straps and supports that held everything together.

'Um, actually, I don't—'

'Excellent,' Logan said, scraping a chair across the floor and sitting himself down. 'I won't keep you long. We'll arrange for you and me to have a more… *robust* discussion down at the station, but for now, there's just a few things I'd like to know.'

'Right. Uh, OK. Yes,' Ross babbled. 'It's just—'

'Why did you run away?' Logan asked. 'I suppose that's my biggest question right now. After "why did you kill Fergus Forsyth?" I mean. But we'll come to that.'

'I didn't! I didn't!' Ross protested.

'You didn't what? Run away?'

'Kill Fergus!'

'Like I said, we'll come to that,' Logan reiterated. 'All in good time. You did run away, though. I don't think anyone can dispute that.'

'All right, yes, I did run away, but I didn't kill—'

'Can you tell me why you did it?' Logan asked. 'Ran away, I mean. We'll get to the killing Fergus bit later, as I say.'

'I didn't kill him!'

'One thing at a time, Mr Lyndsay, please,' Logan urged. 'At your house. With my detectives. You made your excuses to leave the room, then you climbed out the window, and you made a run for it.'

'I mean—'

'How did that work out for you?' Logan asked, then he rapped his knuckles on one of Ross's leg bracings, drawing a little yelp of pain.

'I panicked, all right?' Ross cried. 'It was stupid, I know. It was really stupid, but I panicked. I panic. It's a condition. It's on my medical records. Panic attacks. Anxiety. I have a disorder!'

Logan made a show of taking out his notebook. He licked the end of his pencil, positioned it over the pad, then gave Ross a chance to try that again.

'You climbed out of a window and fled a police interview because of a disorder?'

'Yes!'

'What's the disorder? Itchy feet?'

'What? No! I told you. Anxiety. I get… when I get stressed, I don't think straight. Everything gets heightened.'

'Good job the window didn't get heightened. You might've broken your other leg,' Logan said. 'Why were you so anxious? You weren't a suspect. Note the use of the past tense there, Mr Lyndsay? You *weren't* a suspect. Thanks to your actions, you are now.' He smiled thinly. 'How does that affect the old anxiety levels?'

'Oh, God,' Ross gasped, letting his head sink back onto his pillow.

'Like I say, though, we'll get to how you killed Fergus eventually,' Logan continued. He indicated his notepad. 'So, just to clarify, you want your statement to say that you fled the interview because you panicked? That sound about right?'

'Yes! I mean, no. I mean… when you say it like that, it sounds…'

'Pathetic? Unbelievable?' Logan nodded. 'You're not wrong, there. So, how else would you say it, Mr Lyndsay? Why should I say you went on the run right after the violent and brutal murder of your flatmate? Because, between you and me, it'll have to be a belter of an explanation.'

'I need… I need some painkillers.'

Ross's hand reached for the call button that he'd left hooked to the side of his bed. Logan knew he'd left it hooked to the side of his bed, because he had moved it as soon as he'd entered the room. It was now hanging from the bottom end of the bed, well out of the patient's reach.

'I'm sure that can be arranged, Mr Lyndsay,' the DCI said. 'Just as soon as you tell me, in your own words, why you climbed out of your bedroom window and attempted to go on the run, rather than answer a few simple questions about your relationship with Mr Forsyth.'

'I just… I just… I just…' Ross's voice became higher with each repetition of the phrase, then his diminutive frame seemed to sink further into the bed, and he let out a little sob of defeat. 'We'd had an argument. About money. He owed rent.'

'When was this?'

'Morning before yesterday.'

'So, the day he died,' Logan pointed out, then he made a little circling motion with the end of his pencil, encouraging Ross to continue.

'He'd promised me he was going to pay me two weekends ago. Then he said it would be last weekend, and when he didn't...' Ross sniffed and wiped his nose on his bare arm, almost dislodging a drip-line that was affixed to one of his veins. 'I don't like confrontation. Can't stand arguments. But I needed the money. I pay all the bills. Council tax. Everything like that. Internet. Everything. Sky. Everything.'

'But he stopped contributing?' Logan said. 'God. I'd have been raging, if I was you.'

'He was late before, but never this late. So, I told him... I told him he had to move out. We had a big shouting match about it. He was really angry at me, but I stood my ground. I'm not usually good at that, but I was in the right. I knew I was in the right, so I didn't back down.'

The momentary look of pride on his face melted away and twisted into something more like shame.

'And, well, I said some things I regret,' he added.

'Such as?'

'Just... things.'

'Things like what, Mr Lyndsay?' Logan pressed.

Ross made a sound that was not unlike the whimper of pain he'd given earlier. 'I told him, "why don't you just fuck off and die?"' he said, self-censoring by silently mouthing the swear word rather than saying it out loud. He wasn't sure what the protocol was about cursing in front of police officers, and reckoned he was probably in quite enough trouble, as it was.

Logan's chair gave a little moan as he shifted his not-inconsiderable weight forward on it. 'I think it's important I clarify that. You're saying that you told Mr Forsyth to "fuck off and die"?' he asked.

After approximately one-third of a second of stoicism, Ross relented and nodded.

'On the very day that he fucked off and died?'

Ross continued to nod. He was biting down on his bottom lip, fighting a losing battle against the onslaught of tears that were currently troubling his internal flood barriers.

'Sandra heard. Our neighbour. Across the way. She heard me say it.'

'Your neighbour was there?' Logan asked.

'No. She was in her house. But she gave me a look. When I was going to work. Like a...' He pulled his face into a disapproving, down-the-nose sort of squint. 'She'd never looked at me like that before. Never. So she must've heard me. She must've.'

His defences fell then, the tears forcing their way out through his tear ducts and cascading down his reddening cheeks.

'That's why I ran. Because... because she'd heard me tell him to go and die, and... and if she told you that. The police. If she told the police I'd said that, and then he did, and then... you wouldn't believe me if I said I hadn't done it. You'd think it was me. But it wasn't! It wasn't!'

The door opened at the back of the private room, and a male nurse poked his head around the frame. 'You all right, Ross, you sound...' He stopped when he saw the brute of a man sitting at the side of the bed. 'Sorry, visiting hours aren't until later,' he said, his warm tone cooling so rapidly you could almost hear the pings. 'Can I help you?'

Logan stood. Turned. Made himself as large and imposing as possible, in the hope of quashing any challenge before it could get underway. He produced his ID and handed it over.

'Detective Chief Inspector Jack Logan. I'm just asking Mr Lyndsay here a few questions.'

The nurse took the warrant card and studied it, then handed it back. 'And you've had permission from the consultant?' he asked, unconcerned by the size of the man looming over him.

Logan shouldn't have been surprised. There was very little that would faze an NHS nurse. After a couple of years on the job, they'd seen everything, dealt with everyone, and had developed a mental armour thick enough to rival that of any copper's.

'It's just a quick chat,' Logan said, but he knew the game was up from the way the nurse stepped back, granting the DCI unfettered access to the exit.

'Well, you'll have to continue it another time, after the consultant's given his permission.'

Logan returned his ID to his pocket. 'Where do I find the consultant, then?'

'He'll be on the ward just before lunchtime. He won't be round to see Mr Lyndsay until after two. I suggest you call in after that.'

Logan thought about arguing, but he'd be on a hiding to nothing. There was no point in standing here arguing. There were plenty of other things to be getting on with.

Besides, the man in the bed wasn't going anywhere.

'Thanks. I'll do that,' Logan told the nurse, tucking his notebook into his pocket alongside his warrant card. He turned back to Ross and fired him a look that made it clear the conversation was far from over. 'And I'll look forward to continuing this in a more formal setting later, Mr Lyndsay. I suggest you use the time to get your story straight.'

He stepped out of the room, then about-turned and entered again.

'Oh, and you'll probably want to get yourself a good lawyer.'

Chapter 18

Moira Corson leaned on the reception desk, on the opposite side of the glass, her face completely impassive and yet, somehow, simultaneously filled with contempt.

'What do you mean "name"?' Logan asked. 'You know my bloody name. I've been here dozens of times before.'

Without shifting her gaze from his, Moira tapped the paper that was attached to the clipboard she held balanced on one arm.

'Name,' she repeated.

'Jesus.' Logan pinched the bridge of his nose, exhaled, then elected to offer no further resistance. 'DCI Jack Logan.'

Her eyes crept down. She wrote his name in meticulously neat block capitals, spelling out the full 'Detective Chief Inspector' rather than using the abbreviation, like any other normal person on the face of the bloody planet would have.

'Purpose of visit?'

'Murder investigation,' Logan replied.

Moira made no move to write. 'Can you elaborate?'

'For God's sake, woman!' Logan spat, which was met with an utterly impassive look. He sighed, then explained further. 'I'm leading the investigation into the murder of Fergus Forsyth. We're setting up the Incident Room down here, to be closer to the site and to potential witnesses,' he said. 'Happy?'

Moira looked down at her clipboard.

Then she looked up again.

'That's too long for the box.' She clicked the end of her pen. 'I'll put "murder investigation".'

'Is this a wind-up?' Logan demanded. He pointed up to the security camera watching the reception area. 'Is this on the bloody telly?'

'—sti—gay—shun,' Moira said, seemingly dictating the words phonetically to her own hand. She read the next question aloud. 'Time of entry?'

Was that one rhetorical?

Surely, that was rhetorical?

The way she was looking at him suggested it wasn't.

'Well, now, obviously,' he snapped.

This, apparently, was not good enough.

He resisted for as long as he could, loathe to give the old cow the satisfaction.

Eventually, though, he relented. It was that or stand there all day.

'Ten-forty-seven,' he said.

She waited.

Logan rolled his eyes.

'For fu—*A.M.*'

Moira wrote the time in the box. Logan leaned closer to the glass, watching her.

'Mind and just put A.M. Don't write bloody... *ante meridiem*, or whatever it is.'

Moira's gaze crawled up from the page. 'What?'

'Nothing. Just... nothing,' Logan sighed.

'Aunty what?'

'Forget it. Just... can I go through?' He edged his way over to the door. 'I'll just... I'll go through.'

'Contact telephone number?' Moira asked.

Logan grabbed the handle of the door and rattled it. 'This one. The one here. Just put yours. I'll be in this building. I'll just go through, if you can push the buzzer there. If you can just buzz me in.'

'I can't put mine. Contact telephone number?' Moira said again.

With a groan, Logan reluctantly released his grip on the handle and trudged back to the reception desk, fishing out a business card with his phone number on it. He couldn't recite his phone number from memory, and didn't trust people who could. They obviously had too much bloody time on their hands. Either that, or they were robots.

He had just started to read the number aloud when the door he'd just been heaving on opened.

'All right, boss?' asked Tyler, the door already swinging closed behind him.

Logan lunged. His fingers brushed against the handle, but then the door settled back into its frame with a solid thunk.

'No!' he ejected, the sound coming out as something not unlike a sob. He rounded on Tyler, eyes flashing with fury. 'You bloody idiot! What'd you let that close for?'

Tyler glanced back at the door, frowning. 'We can just buzz in again, can't we?'

'Not until I finish filling in this bastard form!'

Tyler looked over to the front desk, and the woman scowling at them through the glass. 'Oh. Right. Aye. We just came in the back door when a couple of Uniforms were heading out,' he explained.

Behind the barrier, Moira reached down out of sight, then produced a second clipboard. She sat both side-by-side on the reception desk, fixed Tyler with the same impassively resentment-filled look, and in a dry, disinterested voice said, 'Name?'

—

'Christ Almighty. She's got worse,' Logan remarked, storming into the Incident Room and claiming a chair with a well-aimed throw of his coat.

'Who's that?' Ben asked. He was fiddling with the height adjustment of his own chair and was currently perched so high on it that his feet couldn't touch the floor.

'Moira on the front desk,' Logan said, still seething over the encounter. 'I mean, she was always a pain in the arse, but Jesus Christ. It's like she's had an upgrade.'

'That'll be the new Chief Inspector. You'll know him. Alisdair Lyle. Complete and utter—' Ben began, then a careless lifting of a lever dropped him a foot and a half in a fraction of a second. He sank out of sight behind a computer monitor, before stopping with a gasp, a thud, and a 'fuck!'

'Careful, man!' Logan said. 'If you give yourself a heart attack by pissing about with your chair, Mitchell will never let me hear the end of it.'

Ben's head slowly reappeared as he cranked himself back up to a more practical height. 'Speaking of Mitchell, she rang looking for you.'

Logan sat at his desk and busied himself by fishing in his pocket for his notebook. 'Did she?'

'Just after we arrived. Phone rang maybe a minute or two later. Spooky timing. I swear, she's got eyes everywhere, that woman.'

'And you answered, did you?' Logan asked, flipping through the pages of his pad as nonchalantly as possible.

'I did, aye. She wants you to give her a ring as soon as you're back in the office. She didn't sound particularly happy,' Ben said. He winced. 'In fact, I'd say she sounded decidedly unhappy.'

'No change there, then,' Logan remarked.

Ben nodded slowly. 'Anything you want to tell me, Jack?'

'There is, actually,' Logan said. He jabbed a thumb over his shoulder, indicating the door. 'What's the big idea sending Tyler to JJ's for bacon rolls without waiting for me to get back? That's a low blow, Benjamin. And after me sticking my neck out for you.'

'We didn't know how long you'd be,' Ben protested. 'We thought we'd get the grub in now, and we could always send Tyler over again later, when you got back.'

Logan gave a tut of admonishment, then looked around at the rest of the room. Jackets and mugs marked the desks the others had already set-up shop at, but the detectives themselves were conspicuous by their absence.

'Where are Hamza and Sinead?' he asked. 'Did they head back up the road last night?'

'No. Stayed down. I've sent them into the school to talk to the headteacher. See if we can find out any information about Fergus's next of kin.' Ben checked his watch. 'Reckon they should be back shortly.'

'So, what… you weren't getting them rolls, either?' Logan asked.

Ben shifted around on his chair, still fiddling with the height adjustment. 'Well, I mean… again, we thought they could get something later. When they were back. They could be a while yet.'

'You just said they'd be back shortly!'

'Aye. They might be. But they might not. And, well, Tyler and I both missed breakfast, so…'

'I don't even want to hear it,' Logan said, raising a hand for silence. He gave a slow, disappointed shake of his head. 'You selfish pair of bastards,' he muttered. 'And after me putting my neck on the line for you, an' all…'

–

The last time Sinead had been in this office, it had been for fighting. Shari Woods in the year above had got wind that her sort-of-boyfriend, Simon Reid, fancied Sinead and—despite the fact Sinead had never so much as spoken to Simon in her life— Shari had tried to exact revenge by flushing Sinead's head down one of the girls' toilets.

Shari had been a big lass. Determined, too. But driven by the desire *not* to have her head flushed down one of the girls' toilets— or any toilet, for that matter—Sinead had fought back. A nose had been broken. Blood had been spilled. None of it Sinead's.

She still remembered her parents turning up. The look of embarrassment on their faces. The long ride home in silence.

They'd made her write an apology letter to Shari. They'd driven her round to the girl's house next day to deliver it, only for the bitch to rip it up in front of her.

Shari's dad had come out. Voices had been raised. Accusations and insults hurled. Sinead's dad didn't throw the first punch, but he'd thrown the last one.

After that, they'd gone to McDonald's, eaten McFlurries, and laughed more than they'd laughed in years.

The office had seemed bigger then. Now, it felt stiflingly small.

She hadn't encountered Bryan Stannard, the new headteacher at Lochaber High School, as he'd only taken up the role in the last few years. He was an immensely heavy-set man with wild greying hair, hands like bin-lids, and a shirt that was two sizes too small around the neck.

He wore dark-tinted glasses—presumably because of some sort of eye condition, because they in no way made him look cool—and a tie the colour of custard.

It struck Sinead as an unlikely colour choice for him. Everything else about his attire was stern and unwelcoming, and this impression was backed up by one of the best examples of 'resting bitch face' the DC had ever seen.

She suspected that someone else had suggested the tie to him, perhaps in an attempt to soften his image and make him seem marginally less terrifying a figure to the younger pupils.

It hadn't worked. If anything, it just made the rest of him seem even more sinister and threatening by comparison.

His weight was clearly putting pressure on both his chair and his lungs. He creaked and wheezed like an old accordion as Hamza broke the news that the PE department had a new staff opening.

'Beheaded?' Mr Stannard said with a gasp that might have been shock, but may just have been the air struggling to get through his collar-constricted windpipe. 'In what sense?'

Hamza, to his credit, didn't skip a beat. 'In the literal sense, I'm afraid,' he clarified, although quite why this needed any clarification, he had no idea. 'In the sense that his head was removed from his body.'

The headteacher's chair groaned like the deck of a ship on rough seas. 'I say,' he muttered. 'That's… I don't quite know what to say about that. God. Poor Fergus. What a way to go.' He considered the surface of his desk for a while, the varnish marked with a million scuffs and scratches. 'How absolutely awful. Do you know who did it?'

'We've just opened the investigation, but we're pursuing a few leads,' Hamza said, exaggerating a little to make it all sound a little less hopeless. 'But we're struggling to build up much of a picture of Mr Forsyth's life. Relatives. Friends. Where he's originally from. That sort of thing. We hoped you might be able to help.'

Mr Stannard appeared shocked by the very suggestion. 'Me? I mean… I don't tend to socialise with the teaching staff or get to know them on a personal level, but I suppose—'

'The school in general, we meant,' Sinead interjected. 'Surely, someone here talked to him? Knew him a bit? He must've had friends.'

'Oh! Right, yes, I see!' Mr Stannard said, chest wheezing with relief. 'Yes, I can absolutely find someone who can…'

After a couple of aborted attempts, he leaned his bulk forward enough to push the intercom button on his desk phone. It rang for a couple of moments before a young woman's voice crackled out from the speaker.

'Yes, Mr Stannard?'

'Ellie. Is it Ellie?'

'Yes, Mr Stannard.'

'Ellie. Do me a favour and track down Mrs Robertson, would you?' the headteacher asked. He flicked his eyes from the phone and tick-tocked them between the detectives sitting across from him. 'There's someone here who'd like to talk to her.'

Chapter 19

'Shite.'

Logan looked up from his desk and over to where DI Forde was sitting with the index fingers of both hands poised over the keyboard of his computer.

'What's wrong?'

'Hm? Oh. Nothing,' Ben replied. He rolled his tongue around in his mouth for a while, then whispered, 'password, password', just loud enough for the DCI to hear.

'Have you forgotten your password?'

'Not forgotten, no. Just... misplaced it in the old mental filing cabinet. It'll come to me, though.'

Ben leaned back and looked up at the ceiling. He was unlikely to find his login details written up there, he knew, but he felt that the change of scenery might help trigger something.

The only thing it triggered was a mild sensation of vertigo, so he stared down at the keyboard instead, and pecked at a few of the keys with a sense of resignation.

'This isn't it. I know this isn't it,' he said, then he clicked the mouse button. 'Oh ho!'

'Is that it?' Logan asked.

'No,' Ben said, visibly deflating. 'I thought it was for a second, but it's chucked me back out.'

He threw a glassy-eyed gaze in Logan's direction, sucked in his cheeks like he was trying to pass himself off as a fish, then whispered, 'password', another three or four times.

'You can get it reset,' Logan reminded him.

'That's admitting defeat,' Ben said. 'I'm not doing that. I'll get it. Just give me a minute.'

Logan turned his attention back to his own screen. He'd pulled up what they had on Ross Lyndsay. This hadn't taken long, as they didn't have very much worth mentioning.

He had no criminal record. No parking tickets. No speeding fines. No D&Ds. Nothing. He was, by all accounts, a model citizen.

Tyler had sent a couple of emails to Lyndsay's employers before heading home yesterday evening, and the replies had come to the shared mailbox while Logan and Ben were driving down the road.

Nobody had any complaints about his work or his attitude. Nobody was aware of any skeletons lurking in his closet.

Yes, he could be a bit highly-strung, both employers agreed, and he'd once had a full-blown panic attack over a spilled pot of soup in the hotel kitchen, but he was a nice guy. Harmless. Salt of the earth.

He was also, Logan had been quick to note, about the size of a Hobbit. Fergus Forsyth was considerably taller, even without his head.

On the one hand, this made him a more likely suspect. Unlike Logan—or anyone of a normal height and build, for that matter— he would be able to move around freely in the tunnel below the well.

On the other hand, could he feasibly have lugged Fergus's corpse out of a car at that layby, over to the well, and down the slope, before dumping him there in the space below the well?

Not on his own, certainly. Not without help.

Which didn't rule him out, of course. He might still be involved.

But Logan wasn't feeling it. He'd give him both barrels of the full interrogation treatment, of course, but his instincts told him that Ross Lyndsay almost certainly wasn't the man they were looking for.

He clicked over to a scan Sinead had made of the note-book they'd retrieved from Fergus Forsyth's drawer. There were a couple of pages filled with handwritten dates that stretched back just under two years. The writing was bunched together, one line below the other, but the dates themselves were spaced out by a few weeks at a time in the early days, then gradually became more regular until they were twice a week, Mondays and Thursdays.

They stopped a couple of months ago, and the pages that followed had all been blank.

There were a couple of numbers written on the first page—a phone number, which had turned out to be Fergus's own, and an eight-digit string of letters and numbers that was presumably the password for something.

Probably not the one Ben was looking for, though.

None of it made sense yet, but Logan got the feeling it might turn out to be an important piece of the puzzle.

'Got it!' Ben announced. He clasped his hands and shook them in the air above his head, celebrating this minuscule victory. 'I'm in.'

'Well done. Was it "password"?' Logan guessed.

Ben gave a snort, protesting just a little too much. 'No. Of course not,' he said, then he hastily clicked the mouse a few times and had a quick scan of the inbox. 'Email in from Ross Lyndsay's boss at the primary school.'

'Seen it,' Logan said.

'And one from his other boss at—'

'Seen that one, too.'

'Oh, well, aren't you on the ball this morning?' Ben retorted. 'Have you called Mitchell back yet, by the way?'

Logan shot a sideways glance at the mobile phone on his desk. He'd been expecting to have had several missed calls from the Detective Superintendent by now, but there were none.

He wasn't sure if this should make him feel better or worse.

'Not yet. I'll get to it shortly.'

'Wouldn't say boo to a goose,' said Ben.

Logan frowned as he replayed the sentence in his head. 'What?'

'Ross Lyndsay. Reading the emails here. Sounds like he wouldn't say boo to a goose,' Ben clarified. He clicked out of the inbox and turned his attention to the shared folders where the case files were stored. 'Mind you, always thought that was a strange saying. I mean, who would? Vicious bloody things. Geese, I mean. They can break your arm.'

'You're thinking of swans,' Logan corrected.

It was Ben's turn to frown. He shook his head. 'It's geese.'

'It's not. It's swans.'

'*Wouldn't say boo to a swan*? Nobody says that.'

'No, I mean… forget it,' Logan said, just as the door to the Incident Room opened, and both detectives' stomachs grumbled at the thought that Tyler had made it back with the food.

They were both disappointed, and at least one of them physically recoiled when they saw Moira Corson looming in the doorway.

'The Chief Inspector wants to see you,' she declared in a voice that could not have sounded less interested if she'd tried.

'Who? Both of us?' asked Ben.

Moira shook her head, raised a hand, and pointed in Logan's direction like someone out of *Invasion of the Body Snatchers*. 'No. Just him.'

'Oh, thank God,' Ben whispered. He grinned at Logan and gave him an encouraging wink. 'Nae luck, Jack!' He laughed. 'You be sure to give young Alisdair my best, and I'll look after your bacon roll if Tyler turns up before you get back.'

—

The office Sinead and Hamza had been shunted into was smaller than the headteacher's and felt like it served less of a specific purpose.

Mr Stannard's office had clearly been meant for him and him alone, from the family photographs on the shelves, to the risers under the desk that lifted it to a more practical height for his bulk.

There was nothing to indicate that this room had any fixed owner. It was the most generic office either detective had ever set foot in, and considering they both worked for Police Scotland, that was really saying something.

There was nothing personal anywhere in the room, just a desk, three chairs, and a bookcase filled with box files at the bottom, and books at the top. The labels on the box files all read, 'Paperwork', and while Sinead couldn't make out the names on the spines of the books on the upper shelves, she reckoned there was a pretty good chance they were all called, 'Reading Material,' or something equally as vague and uninteresting.

It was an office that had been assembled based solely on the dictionary definition of the word, each component slotted neatly into place with no real understanding of why.

Ironically, the woman sitting behind the desk felt like the perfect inhabitant of a room like this one.

She had introduced herself as Mrs Robertson, warned them that she had very little time to spare, then ushered them into the office and ordered—not invited—them to take a seat.

There had been no need for the introduction from Sinead's point of view. She had spent six years in Lochaber High School, and while she'd had no direct run-ins with Cops and Robertson, the depute head had been a constant presence throughout the DC's school career.

She sat across from them now, her hands shoulder-width apart, palms flat against the desktop. There was something oddly disconcerting about the pose, and both Hamza and Sinead continually felt their gazes being drawn to her hands, as the subconscious parts of their brains worked to figure out why anyone would ever sit in such a way.

Anyone who wasn't playing the title role in a *Hammer House of Horror* movie, anyway.

She had seemed largely unsurprised by the news of Fergus Forsyth's death. The murder part had raised an eyebrow, and the decapitation had brought the other one into line.

She'd known something was up, though. No-shows were rare among the teaching staff, she'd explained. Oh, sure, they pulled sickies regularly, but they always phoned in, usually laying it on far too thick as they coughed or whimpered their way through the call.

They all knew better than to just fail to show up. 'Death' was pretty much the only explanation Mrs Robertson would accept in such instances, so it was just as well for Mr Forsyth that he fell into that category.

'You don't seem particularly upset,' Sinead felt compelled to point out.

'I'm not,' the depute replied, with a level of frankness that caught both detectives off guard. 'I didn't know him. We weren't friends. He was a subordinate who worked in the same building. That's all. While I am, of course, sad for him and anyone he left behind, I don't have the luxury of moping around, grieving. My thoughts must now turn to finding a replacement, and keeping the department going for the next few weeks.'

Sinead and Hamza swapped looks that spoke volumes. Mrs Robertson didn't fail to pick up on them.

'Does my attitude shock you?' she asked.

'It just seems... a young man died. A member of your staff,' Hamza said. 'And you just seem a bit...'

'Annoyed,' Sinead concluded.

'I am. I'm livid,' the depute head agreed. 'Frankly, it's a massive headache for me, at a time when we're already short-staffed. We've got exams starting in just under a month. There's no way we'll fill his position in time.' She sighed and looked out the window to where a sports field lay just beyond the car park. 'Thank God it's just PE. If it had been a proper subject... I shudder to think.'

'Yeah. That would've been tragic,' Sinead said, making no effort to hide her distaste.

'Was there something you specifically wanted?' Mrs Robertson asked. She checked the clock on the wall above the door. 'I'm supposed to be covering a class in fifteen minutes. One of those coughers who over-egg the pudding.'

Sinead couldn't formulate a question without swearing, so bit her lip and nodded for Hamza to take the reins. The coldness of the heartless cow on the other side of the desk was incredible. There wasn't even a pretence of concern or empathy. Not so much as a flicker of pity or regret.

'Can I ask when you last saw Mr Forsyth?'

Copsand narrowed her eyes a little as she turned her attention to Hamza. 'Why do you ask? Am I a suspect?'

'No. Of course not,' Hamza assured her. 'We're just trying to establish time of death.'

'I thought you had people for that sort of thing? Gadgets and whatnot?'

'I think you might have watched too much TV, Mrs Robertson,' Hamza said.

'That's very unlikely. I don't own a television,' the depute head replied, with an air of superiority that told them she believed herself far the better person for it. 'Mr Forsyth had a class on Monday afternoon. Last period. He delivered it, as planned, then presumably left soon after.'

'And school finishes…?'

'Three-forty,' Sinead said, earning herself a fleeting puzzled look from Copsand.

'Yes. That is correct,' the depute head confirmed. 'The last bell goes at three-forty. I ask all teaching staff to remain on the premises until four, but some of them are a law unto themselves.'

'Is that how you'd describe Mr Forsyth?' Hamza asked.

'No. I wouldn't describe him as anything. He was a PE teacher. He could run, jump, and throw a ball. The pupils liked him, I believe. But that's essentially all I know of the man. You asked when I last saw him? Last week, sometime.'

'I thought you said—' Hamza began, but Copsand responded before he could get to the end of the sentence.

'I said he taught last period on Monday. I know that for a fact. I don't have to have seen it with my own two eyes to confirm it,' she explained. 'If you're asking when he left the premises, I'd have to say between three-forty and four, and likely leaning towards the former. If you want to know anything else about him, I'm afraid you've come to the wrong person.'

Sinead couldn't believe the coldness of the old cow. She remembered now why nobody had ever had a good word to say about her during Sinead's six years at the school.

'We were also hoping you'd be able to give us details of his next of kin,' Hamza said. 'Maybe former employers. Past addresses. Anything that would help us build up a clearer picture of who Mr Forsyth was.'

The depute head tutted. 'The office staff could have helped with that. There was no need to call me in and waste my time.'

'We didn't call you in,' Sinead said, unable to hold her tongue any longer. Her tone was sharp and abrupt, and made Hamza turn to look at her in surprise. 'Your boss did. He told you to help us. Not the office staff, *you*. So, forget your next class. They're having a free period. You, Mrs Robertson, are personally going to get us the information we need to help us find out who killed one of your teachers.'

Copsand sucked in her cheeks, but said nothing. Not for a while. Instead, she studied Sinead with a sort of detached fascination. It was the sort of look that the weird kid in class might give a fly whose wings he'd just pulled off, as he watches it explore its new flightless, agonising reality.

'What did you say your name was?' she finally asked.

'Detective Constable Bell.'

Copsand clicked her tongue against the back of her teeth and gave a nod. 'Sinead Bell? The one whose parents died a few years back? That's you, isn't it?'

Sinead swallowed. Her hands gripped the arms of the rickety old chair she sat in. 'Yes. That's me.'

'You used to go here. I remember you in Advanced Higher English. Bright girl, if I recall,' the depute head remarked. She flicked her gaze from Sinead to Hamza and back again. 'And yet, here you are.'

She hadn't once moved her hands from their spot on the table, but slapped out a quick drumbeat now. Thump. Thump-thump.

'Here's what's going to happen, Sinead,' she announced, smiling for the first time since she'd introduced herself. It was a rough draft of a smile at best, though. A hurried, scribbled attempt that needed a lot of work before it would convince anyone. 'I'm going to personally ensure you get the information you need from the office staff. I'll make certain it's their number-one priority, despite the hundred and one other things going on that are fundamental to both the running of this school, and the safety and well-being of our pupils.' She hitched the smile wider. This only made the whole awful arrangement of her features look worse. 'How does that sound?'

'We appreciate that,' Hamza said, getting in there before Sinead could say anything they both might regret. 'I'm sure we all want the same thing—to make sure Mr Forsyth's killer is brought to justice.'

'Yes. Quite. Of course,' agreed Copsand with a dismissive wave of a hand that made it very clear that this was way down near the bottom of her list of priorities.

Breaking contact with the table seemed to free her to stand up, and she did so with a series of rigid bending motions that made her look like she was powered by pistons.

'Do you want my advice?' she asked, once she'd pushed the chair back under the desk. She didn't wait for either of them to reply before continuing. 'Talk to Lana Lennon.'

'Mrs Lennon?' Sinead asked. 'As in the English teacher? That Mrs Lennon?'

'Yes. Her,' Copsand confirmed. 'I don't share gossip, so please don't say you heard this from me, but I have it on very good authority that she and Mr Forsyth were close. Extremely close. If you know what I mean?'

'They were in a relationship?' Hamza asked.

'Mrs Lennon's married, isn't she?'

The deputy head raised both hands like she was stopping traffic. 'Like I say, I don't share gossip. But if you want an insight into the coming and goings of Mr Forsyth's life, I can think of no one better to talk to.' One of the raised hands became a pointing finger, which she waved at them both in warning. 'But *after* school. PE. might not be important, but English is, and those children are preparing for the most important exams of their school career. You can have her home address. I suggest you talk to her there.'

'Thank you. We'll do that,' Hamza said.

'Good. I appreciate it,' Mrs Robertson said. 'And now, I wonder if you'd be so good as to do me one other small favour…?'

Chapter 20

The Chief Inspector was all handshakes and smiles when Logan eventually made his way to the office. He sprang from his chair like a sprinter off the blocks, and for a brief, terrible moment Logan was convinced the bugger was going to try to hug him.

Instead, he settled for one of those two-handed grasping handshakes, and the sort of joy-filled look that Logan usually only saw on the faces of parents whose kidnapped child he'd just dropped off back home.

While the name on his warrant card may have been Alisdair Lyle, Logan and most of the rest of the force knew him by something very different.

He'd come from a deeply religious background and used to hum hymns most of the year-round, except at Christmas, when he'd segue into carols for a few weeks.

As a sergeant, and later as an inspector in the drug squad, he'd paused many an operation to have 'a quick word with God', where he asked the Lord to watch over him and the other officers as they smashed in the doors of a suspected dealer's house, and kicked the living shit out of all those inside.

And so, one element of his nickname had been secured. It was his struggles with his weight—and one part of his physique, in particular—that had contributed the second part.

Praying Mantits was a particularly harsh name to be saddled with, Logan had always thought, even for the polis. It was often shortened to just 'Mantits' for the sake of brevity. So much so, in fact, that the 'Praying' part fell mostly into obscurity.

This felt particularly unfair, considering that the Chief Inspector had managed to get his fluctuating weight under control in recent years, but still remained a devout follower of the Christian faith.

Still, they couldn't exactly call him 'Praying'. It just didn't stand up on its own. And so, 'Mantits' he was, and forever would be—an everlasting reminder that he was once twice the man he now was.

'Great to see you, Jack! Great to see you! You're looking well!'

'Cheers,' Logan said. 'Eh... you too.'

'Och, away with you,' Mantits laughed. 'I am not! Do you think so? The wife's had me trying moisturiser, would you believe? On my face. Feel that. "Lot of old bollocks," I told her, but it works.' He presented a cheek to Logan, and nodded encouragingly. 'Feel that.'

'Sorry?'

'Go on. Have a feel.'

Logan got the sense that this would not end until he did as requested. He prodded the tip of a finger against the Chief Inspector's offered cheek, more forcefully than Mantits had likely been expecting.

'Aye. Very good,' he remarked.

'It's made with cucumber,' Mantits said, dropping his voice like he didn't want anyone else hearing of such lavish extravagance.

'Right,' said Logan, because he had absolutely no idea what else to say.

'I can get you some, if you like. I'm sure I've got a sample pot you can have.'

Logan shook his head. 'I'm fine.'

'No?' Mantits took a long appraising look at Logan's face. 'Not even around the eyes?'

'I'm fine, Alisdair,' Logan said. 'You wanted to see me?'

'Yes! I did! And here you are!' Mantits laughed. 'God. It's just like old times, isn't it? Me and you. Side by side. Like *Cagney and Lacey*, or *Starsky and Hutch*.'

Logan became aware that his brow was furrowing, and course-corrected before Mantits broke out the moisturising cream.

'Did we ever work—?'

'*Dempsey and Makepeace*. That's another one,' Mantits said, beaming from ear to ear. 'Remember them? Michael Brandon and Glynis Barber? He was from New York. She was... well, I don't know where she was from. Good show, though. Great chemistry.'

Logan waited until he was sure the Chief Inspector was done, then continued with his question. 'Did we ever work together?'

'Not directly. No. Obviously. But I don't know about you, but I always felt there was a sort of spiritual connection. Two rough-and-tumble Glasgow boys from the wrong side of the tracks, making it good in an unfamiliar world.'

This time, Logan couldn't prevent the frown from taking over his forehead. 'You're from Glasgow?'

'Of course! Can't you tell by the accent?' laughed Mantits. He adopted a style of intonation that was both guttural and nasal at the same time, and nothing whatsoever like his real voice. '*Watch oot! The weans are in the water.*' He held his arms out at his sides, his point apparently proven. 'See?'

'Oh aye. I hear it now, right enough,' Logan said.

The accent had not been from Glasgow. It had barely been from Scotland, in fact. It was Mel Gibson in *Braveheart*. Worse than that, even. It was Russ Abbot as CU Jimmy, all ginger hair and gibberish.

Still, the last thing Logan wanted was to get into a conversation with the man about it. Or about anything else, for that matter.

'What was it you wanted to see me about, Alisdair?' he asked. 'I'm in the middle of a murder investigation.'

This only made Mantits smile wider. He sat on the edge of the desk, gripping the top with both hands, and gave a wry shake of his head. 'Jack Logan,' he said, almost wistfully. 'Do me a favour, will you?'

'What's that?'

'Never change.'

'Eh... aye. Fine.'

'Oh, and one other thing,' Mantits continued. 'We're doing things very much by the book here now. Crossing the Is and dotting the Ts.' He laughed at that and gave another shake of his head, like he couldn't believe the stuff he came up with sometimes. 'If there's a form to be filled, I expect you to fill it. If there's a report to be filed, or a resource request to be made, or an interview room to be booked, we'd all very much appreciate it being done. We're all skinny sailors here, Jack. Do you know why?'

Logan blinked slowly, steeling himself for the inevitable punchline.

'Because I run a tight ship,' Mantits declared, then he followed up with a 'badum-tish' because it was evident that no other bugger was going to. 'You and your team tick the boxes and file the paperwork, and we'll be skinny sailors sailing smooth seas. I bet you can't say that five times fast, can you?'

'No,' Logan immediately replied, brushing right past it. 'Is that us, then?'

'That's us. Back to it, we go!' Mantits chuckled. He jumped up and pumped Logan's hand again. 'Great to see you, Jack! Really great to see you!'

'Aye. You too, Alisdair,' Logan said, taking his hand back.

'And I'm going to bring you in that sample pot of cream,' Mantits insisted. 'And I'm not taking no for an answer!'

–

Logan returned to the Incident Room to find the whole team assembled around Ben's desk. Hamza and Sinead still had their jackets on and stood with their backs to him as he entered. Tyler loomed behind DI Forde's chair, more or less bouncing from foot to foot as if warming up for a run.

The smell of hot, buttery bacon rolls had entangled with the air in the room, making Logan's mouth water and his stomach rumble. He'd hate to be Sinead and Hamza, who had both been stiffed on the JJ's run, and would have to sit and watch while the other three got stuck in.

'That our rolls here, then, is it?' Logan asked, making it very clear to everyone within earshot that his name was on one of them.

'No. I mean, aye, boss. They are,' Tyler confirmed. 'But there's a bit of exciting news.'

'Oh aye?' Logan asked, suspecting there would be very little in that moment that could excite him more than floury bread and crispy bacon. 'And what's that?'

'There's a cake shop!' Ben announced, with near-childlike glee.

'A cake shop?'

'Next to JJ's, boss. Right next door, in fact,' Tyler said. 'They do all sorts. Brownies. Blondies. Cookies. Cakes, obviously.'

'Oh. Right,' Logan said, doing his best to sound disinterested. He sniffed. He shrugged. He made the vaguest of waving motions with a hand. 'Did you get any?'

Sinead and Hamza both stepped aside. There, on the table, sat a large white box with a clear plastic window in the top, and a selection of colourful goodies inside.

'Aye, boss,' Tyler said with a grin. 'You can say that again!'

–

Once the rolls were eaten, the cakes all squared away, and all but a few dregs of tea and coffee drunk, the focus finally turned back to the murder of Fergus Forsyth.

As she didn't have a roll—something she made clear she was going to have words with Tyler about at a later date—Sinead had spent some of the time collating the latest findings on the Big Board.

Mostly, these were focused around the victim, and the new information she and Hamza had brought back from Lochaber High School. The school office still had his CV and original application on file, along with a scanned copy of his teaching qualifications, and a note of his emergency contact.

Unfortunately, the emergency contact was Ross Lynsday, so that wasn't particularly helpful. He had just one named reference—the head of PE at the school in Dumfries where he'd done his probationary years after leaving university—and the only address the school had for him was the house he shared in Invergarry.

'Doesn't exactly paint a vivid picture of a young man's life, does it?' Logan said, picking crumbs of Maltesers rocky road cake from where they'd landed on his shirt, and tossing them into his mouth. 'This can't be all we've got.'

'It's most of what we've got from the school, sir,' Hamza confirmed. 'But we're waiting for a dump to come through from his bank and mobile provider. The school did have a note of his doctor's details, so we'll get onto there, too. Medical records should hopefully date back, so we can see where he used to be enrolled, and we'll check with his old uni, too. They're bound to have something.'

That sounded more promising.

Marginally.

'We did hear something interesting from the depute head,' Sinead said. 'There are rumours among the staff that Fergus was in a relationship with an English teacher at the school. A married English teacher.'

'Really?' said Logan, pausing his de-crumbing for a moment while he gave this some thought. 'You're right, that is interesting. Did you speak to her?'

'No. Thought it might be better if you did it, sir,' Sinead said. 'She used to be my teacher, so I thought maybe best if I wasn't involved.'

'Also, the scary depute head lady told us to wait,' Hamza added.

'And that, yes,' Sinead said. 'That also.'

'What's she like?'

'Terrifying,' Hamza replied. 'I think she's a robot of some kind.'

Logan shook his head. 'The English teacher.'

'Oh. Right. Aye,' said Hamza, before handing over to Sinead.

'I only had her for a couple of years. Third and fourth year,' Sinead said. 'She was… fine. Friendly enough. Got a bit stressed out sometimes. Lost it once or twice with some of the noisier lads, but it was a good class, by and large.'

'Did she like you?' Logan asked.

'I mean… I think so. I don't think she disliked me.'

'I can't imagine anything worse than being a teacher,' Tyler remarked. 'I couldn't do it. I'd be screaming my head off all the time. Some kids are just bastards. There was this right mouthy wee arsehole in my year. All the teachers hated him.'

'No need to be so hard on yourself, son. I'm sure you weren't all *that* bad,' Logan told him, beating Ben to the punch by mere fractions of a second. 'Did we get an address for your English teacher?'

'We did. She's out at Spean Bridge,' Sinead said.

'Good. I'll go round and see her this evening. But I want you there, too,' Logan told her. 'Familiar face might get her talking.'

Sinead nodded. 'If you think it'll help, sir.'

'Christ knows. Worth a try, though,' Logan said.

'We checked the car park for any sign of the victim's motorbike, too,' Hamza said. 'Nothing there. Looks like he definitely left the premises on Monday and never came back. We've got Uniform trying to track it down. It's bright yellow, so pretty distinctive. We're hoping that it'll maybe help us piece together his movements after he left the school on Monday.'

'Right. Good. Keep me posted,' Logan instructed. 'Tyler, any joy with that key?'

'Nah, nothing, boss. Not yet. Dave's still working on it up the road, but we're not making a lot of progress so far.'

'What's your current theory?' Ben asked.

Tyler's expression became immobile, like he'd pulled on a mask of his own when no one was looking, and was now hiding behind it.

'My current theory, boss? Well, eh… I think it, like—the key, I mean—I think it probably unlocks, like… something… that's, you know, previously been locked. Like, it'll open a box, or a safe, or a… thing.' He looked at the senior detectives, swallowed, then added, 'Or maybe a drawer. That's the current theory, at least.'

'Well,' said Ben, after a lengthy uncomfortable silence. 'I'm glad to hear you've got it well in hand.'

'Have you tried a locksmith?' Sinead asked.

The reaction from Tyler suggested this word was new to him. 'A locksmith?'

'Aye. They tend to know about keys,' Sinead pointed out.

Tyler turned his gaze to the window. The light from it pushed the shadows from his face like the rising sun sweeping across the surface of the earth.

'A locksmith,' he whispered, as if afraid that saying it too loudly would scare the idea away. 'That's what I should do. I should ask a fucking locksmith! They know about keys. You're a genius!'

Sinead winked, made a clicking noise out of the side of her mouth, and fired a finger gun in her fiancé's direction. 'Any time,' she said. 'And since I helped you out, I need you to do something for me, too.'

Tyler opened his mouth to make a comment that he real-ised was completely inappropriate for the current company, and aborted just in the nick of time. Instead, he said, 'What would that be?'

'It's not until tomorrow morning. And it won't take long,' Sinead said.

Tyler didn't like where this was going. She was already working hard to soften the blow. Whatever she was going to ask him to do, it was going to be big, and he almost certainly wasn't going to like it.

'Spit it out,' he said. 'What is it you're after?'

'The school wants to do an assembly tomorrow morning. About Mr Forsyth.'

'What?' Logan spat. 'They're not bloody announcing it, are they?'

'It's a school, sir. Rumours are already starting to spread about what happened, so they reckon it's best to get on top of it. Control the narrative, sort of thing.'

'It's going to be all over the papers by tomorrow, anyway, Jack,' Ben pointed out. 'You think the two journos up the road are the only ones onto the story? The Well of the Seven Heads is crawling with the bastards. The coffee shop's never been so busy. I expected it to be on the front pages today, but some scandal about some MP has kept it off. That won't last, though.'

'Is that the crocodile clips on the cock guy?' asked Hamza.

Ben's chair gave a high-pitched squeak of surprise as he turned sharply to the DS. 'What?'

'The MP,' Hamza explained. 'He was caught with a prostitute. She'd put a load of crocodile clips on his cock and balls.'

'*Crocodile clips?*' Ben looked around at the faces of the others, meeting each of their eyes in turn. 'On his... *lad?* Not on purpose, surely?'

'Tricky thing to do accidentally, so I think it probably was on purpose, boss, aye,' Tyler said.

Ben crossed his legs. 'Why in the name of Christ would you attach...? Are we thinking of the same thing? Crocodile clips? Like, springy wee...? With the teeth? That sort of crocodile clip?'

'That's the one, sir,' Hamza confirmed.

Ben sat back. His eyes darted left, right, up, down, as his brain struggled to come up with a rational explanation for such behaviour, but it fell well short in the end.

'On his *bits?* Why?'

'I suppose it's just what he's into,' Hamza said.

'But how?!' Ben cried. 'How do you figure out that sort of thing's your cup of tea? I mean... I just don't...' He shook his head. 'I tell you, he should get together with the ginger up the arse fella. Swap notes. I bet they'd get on like a bloody house on fire.'

Sinead quietly cleared her throat. 'Um, I think maybe we're getting a bit sidetracked here,' she suggested. 'The point I was making was that, yes, the school wants to do an announcement for pupils and staff. If it's in the papers tomorrow, gossip will go through the place like wildfire. They want to put a lid on that before it gets out of hand.'

Logan gave a grunt of resignation. 'Aye. Fine. Hopefully, we can get in touch with next of kin by then.'

'So, eh, what's all this got to do with me?' Tyler asked. 'What's this favour you're after?'

Sinead smiled sweetly. 'They asked if one of us could be on hand to answer a few questions, and maybe provide some reassurance,' she said.

'And we put your name down,' Hamza added, unable to hold it back any longer.

Tyler sat up sharply, taking on the look of a meerkat that had just witnessed something traumatic. 'What? No! *Me*? No!' he protested. 'Boss, tell them! I can't do that! I can't stand up there and talk in front of a bunch of teenagers. Not by myself!'

'Relax. Don't worry. You won't be by yourself, son,' Logan assured him. 'Ben and I will be there, too.'

'Oh, thank God,' Tyler wheezed. 'Cheers, boss.'

His relief was short-lived.

'We'll be up the back watching,' Logan concluded. 'Because I don't know about you, Benjamin, but I would not miss this for the bloody world.'

Chapter 21

Logan's request to have Ross Lyndsay brought into the station for a formal interview was rejected by the consultant in charge of his care. Instead, a solicitor attended the hospital, and the interrogation took place gathered around the bed, with Ross propped up on a couple of thin pillows, and Hamza recording everything on his phone.

The solicitor was new to the area, but not new to Logan. He'd been based in Inverness until a few months ago, then had taken a more senior role at a different firm down here in the Fort. His name was Lawrence Cairns, and he wore the same annoyed expression he'd had on his face when Logan had first met him.

That had been during one of his early cases in Inverness, when a nurse had been found murdered near Raigmore Hospital. Logan had been equal-parts impressed and horrified by the eerily unnatural whiteness and uniformity of the solicitor's teeth. If anything, they'd only grown whiter in the time between then and now, to the extent that they drew the eye of everyone else in the room whenever he opened his mouth.

Logan made the necessary introductions and opening statements for the recording, and was about to get started on his questions when Cairns jumped in.

'I'd like to clarify now that my client is not under arrest. Correct?'

Logan sighed inwardly. The bugger was already trying to make his presence felt, and they hadn't even started.

'That's right,' he confirmed.

'He has requested privately that...' Cairns hesitated like he couldn't quite believe what he was about to say. '...you don't accuse him of killing Mr Forsyth, or saying anything that suggests he was in any way responsible for his death.'

Logan shifted his gaze from the solicitor to his client and back again. Their expressions could not have been more different. Ross's was wide-eyed and hopeful. His brief, on the other hand, clearly knew full well what the only possible response to such a request would be.

'Obviously, I can't promise that. If I think he did it, I'll say so,' Logan pointed out, addressing Cairns directly. 'If you could pass that message on to your client, that would be appreciated. We'll wait.'

Cairns gave a jaded, half-hearted sort of a shrug in Ross's direction to indicate he'd done as he'd been asked, and that it had failed as predictably as he'd almost certainly explained it would. Then he flipped open a leather folio, turned to a page halfway through the notepad, and sat poised with an expensive silver pen held at the ready.

'How's the leg?' Logan asked.

Ross's eyes narrowed as he tried to work out if this was some sort of trick question. And, if it was, how he could avoid falling for it.

'Broken,' he eventually said. 'Really broken. And painful. I could sue.'

'You could try,' Logan said. 'I'm sure your man here would know more about that sort of thing than me.' He shrugged. 'But from what I understand, you jumped out of the bushes where you'd been trying to evade capture, and right into the path of a polis car, doing several thousand pounds worth of damage in the process. Maybe we should be the ones suing you. What do you think, DS Khaled?'

'It's going to be an expensive repair, right enough, sir,' Hamza said. 'Don't see why the taxpayers should have to pay for it.'

'I'm not really going to sue,' Ross said, laughing it off. At least, the noise he made was an approximation of a laugh, even if it fell short of the mark. 'I'm just kidding.'

'Right. I see. Still, good that you've kept your sense of humour, Mr Lyndsay, given the circumstances.'

Ross's not-quite laugh dried into a croak. 'No. You're right. Sorry. I'm just... I'm nervous.'

'And why's that?' Logan asked. 'You told me earlier you weren't involved in Fergus's death.'

'I wasn't! I definitely wasn't!'

'Then what's with all the panic?' Logan pressed. 'Innocent people aren't scared of talking to the polis.'

This wasn't even remotely true, of course. He'd seen grown men fall over in a dead faint at the very thought of being taken into the station for questioning over the most mundane of charges. He'd seen people burst into tears at the side of the road when pulled over for a random blood alcohol test, and some of them hadn't touched a drop in months, sometimes years.

Some people just got antsy around authority figures.

But Logan wasn't going to let the bugger off the hook that easily.

'I just... I told you, I think. Didn't I tell you?' Ross asked, fully aware that he had, but worried the DCI might have forgotten. 'I get nervous. It's a condition. It's an anxiety disorder. I get really nervous. Look.' He held up his hands to show the sweat-sheen that glistened on them. 'See? Soaking. It doesn't mean I'm guilty.'

'It doesn't mean you're not, either,' Logan pointed out, then he pressed on before either the man in the bed or his legal counsel could object. 'Do you mind telling me where you were on Monday around four-thirty in the afternoon?'

'Four-thirty? On Monday?' Ross's lips moved. He counted on his fingers for an inordinately long time.

'It was two days ago, Mr Lyndsay. It shouldn't be that difficult.'

'I'm just... I'm thinking about shifts,' Ross replied. 'I should... I would've been home from school. But was I back out to the hotel?'

'I don't know. That's why I'm asking,' Logan said.

'Sorry, I wasn't asking you, I was just... I was thinking out loud. And no. I wasn't.'

'You weren't thinking out loud?'

'Oh. No. Yes. I was. I wasn't back out at the hotel. Monday, I was… wait! I was! Jenny was sick! She couldn't come in, so I covered her shift!'

Ross sunk back into his pillows with a little chirp of relief. The effort of remembering the events of forty-eight hours previous had taken a visible toll, and he closed his eyes for a moment as he tried to summon the energy to continue.

'I told you I didn't do it,' he muttered, his tone far off and dream-like.

'And what time did that shift start, Mr Lyndsay?' Logan asked. 'Because we spoke to your manager at the hotel, and he claims you didn't make it into work until five-twenty.'

Ross opened one eye. 'That sounds about right.'

Beside the bed, the solicitor rubbed his temples and muttered something very quietly.

'In which case, I'll repeat the question,' Logan said. 'Where were you at four-thirty on Monday afternoon? Fifty minutes before you started work.'

'What? Oh. Sorry. *Four*-thirty?' Ross said, sweat beading on his skin once again. 'On Monday? I was probably… I was probably at home. Yeah. I'd have been at home.'

'Good. Now we're getting somewhere,' Logan told him. 'Did Fergus come home when you were there?'

'No.'

'Did you continue your argument about money?'

Ross side-eyed his solicitor. 'I, uh, I said he didn't come home.'

'I'm well aware of what you said, Mr Lyndsay,' Logan informed him. 'So, you're saying you didn't argue about money that afternoon?'

'No.'

'Just that morning.'

'Uh… yes.'

'When you told him to—and correct me if I paraphrase this slightly—"fuck off and die"?' Logan said. 'You're maintaining that this was the last time you spoke to Fergus or saw him alive?'

'Yes. And just because I said that doesn't mean I did it,' Ross insisted. 'I wouldn't kill Fergus over money!'

'Then why did you kill him?' Logan pressed.

'I didn't!'

'Did you hire someone? Is that what happened?'

'No!' Ross protested, close to tears now. He looked imploringly at his legal counsel. 'Tell him I didn't do it!'

'Obviously, he didn't do it,' the solicitor intoned. 'You're wasting everyone's time here, Detective Chief Inspector, and I think you know that. My client is physically and emotionally incapable of having murdered Mr Forsyth. That much is clear.'

'Yes! Exactly!' yelped Ross, happy to ignore the slight if it meant the interview coming to an end and him no longer being under suspicion. 'How could I have killed him, even if I'd wanted to? Which I didn't!'

Logan rubbed his chin. He'd shaved that morning before coming down the road, so there was a disappointing lack of the usual stubble-scraping sound.

'Then who did?' he asked. 'Who killed him?'

Ross blinked. 'I don't know.'

'You're down as his next of kin. You lived with him. Right now, it seems that you're the world's foremost leading expert on Fergus Forsyth. So, who killed him?'

'I don't know!' the smaller man insisted. 'If I knew, I'd tell you!'

'Fine. Then, why might someone *want* to kill him? Did he have any enemies you were aware of?'

'Enemies? No. Of course not. I mean, he was a high school teacher, so maybe one of the kids?'

'Did he have any other friends he spoke about?' Logan pressed. 'Was he in a relationship that you were aware of?'

'I mean, he had a girlfriend, I think, but I never met her. They used to meet up a couple of times a week. Mondays and Thursdays. He was working most other nights.'

'So, he'd have been due to meet her on the night he died,' Hamza pointed out.

Ross gave a half-hearted little shrug. 'I suppose so. Yeah.'

'Wait... Mondays and Thursdays?' Logan asked. He thought back to the notebook with the dates. 'Every Monday and Thursday?'

'Pretty much, yeah.'

'Do you have a name?' Logan asked.

The man in the bed frowned and glanced uncertainly around at the other men.

'Um, yeah. It's... it's Ross.'

Logan tutted. 'For fu—for the girlfriend, I mean.'

'Oh! Yes, I see. Uh, no. No. No idea. Sorry.'

Logan raised a deeply sceptical eyebrow.

'I don't! He never said. He was pretty secretive about it. I don't think it was that serious, though. At least, I don't think he took it seriously, I'm not sure about her.'

'Where did they go when they were together?'

'I have no idea. Not the hotel. I work those nights, and they never came in. So... I don't know.'

Logan waited until Hamza had finished jotting down some notes before continuing. 'Can you think of anyone else who might have had a grievance with Fergus? Anyone at work, or in the local community?'

'No. No, I can't think of anyone who'd want to hurt him,' Ross said, then a look of shock went zooming across his face, there one moment, gone the next. His features didn't quite settle back into their original position, like they'd been forever changed by some realisation.

'Did something just occur to you, Mr Lyndsay?'

'What? No.' Ross shook his head firmly. Too firmly.

'No? I mean, from where I'm sitting it looked to me like something just occurred to you. How about you, Detective Sergeant?'

Hamza nodded his agreement. 'Definitely, sir. Something *definitely* just occurred to him, I'd say.'

Both men fixed their gazes on the man in the bed. If he could have sunk further into his pillows, he almost certainly would have.

'In a moment, I'm going to ask you that question again,' Logan warned him. 'I suggest this time you consider your answer very carefully before you give it. Do you think I made that clear enough, Detective Sergeant?'

'I'd say you made it very clear, sir,' Hamza replied. 'I can't see how you could have made it any clearer.'

'Thank you,' Logan said. Neither detective had looked at each other throughout the exchange, and Logan leaned forward now, his stare boring into Ross like it was trying to drill right through his face. 'Did something just occur to you, Mr Lyndsay? And please, take your time.'

In the bed, Ross's mouth flapped open and closed a few times, as his eyes searched for support from his solicitor.

'Don't look at him. Look at me,' Logan instructed. 'Who did you think of? Who might have wanted to kill Fergus Forsyth?'

Ross shifted in the bed. 'I doubt... I don't think he'd have wanted to kill him. But Fergus did owe him money. More than he owed me, I mean. A lot more, I think.'

Logan heard Hamza's pen start scraping across the notebook page. He gave Ross a nod of encouragement, urging him to continue.

'He's... if he finds out I set you onto him, though, he'll... he won't be happy.' Ross's eyes burned with fear as they flitted from one detective to the other in a series of twitchy little movements. 'You won't... you won't tell him it was me, will you?'

'He won't know it was you, no,' Logan promised. 'Who did Fergus owe money to, Mr Lyndsay?'

Ross seemed to get into a wrestling match with his own mouth, either trying to spit the name out or swallow it back down. It eventually emerged as the sort of shrill whisper usually only heard in horror movies.

'Dinky.'

Logan's brow wrinkled. 'Sorry?'

'Dinky,' Ross repeated, a little more clearly this time. 'He owed money to Dinky.'

'Who's Dinky?' Logan asked. 'Dinky who?'

'I don't know his second name,' Ross explained. 'He's just... he's a little guy. Smaller than me.'

'Bloody hell, what is he, an elf?' Hamza asked, the words tumbling out of him before he could stop them. He cleared his throat and smiled apologetically. 'Sorry. That was... sorry.'

'He's got dwarfism,' Ross said.

Hamza spoke again before Logan could get a word in. 'Right. And just for the record, what height are you, Mr Lyndsay?'

'I'm five foot. But what's that got to do with anything?' Ross asked.

Hamza shook his head. 'Nothing. Sorry, carry on.'

'You were saying about this Dinky fella,' Logan reminded him.

'Right. Yes. God,' Ross whimpered. 'He's sort of a... bookie, I suppose. Or like, a loan shark, maybe. I've never had anything to do with him, but I've heard stories, and I've seen him about. He's got a house near Letterfinlay. Up on the hillside, overlooking the water. You know the big straight by the loch? There. He lives there. Big white house. Got a metal shed at the side.'

'I think I've seen it,' Logan told him.

'OK, good. But, please don't tell him I told you! Don't tell him I gave you his details.' Tears welled up in Ross's eyes again. 'If he finds out, there's no saying what he might do.'

Chapter 22

The prod from Olivia was hard and sharp. It caught Jonathan almost right in the centre of his chest, and it took all his self-control not to acknowledge the pain of it.

Her features were sharper still. She'd taken to scraping her hair back in recent weeks. It made her look harder. Fiercer. She'd always looked young for her age, but now she looked older. Too old, if anything.

It wasn't just the hair, it was everything. The way she moved. The way she talked. The way her eyes had been shaded in darker. They looked matte these days, not glossy. Jonathan had never seen eyes like them before.

And he hoped that he never would again.

'Where the fuck have you been?' she demanded, pulling him into the doorway of what had once been a TV repair shop, before TVs had become cheap enough to be virtually disposable. Now it was locked and shuttered, but the inset door offered a good place to shelter from the rain, and from prying eyes.

'I got held back after Maths,' Jonathan explained.

'What did I tell you about that?' Olivia hissed. 'Don't draw attention to yourself. You're a model fucking pupil now. All right?'

'I was just talking,' Jonathan mumbled.

'Well don't. Keep your mouth shut. You've got nothing worth saying, anyway.' She prodded him in the chest again, harder this time. Jonathan gritted his teeth, then shot a sideways look at the black SUV parked across the street. 'Don't look at him, look at me,' Olivia instructed. 'Do you have the money?'

Jonathan nodded. 'Yeah.'

'Well, give me it, then!'

The boy stole another quick glance at the car and the skinhead behind the wheel. Then he unzipped his bag, pulled out a thin envelope, and handed it over.

Olivia took it, appeared very disappointed by its lack of weight, then stuffed it into her own bag.

'That's it?'

'So far, yeah. I've still got stuff left.'

'You'd fucking better have stuff left, unless they're all hundred quid notes in there,' Olivia replied. 'I want that stuff shifted by this time next week.'

Jonathan's eyes came dangerously close to popping out of their sockets. 'Next week? But there's loads of it!'

'You said you could shift it,' Olivia reminded him.

'Aye, but not all at once. I've gone round all my usual customers this week already. They're all sorted.'

Another prod to the chest, this one hard enough to make the much bigger boy flinch. 'Then find other customers,' she instructed, swinging her bag up onto her shoulder. 'Or I'll find someone who can.'

She had taken just a couple of steps out onto the street when Jonathan called after her.

'Fine. Do that. I want out, anyway.'

Olivia stopped. Turned. Marched back.

'No, you don't,' she told him.

'Aye, I do,' Jonathan insisted, his chest puffing up. 'I've had enough. It's too risky. I'm out.'

'You can't get out, Jonathan,' Olivia told him.

'Aye, I fucking can. You going to try and stop me like? I'll grass you up. All I've done is sold a bit of puff. You're the one I got it from. You'll be in the shit.'

Olivia shoved him, driving both hands against his chest hard enough to slam him back against the shuttered door.

'Look over my shoulder, Jonathan,' she said, spitting the words into his face. 'See that guy? He's ex-Russian Mafia. You think he's going to let you out? You think he'll just let you go, knowing what you know?'

The skinhead in the car was watching the tussle in the doorway. It was difficult to read his face from that distance, but Jonathan could quite confidently state he didn't look particularly pleased.

'Fine. I'll… I'll grass him up, too,' Jonathan said, which earned him a look of genuine horror from the girl currently pinning him to the metal barrier.

'Don't ever fucking say that to anyone but me,' she warned. 'And I'm going to pretend I didn't hear it. If he thinks for a second that you're going to talk to the police, you're dead. And not just you. Your mum. Your dad. You've got a wee sister, haven't you? He'll kill her first. He'll make you all watch. Worse, he'll make you all *help*. He'll make it look like a murder-suicide. Like your dad did it. Like he enjoyed it. That's why you can't get out, Jonathan. That's why none of us can. Ever.' She released her grip and stepped back, her shoulder slumping as the fight left her. 'No matter how much we might want to.'

'Fuck,' was all Jonathan could think to say about any of that. He felt it so appropriate, though, that he said it again a few times for added emphasis.

'So, same time next week, then?' Olivia asked, brightening again.

Jonathan slowly nodded. 'Um, aye. Aye. Same time next week.'

—

'What was that about?' asked the skinhead in the SUV, as Olivia jumped into the passenger seat beside him. His accent was still mostly Polish, but he'd learned much of his English growing up in Inverness, and a lot of the local twang had crept in. 'Is everything OK?'

'Yeah. He was just being a whiny little bitch,' Olivia said. 'He said he wants out.'

'Oh. Shit. Is that…? What did you say?'

Olivia grinned as she reached into her bag and pulled out the envelope Jonathan had given her. 'I said you were Russian Mafia, and that you'd kill his family.'

'Ha! Seriously?'

'Yep.'

'He didn't believe you?'

Olivia laughed. 'Totally swallowed every word. You should have seen his face. I swear to God, he nearly pissed his pants. It was hilarious.'

The skinhead gave a nervous chuckle. 'God! I actually feel bad for him now.'

'Don't. He's a dickhead,' Olivia said. She took the money from Jonathan's envelope, counted it out, then added it to a much larger bundle in the SUV's glovebox. 'Right then, Borys,' she said, once she'd closed the glovebox door again. 'I'm going to get you to drop me off at my friend's house. But first we've got a few more stops to make.'

She turned and watched the city start to move as Borys pulled away from the kerb. Her reflection looked back at her from the other side of the glass.

'Let's just hope this lot have done a better job than Jonathan.'

Chapter 23

Dinner came courtesy of one of the local takeaways, and was eaten in the Incident Room as they all took turns going over their findings for the day.

Tyler had gone first. Partly, this was because his was a relatively quick and easy update, but mostly because his Chicken Maryland had still been too hot for him to eat.

His choice of food had caused some controversy in the office, after they'd all settled on ordering something from the nearest Chinese takeaway. Logan had been frank and forthright in his insistence that there was something fundamentally wrong with anyone who ordered from the 'Western' section of a Chinese menu, and the others—even Sinead—had been quick to agree with him.

Sinead had agreed more vehemently than most, in fact, and it soon became apparent that this was not Tyler's first offence of this particular crime.

He eventually managed to steer the conversation around to the mystery key. The local locksmith based out on the Claggan Industrial Estate was currently off on holiday—in the Florida Keys, no less, which had amused Tyler no end. He had, however, been able to track down a former locksmith who still lived in the area, and sent him pictures of the key taken from a variety of angles, with accompanying measurements.

The former locksmith had written a lengthy and detailed response, and sent it over within the hour. Unfortunately, the reason for the email's length was the list of possibilities it contained. There were over twenty possible suspects, from padlocks to diaries, all ranked in no particular order because, as he pointed out in the final line of the correspondence, he quite frankly didn't have a fucking clue.

Tyler finished by asking permission to stick the photos of the key on social media to see if some randomer might recognise it. Then he hurried to his desk and got stuck into his now just cool enough to be edible Chicken Maryland which, for reasons not explained on the menu, came accompanied with a small sausage, a slice of cold bacon, and half a banana fritter.

There was some brief discussion about Fergus's mobile phone. Records had been requested from the network, along with any information on his movements in the days leading up to his death. It was hoped that these might open up some new lines of inquiry, but the network was being stubborn and insisting on all the correct paperwork being submitted, so it would take time.

The phone itself remained locked. Tyler had given it to Hamza, as the DS had a better grasp of technology than anyone else in the office, but Hamza had been too afraid of entering the six-digit PIN too many times and locking the phone to do anything with it. Ultimately, it would have to be passed on to the tech bods in the morning, so they could have a crack at it.

There had been a slim hope that Ross Lyndsay might know the PIN code, but he'd insisted that he didn't, and Logan had believed him. It was all numbers, too, so the code in Fergus's notebook wasn't it, either.

The DCI took the floor next, his mouth burning from some of the spiciest Salt and Pepper Chicken he'd ever eaten in his life.

Before he could get started, Ben stopped slurping down Chow Mein long enough to ask if the DCI had called Detective Superintendent Mitchell back yet. Logan pretended he'd forgotten, confessed that he hadn't yet called, and made assurances that he'd do so just as soon as they'd finished the briefing.

Once he had successfully pulled the wool over Ben's eyes, he went back over the Ross Lyndsay interview, with Hamza chipping in occasionally to add further details drawn from his notes.

After they'd recapped pretty much everything that had been said around the hospital bed, there was a general sense of agreement that Lyndsay probably wasn't involved in Fergus's murder.

For one thing, his size went against him—or *for* him, perhaps. He was almost certainly too small to lift a fully-grown adult body even a short distance. Corpses were heavy, awkward things, and lugging them around wasn't an easy task. It needed strength and leverage, neither of which Mr Lyndsay had been blessed with.

Ben had called and spoken to the manager who'd been on duty at the hotel in Invergarry on Monday evening, and she'd confirmed that Ross had turned up for his shift. He hadn't behaved any differently, from what she could tell. Certainly, nobody had remarked on him being quiet or withdrawn. No more so than usual, at least.

He'd been there until late, too. It had been well after midnight before they'd got the kitchen cleaned up and ready for the next day.

Could he have then gone home, removed his flatmate's head with a power tool, transported the body a couple of miles to the well—without owning or having access to a car—and disposed of it, before stuffing the head somewhere?

It was possible. Just very, *very* unlikely.

'Anyone heard of someone by the name of Dinky?' Logan asked.

'No' unless he used to make toy cars,' replied Ben.

'Loan shark. Or bookie. Possibly both,' Logan explained. 'Lives out near Letterfinlay. Apparently, Fergus owed him money. Lyndsay was scared of him when he told us. Worried about what he might do.'

'He might be on CID's radar,' Sinead said. 'Can't say I've ever heard of him, though, and I used to cover up that way back when I was in uniform.'

'Check, will you? Then, Hamza, you take Tyler up and have a word with him. Tonight, ideally. Sinead and I will go chat to that English teacher, and see if she can shed any light on anything.'

'Right you are, sir.'

'Bagsy driving,' Tyler said, spraying banana fritter onto his desk.

'Fine. As long as you don't drive like an old woman like you usually do,' Hamza said.

'I don't drive like an old woman!' Tyler protested. He wilted under the looks this earned from the others. 'OK, but just on the winding bits.'

'Anything you want me to be getting on with, Jack?' Ben asked. There was a hopeful note to the question. An enthusiasm. But there was a wariness to it, too, like he was secretly dreading the answer.

'Aye. Aye. Absolutely,' Logan said, his mind racing. 'You could… eh… oh! I know! If Tyler's up doing the interview, you could put out the social media shout on the key.'

'*Social media*?' Ben replied, screwing up his face at the very thought. 'Me? I'm not sure that's such a good idea.'

'Already did it, anyway, boss,' Tyler revealed.

'Right. OK. Good. In that case, Ben, you could… you could check if any new reports have come in from Shona or Geoff Palmer's team.'

'I looked a minute ago, sir,' Hamza announced. 'Nothing new.'

'Still. Worth checking again,' Logan said. 'You never know if—'

'Nothing, boss,' Tyler said. 'Just did a refresh.'

'Did you? Did you? Thanks for that,' Logan said, glowering at the DC. As this was no different to the expression the DCI usually wore when talking to him, Tyler didn't pick up on it, and simply smiled back in response.

'No bother, boss. You know me, always happy to help.'

'I suppose I could start filling out some of the paperwork. Book an interview room for tomorrow, in case we want to bring someone in,' Ben suggested. 'Keep Mantits happy.'

'Aye!' Logan said, seizing the suggestion. 'Aye, that sounds like a plan. You do that, then maybe head back to the hotel. We did get a hotel, didn't we?'

'Premier Inn,' Sinead confirmed. 'They're even throwing in breakfast.'

Logan nodded approvingly. It was, after all, the most important meal of the day.

'Good stuff. Ben, once you've finished the filing, head back there and get some rest,' Logan told him.

'Rest? Why? I'm no' tired, Jack,' Ben insisted. 'I'm not a bloody invalid.'

'No, I know,' Logan said. 'I'm just… it's your first day back.'

'Second.'

'First *official* day back,' Logan countered. 'No point jumping in headfirst. Ease yourself back in. There'll be plenty of time for you to get your teeth into the other stuff.'

Ben begrudgingly agreed, but it was clear to everyone that he wasn't happy about it. Still, better unhappy than landing himself back in hospital again.

Or maybe even worse next time.

'You can sit in on any interviews we do here,' Logan said.

'Oh, that's very kind of you, Jack,' said Ben, sarcasm dripping from every word. 'But are you sure? I'd hate to be a liability. Don't want me nodding off halfway through.'

'That's not what—' Logan began, but Ben was up on his feet, his nose held aloft.

'If you'll excuse me, I'll go see if I can find those forms,' he announced. 'It'll take these old bones a while to get there, and my eyes aren't what they used to be.'

Logan and the others watched him shuffle towards the door, one hand resting on his lower back. It was only when he'd left that Tyler finally broke the silence.

'Was he really annoyed, or was all that just a wind-up, boss?' he wondered.

Logan shrugged and relinquished a sigh he'd been holding onto for a while. 'Honestly, son? I have absolutely no idea.'

Shona Maguire stood at the window of her cottage, the smell of popcorn drifting through the air around her.

The sun was on the wane, and its fading light danced across the waters of the Beauly Firth just a little way down the hill from where her house stood. Shona wasn't looking at that, though. She was looking for something that wasn't currently there.

Olivia was late. Twenty minutes now. Cancelling the night before was one thing, but being late wasn't like her. At least, it hadn't been like her until recently. She'd always turned up early—stupidly early, sometimes, before Shona had even arrived home from work.

That had changed a few months back. Now every time she visited, she arrived a few minutes later than before. Shona wouldn't have cared, but she'd become more distant over the same time period. Withdrawn. It was like there was always something on her mind these days. Some distraction. Some burden she was having to bear.

It couldn't be easy, of course, with her dad in prison and her mum a useless cow—Olivia's words, not Shona's. She'd been forced to change schools, and there had been some drama involved in the transition, to put it very mildly.

Shona remembered her own teenage years. All the stresses and pressures, both real and imagined. The problems she'd had fitting in.

Whoever said that your school days were the best days of your life hadn't gone to Shona's school. Hadn't walked in her shoes. Hadn't seen what she'd seen, or faced what she'd faced.

And then, of course, there were the Troubles. Like being a teenager wasn't hard enough without an ongoing civil war to contend with.

She shook her head, dragging herself back from the past and into the present, just as a black SUV drew up at the front of the house. It wasn't her usual taxi, but Olivia was in the front passenger seat. The driver beside her was in his mid-twenties,

Shona would estimate. Shaved head. Brow that didn't suggest a deep thinker.

Something about him—everything about him—made her want to step back from the window and draw the curtains shut.

Shona watched Olivia tap her watch, and point to the floor. The skinhead nodded once, waited for her to get out, then pulled a tight U-turn and revved noisily off in the direction of the Kessock Bridge, headed back to Inverness.

Olivia gave a wave as she came up the path, and opened the front door without knocking.

'Hello!' she called, stomping her feet on the mat.

'Hi. I was starting to think you weren't coming,' Shona said, meeting her in the hall.

Olivia frowned. 'Am I late?'

'It's fine.'

'I had stuff I had to sort out,' Olivia explained.

'Still busy, then?'

Olivia smiled. 'Yeah. Yeah, something like that.'

She was being cagey. Her vagueness set alarm bells ringing. 'Is everything OK at home, Olivia?'

'Fine. Yeah.'

'Because if it's not...'

'It is. And it wasn't a home thing. It was a work thing.'

Shona's eyebrows arched. 'Work? I didn't know you had a job. When did this start?'

Olivia shrugged, took off her jacket, and hung it on the peg behind the door. 'Just sort of fell into my lap a while back,' she said, then she rubbed her hands together and sniffed the air. 'Do I smell popcorn?'

'You do,' Shona confirmed. 'Sweet and salted.'

'Get in!'

Before Olivia could head through to the living room, Shona nodded in the direction she'd come from. 'Who was that dropping you off? A friend? He looks a lot older.'

'So are you,' Olivia pointed out.

'Well, yes, but—'

'He's not a friend. He's just someone I work with.'

Shona's eyes crept to the door, like she was trying to see through it and all the way along the road to the bridge. 'Oh. Right. And what's the job? What is it you're actually doing?'

'It's a distribution company,' Olivia replied. 'Small at the moment, but we've got big plans to expand.' She smiled and very deliberately sniffed the air again. 'Now, about that popcorn…'

Chapter 24

DC Neish and DS Khaled sat in Tyler's car, the setting sun skipping across the surface of the unimaginatively named Loch Lochy down the hillside behind them, and a small whitewashed stone cottage nestling amongst the trees fifty yards up the slope ahead of them.

'See? Didn't drive like an old woman, did I?' said Tyler, as he shut off the engine and unfastened his seatbelt.

'Well, you did at the winding bits,' Hamza pointed out.

'Yeah, but I didn't want you throwing up in my car, did I?' Tyler protested.

'I think I'd have been all right. My stomach can cope with speeds greater than twenty-five miles an hour.'

'Bollocks it was twenty-five! And even if it was, some of those bends are pretty hairy.'

'Unlike your chest, ye big Jessie,' Hamza chuckled. He opened the door and wiped his smile away with a rub of his hand. 'Right. Game faces on. You ready?'

'Ready, Sarge,' Tyler confirmed, snapping off a salute.

'You can knock that on the head, for a bloody start.'

'Sorry, Sarge. Don't shout at me, Sarge,' Tyler whimpered, as they both got out of the car. 'I hate it when you stamp your authority, Sarge.'

Hamza gave the DC the finger, then led the way up the track to the ramshackle front gate that led to a garden of weeds, gravel, and dog shit.

A sign on the gate warned them to 'Beware of the Dog', but other than the regularly-dotted shite coils, there was no sign of one.

'Here, boy,' Hamza called in a sing-song voice. 'Heeere, boy.'

'What the fuck are you doing?' Tyler asked.

'Checking if the dog's around.'

'Why?'

'Because it says "Beware of the Dog".'

Tyler tutted. 'It probably just says that to keep Jehovah's Witnesses out.'

'Have you seen the size of those turds?' Hamza asked. 'What dog shites like that? The Hound of the Baskervilles?'

Tyler had to admit that they were sizeable deposits. Whatever breed of dog had left them was likely to be a monster. But they could see a full three sides of the garden, and there wasn't a dog—giant or otherwise—in sight.

Besides, he was still smarting a little from the 'big Jessie' comment and was keen to reassert himself.

'You're worrying about nothing,' he said, reaching for the gate. 'If there is a dog, we'll pat it. All right? We'll calm it down. We're a couple of bright lads, Sarge. I'm sure we'll figure it out.'

The gate gave a two-note creak as Tyler pushed it open. It sounded almost like a trumpet-call—one low note, then a second higher one as the rusty hinges continued to swing.

Tyler was halfway up the path when the fucking thing came careening around from the back of the house, all teeth and drool and eyes like burning coals. It moved like a bullet of furry fury, its paws rarely appearing to touch the ground as it rocketed towards the detectives.

The barking reached them a moment later, as if the dog was travelling too fast for the sound to keep up with it.

Tyler ejected a breathless 'shit!' then raced back out through the gate and slammed it shut a fraction of a second before the dog collided with it.

If the detectives thought the creaking of the gate had wound the dog up, then crashing into the thing drove the animal full-on bananas. It snapped, snarled, foamed, frothed, its lithe, muscular body vibrating with a rage it had no hope of managing to contain, even if the thought had occurred to it.

'Jesus!' Tyler yelped, drawing back from the gate just as the dog tried to force its head through the bars.

'I told you, didn't I?' Hamza said. 'It's on the sign. "Beware of the Dog". I told you.'

'I don't think that's even a dog, though,' Tyler wheezed. 'That's a fucking bear, isn't it?'

This was, of course, an exaggeration. The animal was definitely a dog. Quite what kind of dog, however, was more difficult to pin down. There was some Rottweiler there. A bit of Bulldog, a pinch of German Shepherd, and a liberal sprinkling of *Cujo*, from the Stephen King novel of the same name.

Tyler's notion of calming it down suddenly seemed child-like and naive. It would take more than some soft words and a bit of patting to soothe this beast. An electric net and a tranquilliser dart might do the job, but even that felt like a bit of a stretch.

'If that thing doesn't have rabies, I don't know what does,' Tyler said.

The initial panic of being in the same enclosed space as the animal was fading now that it was safely on the other side of the metal gate.

Given the energy it was devoting to trying to force its way through, though, there was no saying it would remain on the other side for long.

'I have an idea,' said Hamza.

'Is it "call in an orbital strike"?'

'No. I'll distract it, and you go knock on the door.'

'Fuck off!' Tyler cried. 'No chance! It'll eat me alive!'

'Like I said, I'll distract it.'

Tyler's voice ramped up an octave. 'How are you going to distract *that*?'

'I don't know. I could… I could throw a ball for it,' Hamza suggested.

DC Neish scowled. 'A ball? Fuck a ball, maybe if you throw a hand grenade for it to catch, it might slow it down and buy us a few seconds, but a *ball*? I'm not going in there, even if you give it *your* balls to play with.'

'We need to go see if this Dinky fella's at home,' Hamza reminded him.

'Fine. I'll distract it, then, and you be the one to go knock on the door.'

Hamza side-eyed the frothy-mouthed maniac mongrel currently trying to chew through the bars of the gate, then he drew himself up to his full height. 'I'm the one giving the orders around here, sunshine,' he said.

'Oh. It's like that, is it?' asked Tyler. 'That's where we've got to, is it? Pulling rank? Well, what do you think of this?'

Still watching Hamza, Tyler sidestepped along the front fence a few paces, away from the gate. The dog followed, barking and snarling, its coal-black eyes fixating hungrily on him.

Tyler returned to the gate, and the dog did the same, then turned its attention back to trying to gnaw through solid metal.

'It's me the fucker wants, not you. I was the one in the garden,' Tyler pointed out, ashen-faced. 'I'll lead it around the back. You go over the gate and sneak up to the house. Then, phone me when you're ready to come out, and I'll keep it busy.'

Hamza regarded the dog. He looked along the path to the front door. There was nobody at the windows. If someone was home, they were bound to have heard all the commotion out front. Which meant either the house was empty, or whoever was inside couldn't give a shit about who or what his dog chose to set about.

'Right, fine,' he sighed. He undid the knot on his tie and put it in his pocket, then undid the top button of his shirt.

'That going to make you faster, like?' Tyler asked.

'Just… shut up. This is your fault,' Hamza told him.

'How is it my fault?'

'Just go. Get the bloody thing around the back. And make sure you keep it there!'

Tyler nodded, winked, then kicked the mesh fence as hard as he could, rattling it against the posts.

'Come on then, you big hairy bastard,' he spat, dancing along the front of the fence. He thrust a hand over the top, then whipped it away just before teeth snapped shut around it. 'You want me? Come and get me!'

—

'God, he's so shiny,' Olivia remarked. 'He's such a shiny man.'

Shona's mouth was full of popcorn, so she could only nod and make noises of agreement.

'It's like he's been polished,' Olivia continued as, on screen, Arnold Schwarzenegger went trudging through a jungle with a big gun and a facial expression that suggested he'd been heavily constipated for several days. 'Like someone's buffed him up.'

Shona swallowed her popcorn. 'Yeah. I think this is his shiniest role,' she said. 'He's pretty shiny in *Commando*, too, but I think this is peak-shine.' She reached into the bowl and grabbed a handful of popcorn before it was all gone, then gestured to the screen with it. 'Just wait, though. If you think he's shiny, hold on until you see—'

'Holy shit, look at him!' Olivia laughed, stabbing a finger at the telly. A bald black man came staggering out of the trees, his skin sporting such a sheen he could've been made of glass. 'Has he been swimming in baby oil? No wonder the alien can track them down, they're all so shiny they must be glowing!'

Shona dropped her voice into her Arnie impression again. 'Don't make fun of my shiny muscles! Or I'll be back.'

Olivia tilted a hand back and forth, suggesting an iffy performance. 'Three out of ten,' she said, reaching for more popcorn.

'Three? That was a solid six!' Shona protested.

'It was a three. And that's generous,' Olivia insisted. '"I'll be back!" That's six out of ten.'

'That sounds exactly like how I said it!' Shona protested. '"I'll be back!"'

'"I'll be back!"'

'"*I'll be back*!"'

'Meh. Still not great. Maybe five,' Olivia said, then they went back to watching the movie.

They were sitting side by side on the couch, their feet pulled up at their sides, the popcorn bowl sitting between them. There had been no more talk of Olivia's late arrival, of her new job, or her mysterious skin-headed co-worker. And they hadn't even touched on her last-minute cancellation the night before.

For a while, Shona had dreaded Olivia's visits. Their relationship had started from a strange place, with Shona essentially being complicit in her kidnapping. When the girl had continued to invite herself over for movie nights, Shona had initially tried to find ways out of it. Olivia had been tenacious, though, and rarely took no for an answer.

Eventually, Shona had surrendered to her fate, and accepted that weekly movie nights with the teenage daughter of a jailed Russian drug kingpin were now just a thing that happened in her life.

Over the months that followed, though, she'd come to enjoy the visits. Olivia could be good company, and it was always a pleasure to educate the younger generation on some true cinematic greats. Besides, Shona had enjoyed revisiting some long-forgotten classics, too.

She'd always been careful, though, to steer herself away from the role of 'much older best friend' in Olivia's eyes, and tried to position herself as a stable adult figure with concerns for the girl's wellbeing.

As such, she always felt something of a responsibility to be a sounding board for any challenges Olivia might be facing.

Unfortunately, Olivia was rarely forthcoming.

'How was school?' Shona asked, during a lull in the movie's action.

'Fine,' Olivia said with a shrug.

'No drama?'

'Nah.'

'That boy not still bothering you?'

Olivia's hand paused with her popcorn halfway to her mouth. 'Jonathan? No,' she said, after a moment. 'I sorted him out.'

'That's good. But remember… if there's anything… I know it's not easy to tell your mum things, sometimes, so if there's anything you're worried about. Any concerns. If anyone's bullying you, or—'

'Bullying me?' Olivia turned to her, a look of amusement on her face. 'Ha. Nobody's bullying me. Believe me.'

'Right. Good. That's… great,' Shona said, pleased to hear it. 'It's just, you said before that some of the kids were giving you grief.'

'They stopped,' Olivia said.

Something about the way she said it made Shona miss a beat. 'They stopped?'

'I stopped them.'

The puzzled look on Shona's face told the girl she needed more information.

'I had a word with them,' Olivia elaborated. 'We talked it over.'

'Oh! Good! And… what? They just stopped picking on you? Just like that?'

Olivia nodded. Smiled. Or smirked, maybe. 'Yes,' she confirmed. 'Just like that.'

She fished the last of the popcorn out of the bowl, stuffed some in her mouth, then turned back to the screen.

'It wasn't difficult. You can make people do pretty much anything,' she remarked, as several shiny men shot guns at trees on the TV screen. 'You just have to find the right motivation.'

Chapter 25

Logan and Sinead were shown into the neat living room of a compact semi-detached house, presented with tea, biscuits, and an apology for the greeting they'd initially been given.

'Clyde doesn't like visitors. Especially during dinner,' Lana Lennon explained. 'He didn't know you were... if he had, he'd never have spoken to you like... well.'

She smiled apologetically, then hovered by the armchair on the opposite side of the coffee table to where the detectives were sitting, as if waiting for permission to sit.

'That's quite all right, Mrs Lennon. I'm much the same myself,' Logan assured her. 'And it must be a difficult time.'

Lana wrung her hands together. 'Difficult time?'

'Yes.' The DCI waited for some moment of realisation, then continued when it didn't come. 'I understand Mr Forsyth was a friend of yours.'

'Mr... Fergus?' She smoothed down the front of her jumper and shot a wary look at the living room door. 'I don't... sorry, what's this about?'

'You didn't hear?' asked Sinead. 'Sorry, we thought Cops—uh, I mean, we thought Mrs Robertson at the school would've told you.'

'Told me what?' Lana asked. The senior detective's previous words suddenly hit her properly, and she lowered herself onto the armchair. 'What do you mean "*was* a friend" of mine?'

Logan was happy to sit back and let Sinead handle this part. When it came to breaking bad news to people, she was a natural—sympathetic without being patronising, to-the-point without ever being blunt. She knew how to deal with grieving people. God knew, she'd been through it herself enough.

'I'm sorry to have to tell you that yesterday morning Mr Forsyth was found dead,' Sinead said.

'Dead?'

'I'm afraid he was attacked.'

'Attacked?'

This sort of reaction was par for the course, in Logan's experience. He called it 'the echo'—when a person receiving bad news wanted so badly for it to not be true that they turned it around and bounced it straight back, rather than take it in.

'What do you mean, he was attacked?' Lana cried. 'What do you mean he's dead? How? Why? I don't... how can he be dead? How can Fergus be *dead*?'

She realised her tone was creeping higher and higher, glanced at the door, then swallowed as she fought to bring her voice back under control.

'I understand what a shock this must be for you, Mrs Lennon,' Sinead said. 'Mrs Robertson mentioned that you and Fergus were close.'

There was that look again, the eyes going to the door, the moment of panic at what she might find there.

'Would you like to discuss this elsewhere, Mrs Lennon?' Logan asked her.

'What? No. I don't...' Her voice was a whisper now, nothing more. 'I just... God. I don't know why she'd say that. Please don't repeat that. My husband wouldn't... it's not... Fergus was... there wasn't...'

She buried her face in her hands and her shoulders heaved. Logan and Sinead would have been content to leave her there to pull herself together, had a grunt from the doorway not snapped her upright like she was spring-loaded.

'So, what's all this about, then?' Clyde barked.

He'd been drinking. Not a lot, but enough. Logan could spot the signs a mile away.

'Nothing!' Lana practically sang. Her face was a clown-mask, the smile contorting her features into something grotesque in its desperation to please. 'Just... it's nothing.'

'I wasn't asking you,' Clyde told her. 'I was asking them.'

'We're just asking a few questions about an incident connected to the school,' Logan said, getting to his feet. He enjoyed watching Clyde's head tilt back to follow his progress. Although, give the man his due, he didn't appear to be remotely intimidated.

'Christ. What's she done now?' Clyde asked.

'It's nothing like that, Mr Lennon,' Logan said. 'Maybe you and I can have a chat in the kitchen?'

Panic flashed behind Lana's eyes, but Logan made her a promise with a nod and a thin-lipped smile, then gestured for Clyde to lead the way, leaving Sinead and Lana alone in the front room.

'I'm not sure if you remember me, Mrs Lennon,' the DC began. There was no need to go any further.

'Of course I do, Sinead,' the teacher said, mustering an expression that looked fractionally less grief-stricken. 'It's lovely to see you. He won't say anything, will he? To Clyde?'

'No.'

'Are you sure? How can you be sure?'

'Because I know him,' Sinead said. 'He might not look it, but he's a big softy. He could see you're scared. We both can. He won't say anything that could make things... difficult for you.'

Lana still seemed unconvinced, but her hand-wringing became a little less anxious. She nodded. 'If... if you're sure.'

God, she was terrified. Not of Sinead or Logan, but of the man she'd married. As she realised this, half-forgotten memories pinged back to the surface of Sinead's mind.

Mrs Lennon with a black eye.

Mrs Lennon with a swollen lip.

Mrs Lennon holding her ribs, too sore to sit down for the whole lesson.

She'd made her clumsiness a running joke with the class. Her trips and falls. Her knocks and scrapes.

'Two left feet,' she'd say.

'Never watching where I'm going,' she'd say.

'I really should learn to pay more attention!' she'd say.

And they'd smile. And they'd laugh. And they'd think no more about it.

'If he's hurting you, Mrs Lennon, we can help,' Sinead of the here and the now said, desperately trying to compensate for the failings of Sinead of the there and the then.

How hadn't she seen? Why hadn't she said something? Told someone?

'What? No. God, no. He just... he has...' Lana shook her head and clenched her fists down by her side, burying them in so tightly against her hips she was almost sitting on them. 'Fergus. What... what happened? If you can say. Can you say? What happened?'

Sinead was loathe to move on so quickly and leave the domestic abuse discussion behind, but Lana clearly had no interest in discussing it any further.

'He was found yesterday by a tour group,' Sinead said. 'We don't know for sure yet exactly how he was killed.'

'Oh!' Lana perked up at that. 'So maybe he wasn't killed, then? Maybe it was natural causes? Or... or an accident. Could it have been an accident?'

Sinead explained that it was none of those things, then explained why they were able to be so certain.

Lana cried some more at that. And who could possibly blame her?

'Mrs Robertson said she thought you and Fergus were... close,' Sinead said, once Lana had composed herself again. It was a question very thinly disguised as a statement, and Lana's response was instantaneous.

'No! That's not... I don't know what she's talking about! She shouldn't say things like that if they're not... if they aren't...'

From where Sinead was sitting, it looked as if her old teacher's batteries just ran out at that point, or some key in her back stopped turning. She just sat there, frozen, half-sitting on her hands, her eyes misting over.

'Mrs Lennon?' Sinead said. There was no immediate response from Lana, and Sinead was a half-second away from waving a hand in front of the woman's face when she rebooted.

'Yes,' she said, in a voice so faint that Sinead initially thought she might have imagined it.

'Sorry? Did you say...?'

'We were close.' Lana was still keeping the volume down, but there was a strength to her voice now that hadn't been there a moment before. Her gaze flitted to the door again, then up to the ceiling above them. 'You won't tell them, will you? My husband and son? They don't need to know, do they?'

'Honestly? That depends on what happens with the investigation,' Sinead admitted. 'If it's at all possible, then no, they won't. Right now, it's just you and me talking, Mrs Lennon.'

'Call me Lana, for God's sake. We're not in school now, Sinead.'

Sinead smiled. 'Lana, then. Right now, it's just you and me talking. That's all. I want to figure out what happened to Fergus. I want to find who killed him. And I think you probably do, too.'

'Yes. Yes, of course,' Lana said. She inhaled slowly through her nose, closed her eyes, and then breathed out through her mouth until her lungs were almost empty. 'Right then,' she said, opening her eyes again. They were focused now. She was ready. 'Where do you want to start?'

—

'Nice table,' Logan remarked, running the flat of his hand across the smooth grain of the wood.

Clyde's response came curtly. 'You can buy it, if you want,' he said, and Logan wasn't sure if he was joking or not.

'Wouldn't really fit in my kitchen,' Logan said, oddly embarrassed to admit that he had a dining room these days, as if this revelation would open him up to a ribbing from this total stranger.

'Well, if you know anyone, I'm doing them cheap. They're solid, too. None of your shite,' Clyde said, and Logan recognised it as a sales pitch.

'What, did you build it, or something?' he asked, taking a seat in one of the matching wooden chairs. The set was solid and rustic, and if Logan had been in the market for a dining room table and chairs, he'd have been tempted to take a punt.

Clyde confirmed with a nod and a shrug, then looked to the door that led out into the hall and tilted his head, straining to make out the quiet murmuring from the living room.

'You couldn't stick that kettle on, could you, Mr Lennon?' Logan asked. 'Been a long day.'

Clyde didn't hide his irritation as he filled the kettle from the tap, slammed it back onto its base, and slapped the button down. The fill-level window lit up, and an almost inaudible rumble indicated the water boiling process had begun.

That should drown things out for a while.

'You've got a workshop, then?' Logan asked.

'What?'

'For the woodwork. I assume you don't build them here?'

'Oh. Right. Yes.'

'What other stuff do you make?'

'Anything. Why?'

Logan ran his hand across the table again, taking time to examine the edges. 'It's good work. What sort of tools are involved in making something like this?'

'Look, just get to the fucking point, and tell me what all this is about,' Clyde barked. 'You're not here to talk about tables.'

'No,' Logan admitted.

'So, why are you here? What's the silly bitch gone and done now? Speeding, was she? Hit another car and drive off, did she? Fucking hell. More stress. Just what I bloody need. I'm already shitting blood.'

'Sorry?' asked Logan. He'd never heard that particular euphemism for being stressed before. 'Is that a local phrase, or...?'

'No. I'm shitting actual blood. Out of my arse. At work today. And now this!' He shook his head. 'More fucking stress. You married?'

'Divorced,' Logan said.

'Aye, well, you want my advice? Keep it that way,' Clyde said. 'First time's bad enough, second time's worse. First one was a headache, but this one? Fuck me. Talk about stress! And me shitting blood, and all.'

The kettle was coming to the boil. Logan waited for it to finish before continuing the conversation.

'Thanks for the advice. And don't worry, your wife hasn't done anything wrong, Mr Lennon. Nothing to stress about,' he said. 'We're talking to all the teachers in the school about an incident that occurred involving another member of staff.'

Clyde sneered. Either he thought Logan was lying, or he was furious his night had been interrupted over something so trivial.

'I'd love that cup of tea now, if you don't mind,' Logan told him.

There was some muttering, some thumping of mugs and cupboard doors, and some sloshing of hot water, then Logan's tea was presented to him, teabag still bobbing around on the surface, a teaspoon sticking out of the murky liquid like the neck of the Loch Ness Monster.

Clyde himself didn't partake. Instead, he opened the fridge, removed one of several cans of Tennent's Lager, and scoofed down a series of long, thirsty gulps.

'Has your wife ever mentioned Fergus Forsyth, Mr Lennon?' Logan asked, plunging his teabag down to the bottom of the mug with his spoon.

Clyde burped. 'Fuck. You mean the PE teacher?'

'She's spoken about him, then?'

'No.' Clyde pointed up to the ceiling. 'But he goes on about him non-fucking stop.'

Logan followed the other man's finger. 'Who?'

'Bennet. My boy. Lazy little shit. Won't do a bit of exercise, just sits on his arse playing stupid bloody games, but hero-worships that fucking PE teacher, all the same.' He took another gulp of lager, then adopted a high-pitched, whining voice. '"Oh, Fergus is so funny! You should've heard what he said in class today!"' With his free hand, Clyde fired off a wanking gesture. 'I mean, *fuck off*!'

'Fergus?' Logan asked, the word jumping out at him. 'He calls him by his first name?'

'They all do! It's his whole fucking "down with the kids" bullshit,' Clyde said. 'Wanker. Wants to be their mate, that's his problem. You don't earn a teenager's respect by being their fucking mate!'

'Spare the rod, spoil the child,' said Logan.

'Exactly! Ex-fucking-actly!' Clyde said, pointing at Logan like they were comrades in arms. 'Course, you can't say that now, can you? Discipline's a dirty word. Supposed to let them say what they want to you, and just grin and bloody bear it. Meant to let them come home late, go where they want, talk to fucking whoever. Madness. I had many's a thick ear in my day.' He swallowed down another mouthful and burped loudly. 'Never did me any harm.'

'And what about your wife?' Logan asked.

Clyde paused with his can almost at his lips. 'What about her?'

'She ever need slapped into line?'

Logan was stirring his tea, slowly swirling the bag around in the mug. He had no intentions of drinking it. It was a prop, nothing more. The clink of the spoon on the inside of the cup sounded deafening in the silence of the kitchen.

'Oh, I see what this is,' Clyde muttered. 'Yeah. OK. I see. What's she been saying? What am I meant to have done?'

Logan finished stirring his tea, and set the hot spoon down on the table with a clunk. 'I don't know, Mr Lennon. You tell me,' he said. 'What *have* you done?'

—

Lachlan had made it clear that he wasn't comfortable with this, but Bennet had virtually begged. He stood halfway down the stairs, breath held, weight balanced in such a way that he could beat as quiet and quick a retreat as possible.

He'd been straining to hear the conversation going on in the living room when the big guy had taken Clyde through to the kitchen. It had happened so suddenly that Lachlan had no time to escape, and he could do nothing but stand there frozen like the prey of some apex predator, braced for the snapping of hungry jaws.

They had passed the foot of the stairs without looking up, and Lachlan's heart had started beating again at the sound of the kitchen door closing.

It had been Bennet's idea to listen in. He'd been too scared to do it himself, though. Too worried about getting caught. They'd been friends for a year or so now, and Lachlan had always been the older one. The bolder one. The bigger brother. He could say things to Clyde that Bennet wouldn't dare. And now, it seemed, he was also in charge of the espionage department.

'What are they saying?' Bennet whispered from the top of the stairs.

'I have no idea,' Lachlan whispered back. 'The kettle's boiling in the kitchen, and your mum's talking really quietly.'

'Get a bit closer,' Bennet urged.

'Fuck off! You get a bit closer!' Lachlan hissed back. 'That's the police. I'm not getting mixed up in… whatever this is.' He looked up the steps behind him. 'What is it, anyway? Why are the police here?'

'That's what I want to find out,' Bennet said, but there was something off about the delivery. He knew more than he was letting on, Lachlan thought.

'You don't have *any* idea?' he asked. 'You sure?'

Bennet started to say, 'no', but his mouth clamped itself shut around the lie, turning it into a pained sort of 'nnng' instead. He nodded, just once, then looked down at his feet. The toes hung over the edge of the top step like he was getting ready to launch himself into the abyss.

Or headfirst down the stairs, at least.

Lachlan crept up a step. The voices downstairs became fainter.

'What is it?' he asked. 'What's happened?'

Bennet's lips were sealed shut, but his jaw was moving up, and down, and side to side. The movements became more and more agitated until it looked like he was fighting to contain an increasingly irate wasp.

Lachlan took another step closer. Close enough to notice the shake of Bennet's hands. Close enough to hear the crack in his voice.

'It's that... remember that teacher I told you about?'

'Who? The horrible old cow, or the nice one?'

'The nice one. Fergus.' Bennet looked up, and his eyes were two dark hollows. 'He's dead,' he said. The words were whispered, yet they filled the stairway around them. 'He's been murdered.'

—

Shona Maguire's eyes were watching *Predator*, but her mind was otherwise occupied. Something about what Olivia had said—or maybe the way she said it—was bothering her.

You can make people do pretty much anything. You just have to find the right motivation.

She hadn't sounded like the girl Shona had come to know over the past year and a bit. She'd been smiling when she'd said it, but there had been something cold there. Something almost threatening.

'What about you?' asked Olivia, derailing Shona's train of thought.

Shona blinked. '*What about me* what?'

'How was work? Anything exciting happening?'

'You know I can't really talk about that,' Shona said.

'I heard there was a guy who had his head chopped off,' Olivia said. She shot Shona a sideways look, caught the look of surprise on her face, then went back to watching the screen. 'It's true, then.'

'How did you...?' Shona began, before she shook off the surprise. 'Again, I can't really talk about it.'

'It's fine. I don't care,' Olivia said.

'Where did you hear?'

'Around. Just, you know, sources.'

'Sources?'

Olivia nodded. 'They told me. I hear a lot from them.'

Shona studied the girl's profile. It was giving nothing away.

'Do you?' she asked.

'I do.'

'What sort of things do you hear about?'

Olivia gave a one-shouldered shrug. 'All sorts.'

'For example...' Shona said, teasing the information out of her.

Olivia side-eyed her again for a moment, then went back to facing the screen. 'Like the bodies found in that freezer last month,' she said. 'In the old butcher's shop on the estate. I heard about that. Dealers, weren't they? I heard that serial killer guy did them in.'

'That's what you heard, is it?'

Olivia nodded, just once. 'Yep.'

'Well, you might want to check your sources, then,' Shona said, turning her attention back to the film.

'What? What do you mean?'

Shona smiled enigmatically. 'Just... maybe don't believe everything you hear.'

Olivia's eyebrows almost met in the middle. 'What? But... that's what happened. I know that's what happened. I was... told. They told me.'

Shona's smile broadened further. 'They told you wrong. I mean, you're almost right. You're close, but there's one thing your sources messed up.'

'They can't. How? What is it?' Olivia demanded. She was sitting forward now, the film forgotten.

Shona's smile faded when she saw the worry lines scribbled all over the girl's face. 'It's been in the paper, already, so I suppose I can tell you. There weren't two bodies in the freezer,' she said. 'There was one.'

'One? What do you mean, "one"? How could there only be one?'

'A Latvian guy. But you're right, a dealer, they think,' Shona said. 'Definitely just the one body, though.'

And with that, the bottom fell out of Olivia Maximuke's world.

Chapter 26

Hamza tapped lightly but urgently on the peeling front door of the house, painfully aware that the slightest sound might summon the hellhound. He could still hear it barking and snarling somewhere around the side of the building, along with the sound of Tyler clapping, whistling, and shouting the occasional insult as he goaded the animal on.

'Come on and eat me then, you four-legged bastard' had been Hamza's personal favourite so far, although 'I bet your dad shagged a pug' put in a respectable showing for second place.

There was no sound from inside the house. The door was a decrepit, rotting thing, and the two glass panels fixed into it were weathered by a lifetime of dirt and grime.

Hamza tapped again. 'Come on, come on,' he whispered.

The dog stopped barking.

Hamza went rigid. Held his breath. Performed a series of advanced calculations that took in the distance from the door to the gate, the speed at which he could run, and how far away the dog had sounded, and ultimately concluded that he was in deep shit.

'Oi! Bollock-breath! Over here!'

The barking started up again. Hamza exhaled silently. He was about to knock for a third time when a lock clunked and the door was opened just far enough for a security chain to pull tight.

A face appeared in the gap just a little higher than Hamza's waist height. Despite the relatively short distance between it and the ground, the head appeared to be adult-sized, with a scar on one cheek, and a thick, luxurious moustache like a 70s porn star.

'What you want?' the little man demanded. Hamza had been expecting a helium-style falsetto, but the guy sounded like he'd been gargling with gravel. Shut your eyes, and he was an old-school Glasgow hard man, ready to chib anyone who looked at him the wrong way.

'Uh, hi. Are you...' Hamza almost couldn't bring himself to say the word. Then he remembered the dog, and his sense of self-preservation forced it out of him. '...Dinky?'

'Who's asking?'

Hamza produced his warrant card. 'Detective Sergeant Hamza Khaled,' he said. From the other side of the house, he heard a frenzied howl, and his buttocks clenched so suddenly his arse nearly folded inwards. 'Mind if I come in and ask you a few questions?'

—

A few moments before Hamza got an answer at the door, Tyler was feeling pretty pleased with himself. He'd found his rhythm now and, as a result, keeping the dog distracted was turning out to be a walk in the park.

All he had to do was keep walking, and the mutt would follow. If it started to get distracted, he could wave his arms around, or clap his hands, or make some disparaging remarks about its heritage, and he'd have its full attention once again.

The dog, for its part, was less happy about the situation. Tyler had been called to deal with a few stray dog situations when he was back in Uniform, but this was the angriest bastard of a thing he'd ever seen. And it wasn't even a close-run thing. He had no doubt whatsoever that, given the opportunity, the dog would eat him alive. Literally.

And possibly without having to chew.

He plodded on a little further, keeping one eye on the snarling demon-beast, and another on the house. They were almost around the back of the cottage now, where an old-style

Volkswagen Beetle stood propped up on bricks, most of its parts long-since cannibalised.

The curtains were all drawn, Tyler thought, although the green-tinged grime on the windows made it difficult to say for certain. There was no sign of movement, though, and had it not been for the dog in the garden looking quite so well fed, Tyler would've guessed the place had been abandoned for months.

Shit. The dog!

It had stopped a few paces back, and now stood with its head cocked and an ear pointed to the sky, a growl growing at the back of its throat.

Tyler did a sudden star jump, clapping his hands together above his head. 'Oi! Bollock-breath! Over here!' he yelped.

That did the trick. The animal charged at the fence, teeth bared, long strings of saliva swinging from its slavering jaws. Despite the barrier between them, Tyler skipped back a few steps. Each furious bark shot past him like the crack of a bullet. They echoed off the hillside and rolled away across the bracken and heather.

'Yeah, yeah, very good. Woof, woof, woof,' Tyler mocked. 'Everyone's very impressed by the racket you're making. That was a lie, by the way. Everyone hates you.'

He continued on, headed for the very back of the house—the furthest point from the front door. This time, he side-stepped, keeping a closer eye on the mutt.

With a bit of luck, Hamza would already be inside. Keeping the dog occupied until he had finished asking his questions shouldn't be too much trouble. His mere existence seemed to be enough to hold its attention for now.

'Like taking candy from a baby,' Tyler said.

The next side-step brought him level with a gap in the fence.

Quite a big gap.

Two whole missing panels, in fact.

Tyler stared at the space where that part of the fence should have been. His head shook from side to side, like it was refusing to believe what it was seeing.

The dog stopped barking.

Tyler swallowed, smiled, then took a slow sideways step back in the direction he'd come, hoping that the mutt hadn't noticed the opening.

No such luck.

The dog threw back its head and howled like a werewolf on the hunt. The sound was an ancient, primal thing, and some aeons-old instinct in DC Neish flared into life.

'Oh. Shit,' he whispered.

And then, as the boggle-eyed hellhound launched itself through the gap, he ran.

—

Dinky's living room was, not to put too fine a point on it, a shithole. Not literally—the generous slabs of dog faeces that dotted the garden didn't make an appearance here—but it was, in every other conceivable sense.

Empty bottles and cans lay in puddles on the threadbare carpet. Newspapers were stacked taller than the house's owner, piled up on the floor, the couch, the coffee table, and almost every other reasonably level surface.

Nicotine had yellowed the paintwork, and turned the blue sky of a printed landscape canvas into a sickly shade of sea green.

No wonder the little man sounded the way he did. If he'd been responsible for half the nicotine staining, it was a miracle he had a throat left.

And the smell… God. The smell.

As a child, many years ago, Hamza had taken a sneaky swig from a beer can at a neighbour's Hogmanay party, only to discover that the half-empty can had been serving as a makeshift ashtray for the past half hour.

The living room of Dinky's house smelled exactly like that had tasted—sour, stale, bitter, and eye-wateringly, stomach-churningly awful.

'Take a seat, if you can find one,' Dinky instructed.

Hamza couldn't find one. He didn't look, granted, but even if he had spotted somewhere to sit, there was no way he was letting on. Standing would be fine. Standing would be far preferable to the alternative.

Dinky didn't bat an eyelid when Hamza remained on his feet. He clambered up onto an armchair, shuffled in beside a stack of old *Radio Times*, then sparked up a comically oversized cigarette and clutched it between two stubby fingers.

'So?' the little man said, urging him on with a wave of a hand and a waft of smoke. 'What you want?'

'Are you, eh… are you Dinky?' Hamza asked.

'The fuck's that supposed to mean? What are you saying, exactly? You taking the piss out of my size?' demanded the dwarf. He took a long draw on his cigarette while Hamza hummed and hawed through the beginnings of an apology, then gave a nod of his disproportionately large head. 'Aye. I'm Dinky. What can I do you for?'

Hamza aborted the apology halfway through. There had been no laugh or smile from the man in the chair. No 'gotcha!' or other acknowledgement that he'd been joking. He had just spoken in the same gravelly Glasgow monotone, his expression giving nothing away.

'Right,' Hamza began. 'OK, good, so—'

'Hiya!' said a slurred voice from the couch.

A visibly inebriated older man with a nose so red he could've led a team of reindeer through a pea-souper, leaned out from behind a stack of papers and gave a friendly little finger-wave.

'You all right, pet?' the old man asked, all gums and grin. He had the look of the long-term jakey about him. Too much drink and too many drugs, over too many years, had pickled his brain and shunted him into a sort of docile slow motion, out of step with the rest of the world.

'Uh… aye. I'm fine, thanks,' Hamza said. 'Sorry, who are you?'

'That's Ally Bally,' Dinky announced, which immediately caused the old man to burst into tuneless song.

'Ally bally, ally bally bee,' he sang, still beaming from ear to ear, and holding unflinching eye contact with Hamza. 'Sittin' on yer mammy's knee. Greetin' for a wee bawbee, tae buy wee Dinky's candy.'

Dinky thumped a hand on the arm of the chair and cackled through a cloud of cigarette smoke. 'That was fucking magic, big man! Fucking proud of you, by the way! Fucking proud of the big Ally Bally!' He looked up at Hamza. 'Was that no' pure fucking magic?'

'Aye, it was good, aye,' Hamza said.

This was a lie. It wasn't good. Not by any stretch of the imagination. Not by any known definition of the word.

Mildly unsettling? Oh yes.

But good? Not even close. Not by a long shot.

'Now, what was it you said your name was again?' Dinky asked.

'DS Hamza Khaled.'

Ally Bally gawped up at him in wonder. 'Is that a spaceman's name?' he asked. Quite genuinely, Hamza thought. 'Are you a spaceman, man?' He snorted loudly at that, said, 'Spaceman, man', again, then fell back out of sight behind the stack of papers, laughing away to himself.

'Is this about the cow?' Dinky asked.

Hamza frowned. 'Cow? What cow?'

'Doesn't matter then,' Dinky said. 'So, what's it to do with?'

It took Hamza a moment to remember why he was there, the sheer absurdity of the scene momentarily throwing him for a loop.

'I believe you've had some dealings with a Fergus Forsyth recently.'

'You can say that again. Fucker owes me two grand,' Dinky said. 'Is he in trouble? What's he done? He'd better still be able to pay me back that money.'

'He's dead,' Hamza announced.

Dinky's face tightened, his mouth becoming a thin, narrow slit. 'You are fucking kidding me,' he intoned. 'Tell me this is a fucking joke right now.'

'No joke,' Hamza told him. 'He was attacked and killed on Monday.'

'That selfish prick!' Dinky bellowed. He thumped a child-sized fist down on the arm of the chair, and half a dozen magazines immediately toppled over into his lap. 'He'd better have mentioned me in his will, I'll tell you that much. Two grand he's due me. Two grand!'

'That's a lot of money, Dinky,' the drunk on the couch chimed in.

'You fucking shut up,' Dinky warned him. There was a dangerous glint in his eye, and his face was reddening from the neck up. As dwarfs went, he was definitely Grumpy. 'No one's talking to you, so button your fucking lip! All right?'

'Aye, sure Dinky. Message received and understood,' Ally Bally said, Dinky's sudden change in demeanour sharp enough to cut through his decades-long stupor. He mimed zipping his mouth shut, crossed his arms, then sat back out of sight behind the newspapers once more.

'What did he owe you the money for?' Hamza asked.

'Because I lent it to him. Why else would he owe me money?'

Hamza shrugged. 'I heard a wee rumour that you've been running a bookie's out here,' he said.

'A bookie? Me. Naw. That would be illegal, officer,' Dinky replied. 'Couldn't be having that, now, could we? Naw, me and Fergus just had a friendly wee arrangement between two pals. That was all.'

'You wouldn't have been charging interest, then?'

Dinky snorted. 'I said I was his pal. No' that I was a mug. Aye, there was interest. At a very reasonable rate.'

'Which was?' Hamza asked.

Dinky was not liking this line of questioning. A vein was throbbing on one temple, and he was flexing his fingers in and out, like the motion was the only thing keeping his temper in check.

'I'd have to have a think about that,' he finally said, giving himself a tap on the side of the head. 'Dig around in the old memory banks. See what comes up. If you want to leave your phone number, I can get back to you.'

'Fair enough. What did he want the money for?'

'I don't know. I didn't ask.'

'You loaned two grand to someone and you didn't ask what it was for?'

'No. I didn't. Something about some woman, I think. I don't know. I'm no' a fucking building society. I don't give a shit what it's for. All I care about is that I get it back.'

Hamza nodded. 'Well,' he said, rocking back on his heels. 'I'm afraid that's looking unlikely.'

'Fuck's sake!' Dinky ejected. 'You do someone a favour—you do a good fucking deed—and this is what you get.'

'Favours don't usually come with interest rates,' Hamza pointed out. He had his doubts that the man in the oversized chair would have ever done a genuine good deed in his life.

'You can help people out *and* be a fucking businessman,' Dinky snapped back. 'The two aren't... what is it?'

'Mutually exclusive,' Ally Bally said.

'Fucking shut up,' Dinky barked at him. 'Aye. That's it. Mutually exclusive.'

Hamza pulled a noncommittal sort of face that said he disagreed, but that he didn't want to get into a debate about it.

Instead, he moved on to a more relevant line of questioning.

'Where were you on Monday, Dinky?'

'Same place I am every day,' Dinky replied. 'Right here.'

'All day?'

'All day, every day.'

'And you've got witnesses who'll confirm that?'

Dinky grinned. 'Dozens.'

'Dozens?' Hamza arched his eyebrows. 'Have a party, did you?'

'Every day's a party here,' Dinky said.

Hamza looked around them. Ally Bally was peeking out at him from behind the cover of the newspaper stack, still looking somewhat awestruck.

'Shite party, then,' Hamza remarked.

'It was great craic until you turned up,' Dinky replied. 'Ally Bally'll tell you I was here all day. And I can give you twenty other names who'll all say the same.' He pushed the magazines off him, and they slid onto the dirty carpet with a series of slapping sounds. 'You're barking up the wrong tree, if you think I did Fergus in, pal. That's the last thing I want, swear to fuck. Now, if he'd been kidnapped and tortured, I'd get it. Few fingers cut off, maybe. Coming to me then? Aye. Then it makes sense. But I can't exactly get my money back if he's dead, can I?'

'No. I suppose not,' Hamza conceded.

'Good. Right. So, we're done, then?' Dinky asked.

Hamza shook his head, took out his notebook, and flipped to a blank page. 'I'm afraid not. I'm going to need that list of names you mentioned...'

–

Ten minutes later, Hamza returned to the car, sat in the passenger seat, then almost screamed with fright when Tyler rose up from behind him, his face ghostly white beneath a caked-on layer of mud.

'Is it gone?' the DC hissed. He kept low and peered out through the side windows in the back. 'Is it... is it gone?'

'What? The dog?'

'Yes, the fucking dog! Of course, the dog!' Tyler yelped. He clamped a hand over his mouth and ducked, bracing himself for an attack that didn't come.

'Yeah, he called it in before I left,' Hamza revealed. 'It was actually all right when he brought it in. Quite friendly.'

'Friendly?!' Tyler gasped. 'Try telling that to my arse cheeks! If you can even find them!'

He reached for the door handle, thought better of it, then clambered through the gap between the front seats and slid awkwardly behind the wheel.

Hamza watched all this while biting down on his bottom lip, but the ragged backside of Tyler's trousers tipped him over the edge, and the car began to shake with his silent-but-violent giggles.

'It's not fucking funny!' Tyler protested. 'I'll need to go get a tetanus shot now. Although, how they'll do that, I have no idea, since I've got no arse left for them to stick the needle in.'

'It's not that bad, is it?' Hamza asked.

'No' that bad?! Look!' Tyler angled himself until one buttock was pointing up at the Detective Sergeant. 'Check that out!'

'I'm not going to check out your arse!'

Tyler tutted. 'I sustained a work-related injury. It's your duty to check my arse!'

With a sigh of resignation, Hamza checked his arse.

'There's nothing wrong with it,' he said, once he'd given the offered cheek a once-over. 'I don't think it broke the skin. Maybe a bit of bruising, but that's it.'

'Bollocks!'

'I'm no' checking them,' Hamza said. 'I draw the line there.'

Tyler pawed at his buttock through the hole in his trousers, then checked his hand. 'I was sure it was bound to be bleeding. It felt like the bastarding thing sunk its teeth right in.'

'Looks OK to me. You can always check in the mirror.'

Tyler began twisting his way out of the seat. 'Good idea.'

'No' the rearview mirror!' Hamza said, stopping him before he could go any further. 'Later. In the hotel or something, I mean.'

Tyler stopped, thought this over, then sat down again. 'Aye, that makes more sense, right enough,' he admitted, then he nodded in the direction of the house the DS had just come from. 'Tell me you got something worthwhile, at least. Tell me I didn't go through all that for nothing.'

'Well, it was...' Hamza tried to think of the perfect word to describe the experience, before concluding that a suitable one probably didn't exist. '…interesting. It was an interesting twenty minutes. Let's just put it like that.'

'Aye, well,' Tyler grunted, starting the engine and crunching the car into gear. 'I bet not half as bloody interesting as mine.'

Chapter 27

'So?' asked Logan, as he sat with his indicator flashing at the junction that would take them back onto the A82, and southbound to Fort William. 'She tell you anything?'

'Quite a bit, actually. Aye. How did you get on? How was the husband?'

'Complete arsehole,' Logan said, but he chose not to add anything more for the time being.

'Doesn't surprise me. She's scared of him,' Sinead said. 'He sounds controlling. Violent, too. I'm sure of it, although she refused to say. Not sure we'd get her to even admit what was happening, let alone press charges.'

Logan said nothing, and instead let the look on his face do the talking. He'd lost count of the number of domestics he'd been called in on over the years, all the way from his first days in Uniform to his current role in the MIT. Getting a testimony was often the hardest part. Getting them to stick to their guns and not withdraw the accusations came a very close second.

'I don't get it,' Sinead said as if reading his thoughts. 'Why does anyone put up with that? It's been going on forever, I think. She used to turn up to school all bruises and stuff.' She shook her head. It moved slowly, like it was heavier than usual. 'I just... I don't get it.'

'People are complicated things,' Logan said. 'That's about the gist of it, unfortunately. We do what we can, but, ultimately, they've got to make the decision for themselves. And there are consequences. There's always consequences. You think, aye, husband's knocking you about? His arse is out the window.' He gave a shrug, his shoulders apparently hampered by the same additional weight as Sinead's head. 'But it's not always as easy as it sounds.'

'No. No, I suppose not,' Sinead said, although she sounded unconvinced. 'Anyway, Lana admitted that she and Fergus were—as she put it—in an "intimate relationship". It's been going on for about two years. Started about six months to a year after Fergus started at LHS.'

'Weird pairing, isn't it?' Logan said, flooring the accelerator and powering the car out onto the main road ahead of a camper van that came trundling down the hill on his right. It was only ten miles back to the station. Stuck behind that bastard, it'd take them all night.

'How do you mean?' Sinead asked.

'Well, she's much older than him, isn't she? They're in different departments. PE and English? Not like they'd be working in constant close contact.'

'She said they just clicked right away. Just sort of hit it off. They've been seeing each other regularly since then. Initially, just for sex.'

'And later?'

'She said it'd become more of a relationship. More romantic. They'd spoken about running away somewhere. Her, him, and Bennet, her son.' Sinead glanced down at the notebook in her lap, then out at the dark road ahead. 'She was in love with him. No doubt about it. She reckoned he felt the same about her, too. Recently, anyway. To start with, they'd just meet up for sex. Guess where.'

Logan side-eyed her. 'Where?'

'Well of the Seven Heads.'

'No way. Seriously?'

'She called it their "secret spot". Reckons no one else knew about it.'

'Some bugger clearly did,' Logan replied. 'Did she reckon the husband knew about the relationship?'

'Definitely not, no. She was adamant about that. Says that if he did, he wouldn't have been able to keep it to himself. He'd have lost the plot.'

'How do you mean? Like by cutting a man's head off?' Logan asked. He flexed his fingers on the wheel, then gripped it more tightly. The headlights of the camper van had already been left behind, far back in the gathering gloom. 'He's got a workshop, access to power tools, violent tendencies, and a pretty solid motive.'

'Reckon he's our killer, sir?'

'I'd say he bears some closer scrutiny, put it that way,' Logan said. He caught Sinead stifling a yawn. 'But not tonight. Some of us have a bloody speech to be working on.'

Sinead smiled at that. 'High time, too.'

'We'll look into Clyde Lennon first thing in the morning.'

'Sounds like a plan, sir,' Sinead said. She turned away from the window to the man in the driver's seat. 'After breakfast, though?'

'Oh God, aye. After breakfast,' Logan agreed. 'We're no' bloody savages!'

–

He stood by the window, watching the detectives getting back in their car. Watching them driving off. Watching their lips flapping as they talked about him, and about her, and about everything that had been spoken of in the house.

The room was dark now. The detectives had turned back as they'd reached the car, but they hadn't seen him standing there, hadn't seen him staring.

How much did they know? How much did they suspect? He'd have loved, more than anything, to have asked them, but that would have drawn suspicion. Made him look involved. Made him look guilty.

He'd have to go to the workshop. Tonight. Make sure everything was squared away. Make sure it was all properly hidden.

He couldn't have it all falling apart on him. Not now. Not after all that time spent planning. Not when he'd come this far.

He watched until the taillights had turned out of the driveway.

He waited until the car would be safely on its way down the road.

And then, as the first stars appeared in the darkened night sky, he made his excuses and left.

—

While Ben and Hamza slept, Tyler studied his arse in a full-length mirror, and Sinead did her best not to laugh, Logan sat at the desk in his room with his laptop open. His fingers were poised and ready to type. Unfortunately, his brain wasn't sending them any signals.

He'd given his father-of-the-bride speech some thought over the years. Not a lot, but definitely some. Usually, it was after Maddie had done something embarrassing—like the time she'd knocked over and smashed that vase at a Glasgow School of Art exhibition, or her first ever camping trip, when she'd unknowingly pitched her tent in the same field as a particularly randy shorthorn bull.

Once the drama had all passed, he had always made a wee mental note of the incident. 'Good fodder,' he'd say, for the speech he'd one day be called on to give.

And then, of course, he hadn't been. Not for Maddie, anyway. Not for his wee girl.

He was honoured, of course, to have been asked to fulfil all the fatherly duties for Sinead, and by God, he'd do his damnedest for her.

But it wasn't the same. It wasn't the speech he'd waited his life to deliver.

Someone else had given that. And Logan hadn't known a thing about it.

He removed his fingers from the laptop keys and took out his phone. He felt a surge of hope when he saw he had two missed calls, but it spluttered and died when he discovered that both were from Detective Superintendent Mitchell.

He'd have to call her back tomorrow and take the bollocking that he had coming to him.

Flicking to his contacts, Logan pulled up his daughter's name. Her picture appeared on-screen above her number. She was younger in the photo. Fifteen, sixteen, maybe? Smiling, despite her obvious resentment at having her picture taken.

He tried calling the number. It went four rings before diverting to the answerphone system. He listened to it, thinking of all the things he might say after the beep had gone, but all he could think of were recriminations.

He could almost hear the words coming out of his mouth now. Why hadn't she invited him? Was he really that bad? Did she really hate him that much?

The more he thought, the more he resented the way she'd treated him. He knew, of course, that he was to blame. But... her *wedding*. He was still her dad, and she was still his wee girl.

But she hadn't invited him. She hadn't wanted him there. She didn't even want him knowing.

So, even if he hung on, what would he say?

What would be the point of saying anything?

There was a beep as the voicemail greeting finished. He opened his mouth, but no words came until he thumbed the red button that terminated the call.

'Jesus Christ. Nicely handled, Jack,' he muttered, then he placed the phone down, returned his fingers to the keyboard, and stared at his laptop until sleep eventually came upon him.

Chapter 28

Olivia was halfway down the stairs when she heard the voices in the kitchen. A low murmuring. A man. A woman. Her mother, she thought, although it was unheard of in recent months for her to be up this early. Or, unheard of for her to be able to talk coherently this early, at least. At best, she'd manage a grunt as she knocked back a handful of painkillers and went shuffling back off to bed.

Today, though, she sounded bright. Cheerful, even, like she was happy to see whoever was in the kitchen with her. Like she was greeting an old friend.

Or an old lover.

Olivia waited. Listened. Tried to place the voice. It was too low, though, too hushed, and she got the impression that whoever the man was, he didn't want her knowing he was there.

That he wanted to keep his presence a secret.

It was him. It had to be.

She'd gone home soon after Shona's bombshell the night before. Made some excuse that she now couldn't remember, called Borys, and made the trip home in silence.

It had passed in a blur. The drive. The drop-off around the corner. The walk to her house, the trudge up the stairs, the barricading of her bedroom door. She could recall only snatches of it, like glimpses of open sky above an ocean as she kicked and thrashed and tried not to drown.

One body. Not two.

She'd been sure he was dead. Certain of it. How could he not be?

One body. Not two.

He was still alive. Still out there. He knew what she'd done to him.

And he knew where to find her.

What would he do, if it was him? How would he punish her? How would he make her pay?

He had been dangerous before, but now? After what she'd done?

Olivia's gaze went ahead of her, plotting a route to the door. Down the stairs, quietly. Don't stop to pick up a jacket, just creep past the kitchen door, along the hallway, and sneak out the front. He wouldn't dare come after her at school. She'd have time to think, at least. Time to make a plan.

She had money now. Not much. Not nearly enough, but some. It could buy her time, or protection. Buy her a chance.

Olivia was just passing the kitchen door when it opened suddenly. All the tension she'd been holding in escaped as a little yelp of fright at the sight of the man standing there.

The man with the wide grin and the fluorescent yellow running jacket.

The man she had never clapped eyes on before in her life.

'Oh! Sorry! Didn't mean to give you a fright,' he said.

Olivia regarded him with a look that was somewhere between suspicion and contempt, but leaned closer to the latter. He was in his forties, she estimated, but he looked like he lived well. Or better than most of the men her mother associated herself with, anyway.

Which wasn't saying much.

He had good teeth, nice hair, and an obvious eagerness to please that made him look a touch manic.

'Who are you?' Olivia demanded, then she spotted the strip of white around his neck and laughed out loud at the absurdity of it.

Her mum appeared in the doorway behind him, all tits and teeth and tan, and not one of them natural.

'All right, sweetheart? Have you met Father Conrad?'

'No.'

Conrad thrust a hand out for her to shake. 'Well, you have now. Put it there, young lady!'

Olivia shook the hand. If her mother wanted to get in tow with a priest, and embrace her holy moly, fine. Great, in fact. Maybe she wouldn't lie around wasted half the day, or shack up with anyone who'd have her.

Besides, finding a random priest in the kitchen was a far better outcome than the one Olivia had been expecting.

'We're going jogging,' her mother announced.

'Fucking hell,' Olivia muttered, then she smiled apologetically. 'Sorry. Just surprised. But, you know, in a good way. Have fun!'

Father Conrad raised a hand for a high-five as he passed her in the hall. She returned it, despite the cringe-factor, then stepped aside to let her mum go lumbering past, already looking like she was regretting letting herself get talked into this.

'Have a good day at school, sweetheart.'

'Cheers,' Olivia said.

Her mum jogged out after the priest, and closed the door behind her, leaving Olivia all by herself in the house.

She stood there in the hall, half expecting the door to open and her mum to return with a shake of a head and a 'bollocks to that'.

But the door remained closed.

The house remained silent.

And Olivia suddenly felt very, very alone.

–

Logan was the last one down for breakfast, and arrived at the table just as Tyler, Hamza, and Sinead were mopping up their bean juice and egg yolk with the last of their toast.

'Thought you weren't coming, boss,' Tyler said. He scooted his chair over to make room for the DCI to sit, and let out a grimace of pain as his weight returned to his buttocks.

Logan frowned, opened his mouth as if he was going to ask about it, then shook his head.

Sinead stacked her and Tyler's plates onto a tray, making room for Logan to sit his breakfast down. He'd attacked the buffet as soon as he'd entered the restaurant, loading his plate with the sort of fry-up that could harden arteries at twenty paces.

'Well, how bad is it?' he asked the group in general.

The three of them exchanged some sheepish looks, then Hamza reached under the table and produced a small stack of tabloid newspapers. *The Sun* was on top, which was almost enough to make Logan reconsider his breakfast.

Almost.

'*The Well of Eight Heads,*' he said, reading the headline with a grimace of distaste. 'Well, that's original, isn't it?'

'They're not the only one to run with that,' Hamza said, flicking through a few different newspapers to reveal the same identical text. '*The Star* was a bit more creative, though.'

'I dread to think,' Logan said.

'*Well, Well, Well,*' Hamza read, holding the rag up for the DCI to see. '*Headless Horseman Haunts Highlands.*'

'Jesus,' Logan grunted, liberally sprinkling salt over everything on his plate. 'That's just painful. Did any of them name him?'

'We'd asked them not to, but—' Hamza began.

'Bastards!' Logan swore loudly before the DS could reach the end of the sentence, drawing some dirty looks from the smattering of other guests who'd come down for breakfast.

'Aye. Most of them have put a contact number in for anyone who might know anything,' Hamza said. 'So that's something, at least.'

Logan didn't voice an opinion on this, but from his expression, it was clear he found it a small compensation for naming a murder victim before the family could be contacted.

'They get worse every bloody year,' he muttered. 'They'll have hacked his phone by now, you wait and bloody see. Any joy getting into that yet, by the way?'

Hamza shook his head. 'Don't want to chance messing with it,' he said. 'A few wrong guesses and it'll be wiped, or permanently locked.'

'Best get it handed over to the tech bods,' Logan said. 'Let them handle it.'

Tyler shifted his weight in his chair and let out a little groan. This time, Logan's curiosity got the better of him.

'What's wrong with you?' he asked.

'Got savaged by a dog, boss,' Tyler said.

Hamza tutted. '*Savaged*.'

Sinead rolled her eyes. 'He got *nibbled* by a dog,' she corrected.

'Nibbled, my arse!' Tyler objected.

'Exactly. It nibbled his arse,' Sinead agreed.

Tyler blinked in confusion. 'What? No, that's not what I... I mean *my arse* it just nibbled me. It was a savaging. Big bastard of a thing, too, boss. Have you seen *Ghostbusters*?'

'Course I've seen *Ghostbusters*,' Logan retorted.

'You know the dogs in that? The monster things? It was like one of them big buggers. I thought my time had come.'

'It didn't break the skin,' Sinead pointed out.

'Not for want of bloody trying!'

'When did this happen?' Logan asked.

'Last night, out at that Dinky fella's place,' Hamza said.

'Oh. Aye. Any joy there?' Logan asked, glossing right over Tyler's dog encounter and getting down to business.

'Don't think so, sir, no.' Hamza checked out the room around them. There were only a few other guests currently eating, and if he kept his voice down, none of them were within earshot. 'Weird setup, and I'm positive he's up to something, but he's got an alibi for Monday, and he seemed genuinely furious that Fergus is dead. He'd lent him two grand.'

'Aye, well, he'll no' be seeing that again,' Logan said, stabbing a sausage with a fork and dunking it into the yolk of one of his three fried eggs. 'What was the money for?'

'He didn't know for sure, but reckoned it was something to do with a woman,' Hamza replied.

'Ohm?' Logan murmured, having just bitten the end off the sausage. He waved the fork, urging Sinead to take over while he chewed.

'We spoke to Mrs Lennon. She admitted that she and Fergus were in a relationship.'

'You mean shagging?' asked Tyler.

'I mean they were in a relationship,' Sinead insisted. 'They'd spoken about running away together. The two of them, and Mrs Lennon's son.'

'Reckon that's what he wanted the money for?' Hamza asked.

'Could be,' Sinead replied.

'So... what are we saying?' asked Tyler, leaning over Sinead and using his fork to spear a final lonely mushroom that sat on his discarded plate. 'They make plans to elope, or whatever, they get some money together, and then just before they can do it, *bang*. Someone cuts his head off?'

'Someone who doesn't want them to go,' Hamza reasoned.

'Aye. And here's a twist,' Sinead said. 'Mrs Lennon and Fergus used to meet up at the Well of the Seven Heads. She called it their 'secret spot.''

'That can't be a coincidence. Surely?' Hamza said.

'It's a message,' Logan said, finally swallowing. The others turned to look at him as he started cutting up his bacon. 'Been thinking about it since last night, but Ben said it from the start. The history of the well, it's tied into revenge. That's what the beheadings were all about. Someone wanted revenge on Fergus Forsyth. And I think we now know what for.'

'Sounds to me like it's pointing to the husband,' Tyler proclaimed with an aplomb that suggested he had personally cracked the case. 'We should bring him in. See if he talks.'

'Not quite yet,' Logan said. 'I spoke to him last night. He won't be easy to crack. I'd like to have something more on him.'

'Shite!' Tyler yelped, jumping to his feet with such urgency he almost knocked over the table. A waitress and two other diners shot him disapproving looks, but he completely failed to notice.

'What's wrong?' Sinead asked.

'I'm meant to be at the school in fifteen minutes. For that assembly!'

Logan checked his watch. 'Christ, is that the time?' he muttered. 'Didn't realise I'd slept that... here. Hang on.' His eyes went to the empty chair beside Hamza. 'Has anyone seen Ben?'

—

The pattern had been the same since a few weeks after Alice's death—out like a light by half-past ten, and up with the birds at the first suggestion of morning.

He'd eaten breakfast alone, eschewing the fried options in favour of some fruit and cereal. The negligible price difference between the full and continental breakfasts would've wound him right up once upon a time (just two quid less for the continental? Madness!) but he tried not to let himself get stressed by such things these days.

Even though it was ridiculous.

Almost seven quid for some Weetabix and a banana. Aye, he could've had the muffins and pancakes, but if he did that, he'd have been as well with the bacon and eggs.

He didn't let it get to him, though. It wasn't good for the old ticker.

A fiver. That seemed fair. A fiver for fruit, cereal, and a cup of tea. They wouldn't be losing money at that. Not by a long shot.

But *seven*? Come on, be reasonable.

He chose not to dwell on it. It was what it was.

A bloody rip-off, to be precise.

'You're punishing people for trying to be healthy,' he'd told the waitress, still not letting it bother him one little bit. 'It's like the sugar tax in reverse. Eat less, but pay comparatively more.'

'It's not more. It's two pounds less,' the waitress had insisted.

Ben had then explained the meaning of the word 'comparatively' while simultaneously insisting that it was no skin off his nose, but that he had half a mind to write to the head office to complain.

After that, he'd taken a quick spray of his angina medication, and eaten his breakfast in silence.

Now he stood in the Incident Room, sipping tea as he studied the Big Board. He'd been off for months, and had a lot of catching up to do. It was good to get in early. Get a head start.

He checked the clock. It had barely gone eight.

Christ, he was bored.

He'd already checked the inbox. The report from Fergus Forsyth's mobile phone network had arrived overnight. It was churning out of the printer now, despite the nagging wee notice fixed to the machine instructing him to think of the environment, and only to print when absolutely necessary.

He'd made the executive decision that it fit that criteria. Reading lots of wee numbers off a computer screen gave him a headache. You couldn't scribble on the screen, either. Couldn't underline bits of interest, or make notes in the margins.

Well, you could. Hamza had shown him how on a few different occasions now. There was a button, or an icon, or something somewhere you had to click, and then the pointy cursor would become a flashing line with a box around it, or something like that.

Printing was easier. And if one wee document was going to kill off the polar bears, then they were clearly beyond help as it was.

He finished his tea, set the cup down on his desk, and wondered what else he could make a start on while he waited for the printer to finish. He didn't feel the need to prove himself, necessarily. It wasn't that.

OK, maybe it was that.

He'd been out of the game for a while, and they were treating him with kid gloves. He wanted to show them he was still useful. Prove to them. To himself.

His eyes fell on the mobile phone on Hamza's desk. The victim's phone. They hadn't managed to get into it yet. Hadn't even tried, as far as he knew.

Ben fished his glasses from the top pocket of his shirt, pulled them on, then took a seat at Hamza's desk.

The phone lay there, silently challenging him. Daring him to try.

'Come on then, you bugger,' he told it, flexing his fingers. 'Just how hard can this be?'

Chapter 29

Tyler turned up at the school assembly hall to find several hundred uniformed pupils sobbing in their seats.

Many of them had already heard the news by the time they'd left for school. It had, of course, spread like wildfire, so by the time the morning assembly was called, there wasn't anyone who hadn't heard what had happened to Mr Forsyth.

It had become exaggerated as it had travelled from student to student. Mr Forsyth had been murdered, became Mr Forsyth had been beheaded, became Mr Forsyth had been burned alive, or boiled in acid, or chopped up and eaten—by cannibals in some versions, and pigs in another.

A woman with a particularly severe face glared at Tyler as he sidled onto an empty seat on the stage beside five other members of staff. This was the infamous Mrs Robertson, he guessed, based on Sinead's description. A younger, softer-looking woman was standing at the lectern, addressing the audience, telling them that it was OK to be sad. That it was fine to be upset. To grieve.

Judging by the tears tripping down most of their faces, they were way ahead of her.

It was changed days from when Tyler was in school. As a boy, get caught crying and you were done for. Even if a parent had just died in your arms, get caught shedding a single salty tear and you were royally fucked for the rest of your school career. You'd probably have to change to a new school, in fact, if not a new town altogether.

It wasn't like it had been all that long ago, either. Ten years ago, he'd have been wearing a uniform not unlike these. And now, just a decade later, boys and girls alike were openly sobbing, without any apparent fear of repercussions.

It was bloody weird. Good, he thought. But definitely weird.

And over a teacher, too! Tyler couldn't think of a teacher at his school whose death wouldn't have been celebrated with fireworks and a marching band.

The woman at the lectern encouraged the pupils to talk to each other, and share their favourite memories of Mr Forsyth, then stressed that her door was always open, and handed it over to the depute head.

Mrs Robertson took the now vacant spot at the lectern, barked, 'Quiet!' then waited for the weeping to subside. 'We have a representative from Police Scotland here to talk to us now. Finally,' she said, shooting Tyler a sideways look that almost knocked him off his chair. 'He's going to talk to you about... well, we'll find out. Detective?'

Tyler had hoped for a few more minutes to work out what he was going to say, but several hundred sets of eyes were now watching him, and the weight of their expectation forced him to get to his feet.

'Right. Aye. Cheers,' he said.

'Loud, clear voice, please,' Mrs Robertson instructed.

Tyler cleared his throat. 'Sorry. Is that...? Hello,' he shouted at the audience. 'You, eh... you all right?'

They weren't all right. That much was very obvious. Tyler shook his head, admonishing himself, then tried again.

'Eh, my name's Detective Constable Neish. Tyler. That's... my name's Tyler. I'm, eh, I'm one of the detectives investigating the... sad... the... with Mr Forsyth.'

'His murder,' Mrs Robertson said. 'You can say it.'

'Right. Aye. His murder,' Tyler said. 'We're investigating his murder. So...' Shit! What else should he say? Something reassuring. Something inspiring. '...aye. There you go.'

Damn. Failed on both counts.

'Perhaps you could address some of the rumours that have been flying around?' Mrs Robertson suggested.

'Sure,' Tyler said.

There was a lengthy and increasingly uncomfortable silence until he eventually spoke again.

'I mean, I don't know what they are, so you'll have to tell me,' he said, which earned him another look of irritation from the depute head.

Mrs Robertson addressed the audience. 'What rumours have you heard, children? Quickly. Hands up.'

Forty hands went up. Tyler tried very hard not to groan out loud.

'Go ahead. Choose,' Mrs Robertson urged.

Tyler scanned the front few rows and settled on a ginger-haired lad with his hand thrust so high into the air it was practically pulling him out of his seat.

'Eh, you.'

'Not him,' Mrs Robertson interjected. She pointed to a girl a few seats along. 'Jessica.'

'Is it true someone ate him?' asked a mousy-looking girl with *Harry Potter* glasses.

'Eh, no. That's not true,' Tyler said.

'Alison,' the depute head said, quickly moving on. 'What have you heard?'

'I heard his head's still missing, Miss.'

Tyler nodded. 'Um, yes. Yes, that is true,' he said, shifting uncomfortably. Should he be doing this? Was this right? 'But, I mean, I'm sure it'll turn up.'

More hands went up. Mrs Robertson selected a boy sitting right down at the front.

'Maybe they ate his head, then. If you can't find it, maybe someone ate it.'

There was some murmuring then. It sounded almost excited, like the kid in the front row had blown the case wide open.

'It's, eh, no. No. I'd imagine it's not easy to eat a head,' Tyler said. 'You know, like, the skull, and everything. It's hard, isn't it? I mean, maybe the eyes, or...' *Fuck! What was he saying? Abort!*

Abort! '…like, I don't know, maybe the brain, or whatever. But you can't really eat a head. Unless you're like, a bear, or a lion. Or… which it won't have been. Don't think that.'

He flinched at the levels of gibberish tumbling out of his mouth, but it was like a tap had been opened, then the spigot snapped off.

'So, um, no. No, I don't think anyone's eaten it. I think it's probably fine somewhere. Just, you know… not currently attached.'

Some sobbing resumed at that point. A young voice in the audience whispered, 'Is he saying a lion ate his brain?'

The depute head shouted them all back into silence, glowered at Tyler, then pointed to another boy. He had a different-coloured tie and looked older. Sixth Year, probably. His question was more direct than the others, and delivered in a way that was almost an accusation.

'Do you know who the killer is?'

'Not yet,' Tyler admitted. 'These things take a bit of time. Or, you know, sometimes they don't. It depends.'

'On what?' the boy asked.

'Well… on who done it. And how. And if there were any witnesses, or forensic evidence, or stuff like that?'

'Was there stuff like that?'

'Not really, no.'

'So you don't know anything?'

'We're following up on a number of leads,' Tyler said, recycling a phrase he'd heard used at polis press conferences in the past.

'Like what?' the young man asked. 'What are you *specifically* doing to find the killer?'

'Who, me personally, or…? Oh. The police? Right. I'm afraid I can't go into too much detail at this stage. But we're taking it very seriously. We've got a Big Board full of stuff.'

This was more like it, Tyler thought. This felt like more familiar ground. A few reassurances and platitudes, a promise that they would do everything they could to bring the killer to justice, and he was home and dry.

'What sort of stuff? You mean clues?' asked a girl with a sideways ponytail that made her look demented.

'Well, no,' Tyler said. 'Not *clues*, exactly...'

'What then?' another girl pressed.

'Like... theories. Ideas.' Tyler smiled, still labouring under the misconception that this was going quite well. 'Hunches. That sort of thing.'

'*Hunches*? You don't know anything, do you?' called the boy in the different-coloured tie. His voice was becoming louder, and fraying just a little at the edges. He was sitting alone, Tyler noted, an empty seat on either side of him. 'You don't have any idea what you're doing.'

'Bennet,' said one of the teachers sitting on the stage behind Tyler. She rose to her feet, her eyes ringed with red, a sodden tissue clutched in one hand.

Her tone hadn't been a warning one. It had been pleading. Imploring. Begging him to stop.

'You're just knocking on doors, hoping someone knows something,' Bennet continued, ignoring the teacher's plea. 'Someone killed Fergus, and you're going to let them get away with it!'

'Bennet, please, that's enough!' the teacher urged.

'I suggest you listen to your mother, Mr Lennon,' the depute head hissed.

Tyler, meanwhile, tried to stick gamely to his 'reassurances and platitudes' plan. 'We're not going to let anyone get away with anything,' he insisted. 'We've got multiple lines of inquiry that we're—'

'God. Bennet's right,' a girl chimed in from a couple of rows back. 'You don't have any idea who did it, do you? It could be anyone.'

'Do you even know who did it?' demanded a boy right beside her.

'Well, no, not yet, but like I say—'

'Oh my God! You're totally going to let them get away with killing Mr Forsyth!' a girl near the centre aisle positively shrieked.

Tyler hesitated, sensing the audience's growing discontent. Shite. This wasn't how it was supposed to go. This could turn ugly.

'Well, I mean… it's still early days in the… we're…' He raised his voice further, fighting to be heard over the rising murmur of voices. 'Put it this way, we've got a number of leads that we're in the process of…'

It was no use. There was no stopping it. He could see it approaching like an avalanche.

Grief was giving way to anger, and it was rippling through the audience faster than he could possibly contend with. Faces that had been streaked with tears now wore sneers and scowls, and they were all pointed in his direction.

'Justice for Fergus!' bellowed a boy up the back of the room. A chorus of agreement followed. It echoed off the high ceilings, and bounced around the room, gathering other voices as it went, until the hall shook with the racket of it.

'*Justice for Fergus! Justice for Fergus! Justice for Fergus!*'

'That's enough! Silence!' Mrs Robertson screeched, but it was like shouting into a hurricane.

At least half of the pupils were up out of their seats now. Feet were stamped as the chanting grew louder. A rubber whizzed through the air, narrowly missing Tyler's head.

Some of the younger pupils, alarmed by the chaos, began to stampede. Someone smashed the glass of the fire alarm, and a piercing squawk added its voice to the din.

Tyler turned to find Mrs Robertson glaring at him, her teeth clenched together. He summoned the best smile he could, given the circumstances.

'Right then,' he said, tapping his watch. 'I think I'd probably best be shooting off.'

Chapter 30

Logan, Hamza, and Sinead all arrived at the office to find DI Forde looking grey. Not his hair, which had been grey for a while now, but the rest of him. His face, and his demeanour.

'You all right?' Logan asked, shrugging off his coat. 'You look like you've seen a ghost.'

It was then that the DCI spotted the phone on the desk in front of Ben. Its screen was dark, and there was something lifeless about it. Something terminal.

'You didn't... you weren't trying the phone, were you, sir?' asked Hamza, who had spotted the mobile at the same time as Logan. 'You didn't try and unlock it?'

Ben looked down at the darkened screen, but said nothing.

'Tell me you didn't mess about with it,' Logan said.

'I just... I thought I'd have a go,' Ben said. 'I thought... "it's only four numbers, isn't it? I mean, how hard can that be?"'

'Isn't it, like, ten thousand combinations?' Sinead ventured.

Ben looked up, appearing surprised by that. 'Ten thousand? God. Aye. That's... that's more than I thought, right enough.'

Logan clamped a hand over his mouth, stopping himself saying anything he might regret.

'There's a security function, sir,' Hamza said, eyeing the phone like it was an explosive device. 'Put the wrong code in too many times, and no one can access it. Ever.' He steeled himself before asking the question. 'How many times did you try? Do you remember?'

'I'm not sure,' Ben admitted. 'But, well, it's not asking for the PIN number anymore.'

'Oh, Jesus Christ,' Logan ejected, unable to hold it back any longer. 'What were you thinking, Ben? Why were you pissing about with the thing in the bloody first place? You should've left it for—'

Ben tapped the mobile. It illuminated, revealing a screen filled with app icons. He sat back, smugness oozing from every pore.

'It's not asking for a PIN because I turned it off.'

All three of the other detectives blinked in perfect unison.

'You... you got in?' Hamza asked. 'How did you get in?'

'There's ten thousand combinations,' Sinead said again. 'How did you figure it out?'

Ben tapped the side of his head. 'Mind like a steel bloody trap, that's how,' he said. 'I just put myself into the victim's shoes. Got under his skin. Thought like he thought.'

'What was the number?' Logan asked.

'His date of birth,' said Ben. 'Second thing I tried.'

'What was the first?' asked Hamza.

'One, two, three, four.'

Logan snorted and shook his head. 'The master bloody hacker at work, eh? We'll be losing you to the Pentagon yet.' He gestured to the phone. 'Get anything off it?'

'Not yet. Just unlocked it a minute ago. Thought I'd leave some of the excitement for someone else. You know, with my bad ticker and everything. Wouldn't want to overdo it.'

'All right, point made, Benjamin. Point made,' Logan conceded. 'That was some good work.'

'Oh, I know,' Ben said, tucking his thumbs into a pair of imaginary braces. 'Network report is on the printer, too. Haven't had a chance to look at that, either.'

'I'll get on that,' Sinead said, dumping her jacket on the back of her chair.

'And I'll go over the phone, if you want?' Hamza suggested. 'See what we can get off it?'

Logan nodded. 'Right. Good. And I suppose I should—'

'Phone Mitchell?' Ben prompted.

'That is on the list. That's definitely on the to-do list,' Logan said.

'What's before it?' Ben asked.

'Oh, you know...' Logan began. His lips moved in silent calculation as he tried to come up with a solid excuse for not calling the Detective Superintendent right that instant. 'Well, I mean, the case for one thing! We're about to blow it wide open, thanks to this stroke of genius from yourself. I want to give that my focus and—'

'She told you not to bring me down here, didn't she?'

Sinead looked up from where she was retrieving the bundle of paper from the printer. Hamza paused in his tip-tapping on the mobile's screen.

'What makes you say that?' Logan asked with a sort of practised indifference that had exactly the opposite effect to the one he was hoping for.

'Call it polis instinct,' Ben said.

'First time for everything, I suppose,' Logan replied, deflecting for all he was worth. 'I'll give her a call soon. Find out what she's after. It's probably just about the press. She'll be wanting me to make a statement or some shite.'

Ben sucked in his bottom lip, spat it back out again, then nodded. 'Aye. I'm sure it'll be something like that, right enough,' he said, then the Incident Room door flying open brought the conversation to a merciful end.

They knew something was wrong the moment Tyler entered. He looked agitated, his movements sharp and erratic, his eyes darting at shadows.

'What's the matter, son?' Logan asked. 'Another dog after you?'

DC Neish tried too hard to laugh it off, which only made him appear borderline hysterical. 'Haha. What? Nah, boss. Nah, nothing like that!'

Once again, everyone stopped what they were doing. Tyler squirmed as their stares turned on him, one by one.

'What is it then?' Logan asked.

Tyler laughed again. This one was a high-pitched squeak, like a fork scraping on a plate. 'It's nothing! Nothing. It's...' He flicked his tongue across his dry lips and swallowed. 'It's just... the school.'

'God Almighty. As bad as that, was it?' Ben asked. 'Wish we'd gone in to watch now.'

Logan was still scrutinising the DC. Something was definitely up. Something bigger than he was letting on.

'What about the school?' he asked. 'What happened?'

Tyler wasn't laughing now. He shot a glance around at the other detectives, lingered on Sinead for a moment, then nodded over at the window. 'I, eh, I think you should maybe look for yourself, boss.'

Logan turned, strands of heavy dread weaving together in his stomach as he approached the window. He widened a gap in the blinds with two fingers and looked out at the waste ground across the road from the station, where the foundation of the new hospital was now in place.

'What am I looking at?' he asked.

Tyler swallowed again, loud enough for everyone in the room to hear. 'Down a bit.'

Logan leaned closer to the window. There was a crackle as he widened the blinds further, giving himself a clearer view of the station car park.

'Tyler,' he began, still staring.

'Yes, boss?'

'Why are there several hundred teenagers standing outside the station?'

Everyone but Tyler joined the DCI at the window.

'Jesus,' Sinead muttered. 'They don't look happy.'

'Aye, see, that's the thing,' Tyler babbled. 'You know how I was going into the school to help set their minds at ease?'

'That was the general idea, aye,' Logan replied as, down in the car park, the teenagers began to chant their demands for justice.

Tyler tried to smile, but the best he could do was grimace. 'Aye, well, I don't think it quite went according to plan.'

The press was there. Of course, they were. Logan had seen them gathered out front when he'd driven up to the station, but he'd quickly diverted around the back of the building and used the rear entrance, so he didn't have to talk to the bastards.

He had no choice but to talk to them now, though. And, to be honest, he actually rather enjoyed it.

'Fuck off,' he told them, ignoring their questions as he barged through them like a bowling ball through... no, not skittles. What had skittles ever done to anyone?

Like a bowling ball through shit.

It wasn't as satisfying as it could have been, as it was only a small breakaway pack standing outside the station door. The rest of them had scuttled gleefully over to where the Lochaber High School pupils had assembled and were snapping photos and barking questions while three or four hundred teenagers chanted, 'Justice for Fergus!' over and over again.

'All right, all right, that's enough!' Logan bellowed. A few of the closest kids flinched at the sight of him and became notably less enthusiastic on the chanting front, but most of the mass ignored him.

A TV camera was swung his way. Several flashes went off. His field of view was suddenly filled with microphones, and iPhones, and a tape recorder that even he knew was a bloody antique. He recognised the guy wielding that. *Scottish Daily Mail*. Absolute rodent of a man whose values were even more outdated than his technology.

'How do you respond to these young people?'

'What do you have to say to them?'

'They believe the police are letting the victim down. How do you respond?'

The presence of the TV camera made Logan reconsider the outburst that sat on the tip of his tongue. He took a modicum of pleasure from ignoring them completely, but it wasn't nearly as satisfying as swearing at them would have been. He'd have enjoyed swearing at them. Being sworn at was about all the bastards were good for.

He tried shouting at the teenagers again, but those at the back didn't hear him, which gave those in the front enough confidence to go ahead and ignore every word he said.

He'd have to try another approach.

'Whose car is this?' he barked at the journos, the cigarette packets and junk food wrappers abandoned on the dash telling him it belonged to one of them.

To his joy, it was the relic from the *Scottish Daily Mail* who answered. 'That's mine, why?'

Logan clambered onto the bonnet, then up onto the roof.

'Here! Wait! What are you bloody doing?! You'll dent it!'

'Aye. But think of the picture,' Logan said.

The stunt worked instantly. The sight of a six-and-a-half-feet tall man scrabbling up onto the top of a journalist's shitty car, brought a level of hesitation and uncertainty to the chanting. All eyes were suddenly on him, and when he cupped his hands around his mouth and roared at them to 'shut the fuck up!' then shut the fuck up they did.

'Thank you. About bloody time,' Logan boomed with such ferocity that the whole crowd took a step back. 'Let me start by saying how heartening it is to see so many young people getting engaged in the legal process. And then, let me finish by saying *cut your shite, and go back to your bloody classrooms*. Now.'

'Not until you find out who killed Fergus!' an older boy down the front yelled. His fists were clenched and his eyes were bloodshot. Clearly, he was taking the teacher's death hard.

'We're going to,' Logan replied, still shouting for the benefit of the crowd. He could see a few teachers hurrying along the road from the school, as passing cars slowed to see what all the fuss was about. 'At least, we're trying to. We were just working on a breakthrough now, in fact, when I had to step away to deal with you lot. So you might think you're helping, but you're not. We're not sitting on our arses up there, twiddling our thumbs. We're working hard to find a killer. And we're getting closer. We are. But this…?'

He made a sweeping motion with both arms, gesturing to the crowd as a whole. A few cameras flashed, capturing him in this striking moment of drama. He hoped there'd be something Christ-like about him, standing there addressing the crowd, but suspected he'd just turn out looking like a fat lad on the roof of a car.

'This is just slowing us down. You lot standing out here shouting the odds, you're making it *less* likely we'll find who was responsible, not more. You're helping Fergus's killer. Is that what you want?'

Nobody made a sound. Logan singled out the lad who'd challenged him.

'You. Is that what you want? To help Fergus's killer?'

The boy wrestled with his answer, trying to find some way out of the trap. There was no escape from it, though. There was only one answer he could possibly give.

'No, but—'

'Right. Good. Glad we're in agreement,' Logan barked, cutting him off. 'So, if you want to help us do our jobs—if you really want justice for Fergus, here's what you have to do.' He pointed to the school. 'Piss off, the lot of you. Get back to your work, and let us get on with ours.'

The silence had become something wavering and uncertain now. The tightly-packed throng of pupils started to fan out a little at the edges, like storm clouds drifting apart.

Logan rocked back on his heels, and enjoyed the thu-thunk the car roof made beneath his feet as the metal buckled and then popped back into place.

It was the arrival of the teachers that messed everything up. They came barrelling in at the back of the crowd, all raised voices and angry glares. They identified the troublemakers right away, and started cutting their way through the crowd towards them, as if guided by some laser targeting system.

The troublemakers knew what this meant, and instinctively understood that it was in their best interests to keep the protest going for as long as possible. Sure, they'd have to face their punishment eventually, but 'eventually' was a more appealing option than 'right now.'

They began to chant again and, with a bit of nudging and goading, encouraged the others around them to join in.

'Justice for Fergus! Justice for Fergus! Justice for Fergus!'

'Cut it out!' Logan bellowed, but it was too late. The whole crowd was united in one voice now, and he'd lost the element of surprise that he'd gained from climbing on top of the car.

Maybe if he jumped on it a few times, it would trigger an alarm? That might shut them up.

Be fun, too, to watch the *Daily Mail* man's face.

It was Sinead who stopped him. He didn't realise she was there beside the car until she gave him a tug on the trouser leg to get his attention. She said something, but the racket from the teenagers completely drowned it out.

'Hang on, hang on,' Logan said, stepping down onto the bonnet, then jumping the last couple of feet to the ground.

'You'd better not have bloody dented that, or you'll be paying for it,' the journalist warned him, running a hand across the scuffed paintwork at the front of the car.

Logan held a finger up, indicating that Sinead should wait, then he bent down beside the car, and stood up with a satisfied smirk on his face.

'Your tyre tread's looking awfully low. That's two-and-a-half grand and three points on your licence. Per tyre,' he said. 'Do you want to continue this conversation, or will we both just agree that you should button your fucking cakehole right now?'

He knew what the answer would be, so didn't bother waiting to hear it. Instead, he turned to Sinead, his eyebrows already rising.

'What's up?'

Sinead leaned in and spoke urgently in his ear, loud enough for him to hear, but low enough that the journalists didn't stand a chance.

'Something's come up with the victim's phone, sir,' she told him.

'What is it?'

Sinead glanced at the crowd of school kids, then at the reporters trying desperately to earwig in on their conversation.

'I think you'd maybe better see it for yourself.'

Chapter 31

Olivia stood alone at the back of the school building, away from prying eyes. Paulo, one of the Second Year kids, was meant to have met her there right after the breaktime bell, but the little shit was nowhere to be seen.

She didn't like doing business on school grounds. It was too risky. But Paulo got a lift to and from school every day without fail, and so she had no choice but to make their exchanges on the premises.

He was usually on time. He was usually early, in fact. Generally, he'd be there waiting for her when she arrived, standing stock-still in an attempt to look inconspicuous, which actually had the opposite effect.

Today, though, he hadn't been waiting. Today, he was late.

'He'd better have a good reason,' she muttered, but the sound of her own voice in the silence behind the school made her feel strangely uneasy, and she said nothing more.

She'd left the house early, not sticking around to eat breakfast. Not on her own. With time to spare, she'd walked to school, but had found herself checking over her shoulder every minute or so, eyes scanning the streets and alleyways for any sign of movement. Of danger.

Of *him*.

It scared her how carefree she'd been in recent weeks. How confident that she was in control. How sure of herself she had been as she'd walked those same streets, sat alone in her house, strolled freely around town.

He could have been watching. He could have been anywhere.

She'd picked up the pace and ran the rest of the way to school, not stopping until she was safely inside, surrounded by the smattering of other students who arrived stupidly early for whatever reason.

She had felt safer then. Not *safe*. Not by a long-shot. But safer. There was a strength in numbers. Protection in the anonymity of a crowd.

But now, she was alone. Isolated from her fellow pupils, the teachers, and the other school staff.

She was tucked out of sight around the back of the building, waiting for a boy who should've been there ten minutes ago.

Something was wrong, she could sense it. An ulcer of dread had formed in her stomach, spreading and growing, and consuming her from within.

She held her breath—ten seconds, twenty—listening for the scuff of a footstep, or the click of a gun, or the whisper of a warning on the wind: *I'm back, malyshka. I'm back for you.*

Suddenly, she didn't want to be there. Some alarm bell rang in her head, kicking her legs into action. She set off quickly, hoisting her bag onto her shoulder, her skin crawling across the nape of her neck.

She wanted to be with people. Surrounded by them. Lost in amongst them. The canteen. A classroom. The cloakrooms, even. Anywhere but here, with her heart thumping, her head spinning, and her senses screaming at her that he was watching her. That he was near.

Olivia turned the corner, and almost bumped into him. Her hand came up instinctively, scratching at his face, dragging her nails through his flesh, drawing three bloody lines down his cheek.

He screamed. She blinked. Shook her head. Looked more closely.

Paulo clutched his bleeding face, staring at her through a gap in his fingers, his gaze a mix of confusion, and horror, and fear.

'Shit, shit, ow, ow, *fucking* ow!' he grimaced, dancing on the spot. 'What the fuck? What did you do that for?'

Olivia shot a look back over her shoulder. No one there.

Of course, there wasn't.

She let out the breath she'd been holding, pushed back her shoulders and pulled on a scowl. 'You're late,' she told the boy with the blood on his face. 'I don't like it when people keep me waiting.'

—

Logan sat at his desk with a dozen sheets of ever so slightly warm A4 paper spread out around him. Entries on the phone records had been marked in four different colours of highlighter—something Ben had insisted was impossible to do on a computer, despite having been shown how on three separate occasions now.

The other printouts were screenshots of text messages, blown up by the printer so the edges of the text were slightly fuzzy. It made them look a little sordid, Logan thought, like knock-off DVDs shot on a phone camera in a crowded cinema, and punted three for a tenner doon the Barras.

He'd only been looking over it all for a couple of minutes, but already a narrative was emerging.

It was moments like these that made all the many frustrations of polis work feel almost worthwhile. That piece of the puzzle that made you think aye, maybe you could solve this. Maybe a killer wouldn't go unpunished, and a victim unavenged.

It wasn't the full jigsaw—not even close—but it was an important piece. A corner. A bit of flat edge. A basis on which to build.

Lana Lennon's story held up for the most part. The text messages between them confirmed they'd been seeing each other. Logan could even follow the timeline, see the points when their relationship stopped being solely about clandestine sex and became something else. Something deeper.

It wasn't one way, either. Fergus had often been the one to instigate conversations back in the early days of the liaison, but they always turned quickly to meeting up for a quick shag.

In more recent messages, though, he seemed less concerned about the sex element, and instead came across as genuinely interested in how Lana's day was going.

He seemed worried, too. There were several messages asking if she was OK, if she was safe, if Clyde had been 'keeping the heid'.

An unfortunate phrase, given the ending that had been waiting for him.

There was some talk of running away, but the messages referenced in-person conversations they must've had, and information was sparse. One message did reference Fergus getting hold of a couple of grand, which corroborated what Dinky had told Hamza out at his cottage.

The final few texts from Lana were increasingly concerned, asking where he was, why he wasn't replying, if she'd done something to annoy him or make him angry.

In Logan's experience, this was a fairly predictable pattern of responses from a victim of domestic violence—the assumption that they were somehow at fault, that they were to blame, even for things they had no knowledge of or control over. They had it beaten into them and screamed into their faces so often that they started to believe their own bad press.

'I shouldn't have provoked him.'

'I should know by now how stressed he is.'

'It was my own stupid fault for saying anything.'

The final message from Lana had been sent in the early hours of that morning, long after the news had been broken to her that Fergus was in no fit state to ever reply to her again.

I'm so, so sorry. xx

It was a slightly odd thing to text to a dead man's phone, but then grief made you do odd things. And Lana Lennon would not just have been grieving for the man who had died, she would be grieving for herself, and the life she had lost.

He'd been her chance to escape. Her way out. And now, that door had been slammed shut.

And then, to add insult to injury, had its head cut off.

There was one element of Lana's story that didn't fit with the messages on the phone, though. Her husband *did* know about the affair. It was there in front of Logan, in black and white. He'd sent a text to Fergus's phone the night before the PE teacher's death, revealing that he knew all about the relationship.

He didn't say how he knew, just that he did. He seemed angry, understandably, the message packed with enough expletives to make former Detective Superintendent Bob Hoon blush.

OK, maybe not quite *that* many.

Fergus had written one message back, denying everything, and claiming ignorance.

The follow-up message from Clyde was the paydirt, though. That was the jigsaw piece Logan had been hoping for.

'U R a ducking dead man,' Tyler said, reading the message aloud. 'I'd imagine that's a typo, boss.'

'Really? You think so?' Logan asked, but DC Neish completely missed the sarcasm.

'Oh aye. My phone does it all the time,' he explained. 'I tried to write "fuck sake" in a text to Sinead one time, and it came out as "duck sale".' He looked around at the others and raised his shoulders in a prolonged shrug. 'I mean, why would I be writing "duck sale" in a text message to anyone?'

'Maybe if you were selling a duck?' Hamza guessed.

Ben caught the look of irritation as it flashed across Logan's face. He was still raging about the hundreds of school pupils in the car park, whose chanting was now so loud there was nowhere in the building where it couldn't be heard, and idle discussion about the buying and selling of ducks was not doing his mood any favours whatsoever.

'Doesn't look good for the husband, does it?' the DI remarked, diverting the course of the conversation before Logan had a chance to lose the rag.

'It doesn't paint him in a good light, no,' Logan agreed.

'See? Told you it was him,' Tyler said with a nonchalant confidence that suggested it was all over but the singing. 'I knew it.'

'We don't know anything yet. Not for sure,' Logan stressed. 'Not until we talk to him.'

'We going to bring him in now, sir?' Sinead asked. She was standing by the window, watching the crowd of schoolkids in the car park. The teachers had given up trying to talk them down and now stood together off at one side, either working on a Plan B or just waiting until the pupils got bored, hungry, or both.

Logan took the printout of Clyde's final text message from Tyler and read it again for himself. He scratched his chin, compared the message with the one before it, then gave the nod.

'Aye. Let's bring him in,' he agreed. 'Ben, you book us an interview room for today?'

'I did. Wouldn't want to upset Mantits by not following procedure.'

'Right. Good,' Logan said. Then, 'how many?'

Ben missed a beat. 'How many what? Interview rooms? Just the one.'

Logan stood up. 'Oh well, looks like we'll be pissing on the Chief Inspector's parade, after all. I want Lana Lennon brought in at the same time. We need to stress to her that she's not a suspect, though, and don't say a word about the text messages yet.'

'Oh, great,' Ben groaned. 'Mantits is going to be bloody insufferable.'

'There a reason for bringing her in, sir?' asked Hamza. 'I thought you said her story all matched up.'

'It does,' Logan confirmed. 'But knowing she's being interviewed in the room next door'll give us leverage to use against Clyde. Especially if he thinks she's spilling the beans about everything.'

Tyler clapped his hands and grinned. 'Aw, nicely done, boss. Genius move.'

'Oh, thank you so much, Detective Constable. Getting your approval really means a lot,' Logan replied.

This time, and for perhaps the first time ever, Tyler did spot the sarcasm, but he nodded a chipper 'no problem, boss. Any time', all the same, which irked Logan no end.

'What's with these numbers?' Logan asked, tapping a finger on the list of calls and texts with the four different colours of highlights. 'Lana and Clyde, I'm guessing? What about the other two?'

'We don't know,' Sinead said, turning her head away from the window. 'But he was in regular contact with both.'

'Well, aren't they stored in his phone?'

Sinead shook her head. 'Anything relating to those two numbers has been deleted. No texts, no call records, and they're not in the contacts. Both pay as you go SIMs. We're trying to find out if the owners are registered, but it's unlikely.'

'Did you try calling them?' Logan asked.

'Both switched off. Straight through to voicemail.'

Logan sighed. 'Don't suppose they identify themselves on the message, do they?'

'Default greeting,' Sinead said. 'So, no. Afraid not.'

'Aye. That'd be far too easy,' Logan said.

He looked down at the printout. There were hundreds of calls and texts marked in yellow and green—far more than even the pink highlighter used for Lana Lennon's number, and Fergus had been in touch with her several times each day. Whoever those numbers belonged to, they were important to Fergus Forsyth.

The fact all traces of them had been removed from the phone made them important to Logan, too.

'Keep trying them, when you get the chance,' he instructed. 'I want to know who they are.'

'Will do, sir,' Sinead confirmed.

While they'd been talking, Ben had rolled his chair over to his desk and, after a couple of aborted attempts, logged onto the archaic room booking software. 'I'll get our names in for the other interview room,' he announced. 'Stop that bastard moaning at us.'

Logan pulled on his coat. 'Good. Hamza, you're with me. We'll go bring in the nice Mr Lennon. I'd take Tyler, but his face is too punchable, and Clyde Lennon strikes me as a violent man, so I'm not sure he could resist the temptation like the rest of us do. Sinead, try those numbers again, then see if you can track down his wife, will you?'

'That shouldn't be too hard, sir,' Sinead told him. She pointed down at the car park to where the teachers were making their plans. 'She's standing right outside the front door.'

Chapter 32

Sinead had the easy job: stroll outside, ignore the questions from the press and the baying from the pupils, ask for a quiet word with Lana Lennon, and bring her back inside.

Tyler had offered to come with her, but given his presence at the school had helped kick off the riot-in-waiting currently bubbling up outside the station, Sinead had suggested he hang back.

Logan had then stressed his agreement by bellowing, 'Don't you fucking *dare* go outside!' and shooting DC Neish a look that almost soured the milk in his tea.

There was no need for backup, anyway, Sinead had insisted. She was just popping out for a minute. It was a quick, easy job.

That was the theory, anyway.

She hadn't counted on a couple of factors, though.

Firstly, the pupils had not reacted kindly to her taking away one of their teachers. There had been shouted demands asking Sinead what she thought she was doing. Students had blocked the path as she'd tried to lead Mrs Lennon towards the station's front door. They were big lads, for the most part, all spots and snarls, their gangly limbs pumped up with surging testosterone levels and a desire to look impressive in front of the girls.

That was the first problem, and it led directly to the second.

The press, noticing the commotion, came surging over, cameras flashing and questions being barked. Why was she bringing this teacher in? How was she connected? Was she involved in the murder? Had she killed Fergus Forsyth?

Things had escalated when the journos tried to force their way through the testosterone-pumped teens. Already raised voices, rose further. There was swearing. Threats. A few scuffles and shoves.

'Mum? What's happening?' one of the pupils had yelped. 'What are they doing?'

'It's nothing, Benny. Just… I'm just going to talk to them. That's all.'

Spotting an opportunity, half of the journalists switched targets, and started wading through the sea of uniforms to reach the teacher's son. A girl had been knocked over. A punch had been thrown.

Then, just as things were really starting to deteriorate, the front doors of the station had glided open, and four Uniforms had rushed out like football players coming off the bench.

And that was when everything went to hell.

The Uniforms had waded in. Some of the younger pupils had tried to scatter, but found themselves trapped by the bigger kids up the back. The constables weren't being canny, and a few of the teachers had been quick to object about the unnecessary aggression on display.

The officers—all young lads not long out of training—hadn't taken this well. Warnings were shouted, fingers jabbed, threats were issued.

No one saw whose elbow caught the First Year girl in the face, but her squeal drew the attention of everyone around her. She stood there, hunched over, tears, snot, and blood all tripping over each other in their rush to reach the hand she held cupped below her chin.

'What the fuck?' demanded a boy with a Prefect's tie. He took a swing at a photographer who was lining up a shot of the sobbing eleven–year–old. The punch connected hard, sending the pap and his camera sprawling into the crowd.

'Just keep walking, Mrs Lennon,' Sinead urged, guiding the teacher through the gap in the crowd caused by the rising chaos.

Behind them, she heard fists and feet start to fly, but she didn't look back. Let someone else handle that mess. She had her own job to do.

Mrs Lennon did look back, however, and her face told Sinead everything she needed to know.

'Oh, God. Someone's going to get hurt!' she fretted. 'My son. My Benny's in there.'

'We'll get it under control, Mrs Lennon,' Sinead assured her, hoping she sounded confident. 'Best thing we can do is go inside, and everyone should start to calm down.'

The sentence was punctuated by the sound of breaking glass. A car alarm began to howl.

'You know,' Sinead muttered. '*Probably*.'

Tyler was waiting in reception, holding the inner door open so Sinead didn't have to go through Moira's usual interrogation.

The receptionist didn't seem to care this morning, though. She was too busy watching events unfolding out front, a cup of tea in one hand, a couple of custard creams in the other. It wasn't the sort of thing you got to see every day, and she always took the bus to work, so she had no concerns about her car being damaged and could just enjoy the unfolding spectacle.

'You all right?' Tyler asked, quickly closing the door at Sinead's back. 'Told you I should've come.'

'Really not sure you'd have helped matters,' Sinead told him. She finally chanced a glance back out at the car park. It looked like something from a cartoon now, a big mass of fists and feet. All it was missing was the brightly-coloured *Wham!* and *Biff!* sound effects.

'Are there no more Uniforms?' she asked. 'Not that they helped matters.'

Tyler shook his head. 'No. All out and about. Chief Inspector's calling them back to base. The boss and Hamza both left out the back right after you went out.'

'So... what? It's just us?'

'Pretty much, aye. You, me, DI Forde. Whatshername on the front desk. Manti—' Tyler stopped himself in time, then side-eyed the teacher standing wringing her hands beside them. 'Chief Inspector Lyle. He's here, too, but from what I can tell he's

237

essentially barricaded himself in his office. I don't think he's going to be a lot of help.'

'Great,' Sinead groaned. 'How long until Uniform starts arriving?'

Tyler shrugged. 'No idea,' he said, then he turned to the woman beside them and gave her a big puppy-dog grin. 'You must be Mrs Lennon. I'm DC Neish. Tyler.'

'I know. I was at the assembly,' Lana replied with a frostiness that, all things considered, he probably deserved.

'Right. Aye. Um… fair enough,' he said. 'You want a cup of tea?'

'Not really,' Lana said. 'I'd just like to get whatever this is over with.'

'That's completely understandable, Mrs… Lana,' Sinead said. She guided the teacher to one of the two interview room doors and held it open for her. 'If you want to take a seat, we'll be with you in just a couple of minutes.'

'Do I need a solicitor?' Lana asked.

'You can have one. Absolutely,' Sinead told her. 'But you're not a suspect, if that's what you're worried about. We don't think you were directly involved in what happened to Fergus.'

Lana paused at the door. She turned, worry lines etching themselves across her face. 'What is that supposed to mean?' she asked. 'Not *directly*?'

Sinead indicated the uncomfortable chairs on the right-hand side of the room's large table. 'Please, Lana,' she said. 'If you could just take a seat, I'll be in in a moment to explain everything.'

For a moment, it looked like the teacher was going to object, but then she let her shoulders droop and perched on a chair as instructed.

'Two seconds,' Sinead said, pulling the door closed.

Outside, a second car alarm had now joined the chorus of chaos. The voices of children, teenagers, and adults all shouted and swore. There were panicky cries and bellowed threats, tears shed and punches thrown, as the protest tipped over into a full-on riot.

'I have to say, you've really outdone yourself this time,' Sinead said.

Tyler's jaw almost hit the floor. 'What? This isn't my fault!' he protested.

'It feels like it's probably your fault.'

'Well… I mean… I might have played some small part,' Tyler reluctantly conceded. 'But anyway! I didn't want to do it! You're the one who volunteered me to go in and talk to them!'

Sinead had to begrudgingly concede that this was true. 'Aye. I suppose.'

'I can go out and try again,' Tyler suggested. 'Maybe I can talk them round.'

'Jesus Christ, son, gonnae no'?'

Both DCs turned to see Ben making his way along the corridor towards them. He carried a determined look and a megaphone, and by God, he wore them both well.

'Another few words out of you and they're liable to burn the place to the bloody ground,' he said. He gave the megaphone a jiggle to make sure they'd both noticed. 'Just leave this to me.'

Sinead eyed the loudhailer warily. 'You, eh, you sure about that, sir? It's getting pretty hairy out there.'

'Aye. Got to watch your stress levels, boss,' Tyler reminded him. 'Don't want to overdo it.'

'My stress levels are going to get a helluva lot worse if the bastards come swarming in here,' he pointed out. 'And anyway, that lot? That's nothing. Try Sauchiehall Street at half-two on a Sunday morning, the day after a big Old Firm game, then we'll talk about stress.' He gestured with the megaphone. 'Them out there? A bunch of school kids acting up? Just you watch. I'll have them all eating out of my bloody hand in no time…'

–

If bringing in Lana Lennon had been difficult, fetching her husband was proving even more so. Largely, because they couldn't find him.

They'd checked the house first—a phone call, then a nip round and a knock on the door. He hadn't responded to either one, and a quick check of the door handles revealed that the place was all locked up.

That had left the workshop, then. Logan knew enough about where it was that Hamza could pin the exact address down with a quick Google search. It was tucked away at the far end of the industrial estate just past Corpach on the road to Glenfinnan. He hadn't bothered to put a sign on the outside of the building, but the staff at the gym across the road had assured the detectives they'd found the right place.

The workshop was in a self-contained unit with a bright red door and a roll-down metal shutter covering a second, much larger entrance. Both were locked.

The building had a serious shortage of windows. There were only two that Logan could see, both much wider than they were tall, and situated about ten feet above the ground. Light shone through from the other side, and after a quick search turned up nothing to stand on, Logan clasped his hands together and lowered them to knee level.

'Right. Up you go,' he urged.

Hamza glanced from the hands to the window and back again. 'Sure you can hold me up that high, sir?' he asked.

'I could bloody throw you that high, if I wanted,' Logan retorted. 'Come on. Horse on. I want to see if the bastard's in there.'

Hamza nodded, placed a hand on the DCI's shoulder for balance, then raised a foot. Logan whipped his hands away at the last moment.

'Jesus. Wipe your feet first,' he instructed. 'I don't know where they've been.'

Hamza twisted his leg so he could check the sole of his shoe, gave it a rub on the shin of the opposite leg, then raised an enquiring eyebrow. 'All right?'

'I suppose that'll have to do,' Logan said, adopting the position again. He made no sound whatsoever as Hamza stood on his hands, then gave a grunt as he straightened, hefting the Detective Sergeant up until he was level with the windows. 'Christ, you're heavier than you look,' he admitted. 'Can you see anything?'

Hamza clutched the window ledge and peered in through the glass. The lights may have been on, but from that vantage point, it looked like no one was home.

'Can't see him, sir,' he said. 'But I can't get a good look into the corner. Can you shuffle along to the right a bit?'

With a grimace, Logan shuffled along to the right a bit.

'No, my right,' Hamza said.

Muttering, Logan shuffled back in the opposite direction, one of Hamza's feet balanced on his hands, the other standing on his shoulder.

'Anything?' the DCI asked.

Hamza clung to the ledge and leaned further still to his right, until he could see enough of the workshop to be sure nobody was hiding in the corners.

'Doesn't look like he's here. I mean, there's bound to be a toilet, he might be hiding in there, but there's no sign of him in the main part, and none of the equipment is switched on.'

Logan adjusted his stance, shifting his weight from one leg to the other. 'See anything else?'

'Like what, sir?'

'Like anything that might give us cause to break down the door and go inside,' Logan clarified. 'Like a severed human head, or a big puddle of blood. Either of those would do nicely.'

Hamza had to disappoint him. 'Afraid not. Nothing out of the ordinary that I can see.'

'Shite,' Logan spat. He squatted low enough for Hamza to step safely down onto the ground, then brushed his hands against one another and gave his shoulder a wipe.

'Any idea where he'll be?' Hamza asked.

Logan shook his head. 'No,' he said, taking out his phone. 'But I know someone who might.'

Chapter 33

Tyler confirmed into the phone that he'd ask Lana Lennon if she knew where her husband might be, and then told Logan he'd call back in five minutes.

He and Sinead were in the foyer of the station, close enough that they could rush out and help DI Forde if things should turn ugly, but far enough away that Tyler's presence wouldn't escalate things any further.

Moira Corson stood in front of them, still glugging tea and dunking biscuits. She'd winced as she'd watched Ben go past with his megaphone, before announcing, 'They'll eat him alive' to nobody in particular.

'What's all the noise?' Logan asked from the other end of the phone. 'Is that a car alarm?'

'Uh, yeah, boss,' Tyler confirmed. 'I think... I think it might be, aye. Everything's fine, though. Nothing for you to worry about. It's all under control.'

Logan sighed so heavily that even Moira turned to look back at the phone.

'Tell me they're not all kicking off,' the DCI groaned. 'Tell me they're not going mental.'

Logan and Hamza had taken the back road from Spean Bridge to Banavie, then hung a right and headed out to Corpach, specifically so they'd avoid having to pass the police station. All the cars slowing to get an eyeful of what was happening were causing a bottleneck that the detectives had sought to avoid.

Besides, if a disaster had befallen the place, and Logan didn't know about it, he couldn't be expected to sort it out.

Now, though, with alarms blaring down the phone, and the unmistakable sounds of aggression and violence clearly audible in the background, 'plausible deniability' was looking less and less like an option.

'I wouldn't say they're "going mental", exactly, boss,' Tyler said.

This was true. They had passed the 'going mental' stage and had now 'gone mental', past tense. It was a bloodbath out there now. Pupils were no longer just fighting the press and the Uniforms, some of them had turned on each other. Old rivalries and bottled-up feelings had erupted, and the once clearly drawn sides had splintered until it was essentially every man, woman, and child for themselves.

And DI Forde was striding towards it all, one hand in a pocket, the other swinging his megaphone around by its strap.

'Do you need me to come back?' Logan asked.

Tyler covered the mouthpiece of his phone and turned to Sinead. 'Boss is asking if we want him to come back.'

'Can he bring a water cannon?'

'Can you bring a water cannon, boss?'

Sinead tutted. 'That was a joke,' she said, holding her hand out for the phone.

'Sorry, boss. That was a joke,' Tyler said, keeping the phone to his ear but leaning closer to Sinead to let her know he was going to hand it over just as soon as he was done. 'Here's Sinead.'

He handed it over before Logan could respond, then went back to watching Ben. The DI had arrived at the edge of the battlefield now, and was easily within range of a careless kick or punch.

'Sir. It's Sinead. I think we're fine here. The Chief Inspector's calling in more Uniforms.'

'What the hell happened?' Logan asked.

'Got a bit ugly when I tried bringing Lana Lennon in. All deteriorated quickly after that.'

'You got her, though?'

'We did. Any joy with the husband?'

Logan told her that there hadn't been, and gave her the same instruction he'd already given to DC Neish—to get a list of possibilities of where Clyde might be from his wife, then send it over to Logan's phone.

'You sure you don't need us back there?' Logan asked once Sinead had confirmed the instruction. 'We're not far away. We could be there in three or four minutes.'

Sinead didn't answer. Not right away. Instead, she took a step closer to the front door, a smile spreading slowly across her face.

'What's he doing?' Moira demanded. She sounded annoyed, like what was happening out front wasn't part of the plan, and risked ruining the entertainment.

'He's singing,' Tyler said.

And he was. Specifically, he was singing Lady Gaga's *Poker Face* into a megaphone, albeit in the style of a crooner from the 1950s. He had it down word for word, though, and with each new line, more and more heads turned to look at him, as everyone in the crowd tried to figure out what the fuck this old geezer was up to.

'Eh, no. No, I think we're going to be all right, sir,' Sinead said into the phone. 'It looks like DI Forde has got it all in hand.'

'Ben? Christ. Did Ben go out there?' Logan asked.

'He insisted, aye. He brought a megaphone,' Sinead said.

'A mega—oh. Jesus. He's no' doing the *Time Warp*, is he?'

'Uh, no, sir. It's… he's doing *Poker Face*. Lady Gaga.'

Logan made a sound that might well have been a chuckle. 'It's a crying shame you won't get to see his dancing, but good that he's expanding his repertoire, I suppose. Mad old bugger. Always seems to do the job, though. If you can't beat them, confuse the shite out of them. Works every time.'

Sinead had to admit that it did seem to be doing the trick. The fighting had mostly stopped now, aside from a few fringe skirmishes that teachers were rushing in to stamp out. The press cameras—those that hadn't been smashed to pieces—had all turned in Ben's direction.

Some of the teenagers were laughing, and a few even sang along as Ben Frank Sinatra'd his way through the chorus. He raised a hand above his head and waved it back and forth, urging others to join in.

'That's no' something you see every day,' Tyler remarked.

Sinead said her goodbyes to Logan, hung up, then handed the phone back to DC Neish. 'Right. I reckon he's got it all in hand,' she announced. 'Let's go talk to Mrs Lennon, and see if she knows where her husband is.'

Outside, Ben reached the end of the song, then took a bow. Incredibly, given the levels of violence that had been on display just moments before, there was a smattering of applause from the assembled crowd.

'Thanks. I'm here all week,' he announced through the megaphone, then he stretched up on his tiptoes so he could be seen up at the back. 'Right, can you all hear me?'

There was a general consensus that yes, they all could.

'My name's Detective Inspector Forde. But you can call me Ben, if you like. We're all friends here. I'm second-in-command on the investigation into the death of Fergus Forsyth. The first-in-command, Detective Chief Inspector Logan, is currently out pursuing some very promising leads as we speak. He, like all of us involved, is fully committed to finding out who killed Mr Forsyth. And no' just that. We're fully committed to bringing them to justice, and making sure that they are punished to the full extent of the law.'

There was some nodding from a few of the pupils.

'Why did you take Mrs Lennon in?' asked one of the girls.

From the corner of his eye, Ben saw a couple of journalists start typing her name into their phones.

'We'll be talking to all the teachers,' Ben said. A lie, but his motives were pure. 'Mrs Lennon just happened to be first on our list.'

'She's not a suspect, then?' the girl asked.

Ben chuckled. 'Of course not! Like I say, we'll be talking to all the teachers, and many of you lot, too. We're being very thorough. We're pulling out all the stops to make sure Mr Forsyth gets the justice he deserves.'

He waited for the electronic echo of the megaphone to fade away, then he lowered it and continued without the added amplification, which forced them all to shut up and listen carefully.

'Because it hurts. Losing someone you care about. Believe me, I know,' he said. 'It makes you sad, and angry, and frustrated, and... God. Scared. Weirdly scared. And guilty. And ashamed. You want to blame someone, because if you can blame someone, then you're not blaming yourself.'

The only sound in the car park now was the rumbling of cars passing on the main road. Ben looked to the sky for a moment, as if seeking inspiration. Or maybe reassurance.

'But you're not to blame. None of you. Sometimes, and I hate to say this to you, but sometimes bad things happen to good people. Awful things. And it hurts. And it's not fair. But it's not our fault. Not one bit of it.' He shook his head. 'It's not your fault that Mr Forsyth is dead. Not remotely. So take all that guilt, and shame, and frustration, and fear, and throw it away. Get rid of it. Because it's not your fault.'

He let them think on that for a moment.

'But it's not ours, either,' he continued. 'We're doing everything we can to find who did it. To make things right. You and us? We're on the same side here. We want the same thing. Justice for Fergus.'

'Justice for Fergus,' chorused a few of the teens, but the words were spoken softly and calmly, and not bellowed at the tops of their voices.

Ben nodded at them, then gestured at the car park they had almost completely taken over.

'Do we think this is helping matters?' he asked. 'All this fuss, and fighting, and kicking off at each other. Do we think all this will make it *more* likely that we find Mr Forsyth's killer, or less? Hmm?'

The tone in which he asked the question was utterly sincere. There was no blame or fault implied, and so the question came over as a completely genuine one. Because of this, teenagers who might otherwise have automatically jumped straight into 'angry denial' mode were instead forced to carefully consider their answer.

And the answer, of course, was obvious.

'Aye. Much less. Exactly,' Ben said. 'So, hands up if you think we should be devoting more time to finding the killer, and less time to stopping stooshies in the car park. Come on. Hands up.'

The teachers were first to raise their hands. They thrust them up without any hesitation, a couple of them chiming in with a 'Hear, hear!' and a 'Well said!'

A few older students went next, albeit without the same gusto as the teaching staff. This then, gave some sort of permission to the younger pupils to raise their hands, too.

In moments, Ben was standing before a forest of raised arms. It reminded him a little of those pictures he'd seen of Hitler at the Nuremberg Rallies, but he chose not to dwell on that, and just nodded his gratitude, instead.

'Good. Thank you,' he said. 'Now, if you'd all like to head back to school, we'll get back to work. I'll personally assign a liaison who will keep you up to date, but let me finish by saying this: It might take days. It might take weeks. It might even take longer than that. But we will find who is responsible for the murder of Mr Forsyth. We will find them, and we will charge them, and they will be punished. And that's a promise.'

Somewhere, not too far away, a couple of sirens grew louder. Reinforcements were on their way. Just what Ben didn't bloody need.

He checked his watch, then the megaphone gave a squeal as he brought it back to his mouth.

'Now, bugger off, the lot of you,' he instructed. 'Some of us have work to do.'

Chapter 34

Lana Lennon had no idea where her husband might be. She didn't tend to ask him, and he didn't tend to say. He could be secretive like that. She didn't think he was necessarily up to anything, but he guarded his privacy fiercely, and had made it very clear over the years that where he went and what he did was nobody's business but his own.

Sinead had waited for Tyler to text this information to DCI Logan, then had addressed the elephant in the room.

'Why are you still with him?'

Lana sat back a little in her chair, taken aback by the question. She seemed offended by it. Shocked, too, like the thought of leaving him had never occurred to her.

And then… a softening. The knot of her brow untangled. The outrage she had instinctively tried to summon seeped away again, leaving her smaller than Sinead had ever seen her.

'You know, it's funny,' she said, although her expression said it was anything but. 'Sitting with you two… here… I don't have an answer to that. It's like… you ask me that question when he's around, and I can give you a dozen reasons. And I believe them. Then. At the time. I don't know how, but his… his fucking presence makes me believe it.'

She turned and looked at herself reflected in the interview room's two-way mirror, but didn't make eye contact.

'Ask me now, though, and I honestly cannot think of one good reason.'

'Has he hurt you?' Sinead asked.

'No!' Lana said. Then, 'Yes. But he doesn't mean to. He's not… he's not a bad person. Not really. He's just… he had plans.

We both did. For adventure. For fun. But life gets in the way, I suppose. It's frustration, more than anything. He doesn't mean to be how he is. It's not him. Not really.'

'It is, though, Mrs Lennon,' Tyler said, jumping in before Sinead could respond. 'Frustration's no excuse. Everyone gets frustrated sometimes. They don't all start smacking their loved ones around.'

Lana shrunk further, pulling back into herself, reacting to Tyler's words like they were some sort of accusation. Like he was putting the blame on her for not seeing what Clyde was years ago, for not doing something about it.

'Tyler, why don't you go get us all a cup of tea?' Sinead suggested. He opened his mouth to object, but she gave him a pat on the arm and a smile so loaded with meaning it was a miracle that it fit on her face.

He smiled back, not quite sure why he was being made to leave the room, but accepting that—in this instance, at least—Sinead probably knew best.

'Right. Aye. Tea, Mrs Lennon?'

'Please. Thank you.'

'How do you take it?' Tyler asked, rising from his chair.

'I'm not fussy. Just however it comes,' she replied.

Tyler almost challenged her on it. Surely, she had a preferred way of drinking tea?

Wisely, though, he chose not to comment, and instead promised to bring milk and sugar so she could decide for herself.

Sinead waited for him to leave, then said, 'he means well,' as a sort of unofficial apology.

'He seems… nice,' Lana said, glancing at the door through which Tyler had left. 'Maybe a bit…'

She couldn't find quite the right word. Then again, she didn't need to.

'Oh, he's *definitely* a bit… all right,' Sinead laughed. 'Heart's in the right place, though.'

'Yes. I'm sure,' Lana said, chuckling along.

She'd been doing that since the conversation had started, Sinead had noticed—mirroring. If Sinead smiled, she smiled. Sinead fiddled with her pen? Lana fussed with her fingers. It was a de-escalation technique that officers were taught during training—subtly mimic the behaviour of someone in a confrontation, and they were more likely to like you—but Lana seemed to be doing it instinctively.

A learned survival instinct, no doubt.

'They're all like that at the start, though,' the teacher continued. She was facing Sinead, but she wasn't seeing her. Not really. She was looking through her, through the wall at her back, through time itself, and all its wasted years. 'It's all flowers and picnics at the start. People change, though. They realise that the thing they thought they wanted isn't the thing they actually want.'

'Not always, Lana,' Sinead said. She reached across the table and put her hand on top of the other woman's. 'Not all men are like that. There are good ones. Far more good ones than bad ones. No one has any right to hurt you. Not a friend, not a stranger, and certainly not your husband.'

The teacher's lips thinned. She chewed at her gums, stopping herself voicing something she had been conditioned not to say.

She pointed to the door. 'Are you two…?'

Sinead nodded. 'We get married next weekend.'

'Oh! Congratulations!'

'Thank you.'

'I'm really happy for you, Sinead. I really am!'

She really wasn't. She may have been a good teacher, but her acting was shite.

'Thanks,' Sinead said again.

'You're both so young,' Lana said through a smile that may as well have been made of plastic. 'I mean… that's not a bad thing. Necessarily. It's… God. I'm very happy for you. You make a lovely couple.'

'Thank you,' Sinead said, for the third—and hopefully final—time. She watched as Lana's eyes filled with water, which the teacher tried to subtly wipe away before it could be noticed. 'Are you OK, Mrs Lennon? Lana, I mean,' she asked.

'Fine. God. It's fine. I'm fine,' she replied, her throat tight and her voice hoarse. 'It's just… time goes so fast, doesn't it? Just seems like yesterday that you were sitting in my class, and now… here we are. It all just goes so bloody fast.'

'It does,' Sinead confirmed. 'All just seems like yesterday to me, too. I still remember you quizzing me about *Sunset Song*.'

'You never did read that book, did you?' Lana asked.

Sinead shook her head. 'Absolutely not,' she confessed. 'Couldn't get through the first page. Still, I thought I was pretty convincing.'

'You really weren't.' Lana laughed. 'But I have to give you full marks for effort.'

'I wish you'd done that at the time, then. I might've got a higher pass mark!' Sinead told her. 'Good times, though.'

Lana's smile, which had been gradually warming into something more lifelike, was suddenly struggling to stay in place.

'Yes. Well,' she said. 'I'm sure you didn't bring me here to reminisce.'

'No. Much as I'd like that, I'm afraid not,' Sinead confirmed.

'You want to talk about my relationship with Fergus.'

'We do, yes.' Sinead smiled sadly, and this time it wasn't mirrored back. 'And I'm afraid it concerns your husband, too.'

–

'Shite,' Logan spat, reading Tyler's message.

'No joy, then, sir?' asked DS Khaled.

They were still lurking outside Clyde Lennon's workshop, hoping his van might come trundling round the corner. There was no saying he'd done a runner yet. He might just have nipped out for lunch, or to visit a client. He didn't know the finger of suspicion was pointing at him, so hopefully, he was still somewhere nearby.

'No. She doesn't know where he is,' Logan said, shoving his phone into his pocket. He gave the handle of the main door a rattle, then tried lifting the roll-up shutter beside it. Neither one budged.

'Uniform's keeping their eyes peeled for his van. With a bit of luck, that'll turn up soon.'

Logan grunted an acknowledgement. Down in the central belt, finding the van would've been much easier. There were far more ANPR cameras dotted around, and hundreds of polis cars driving around. Getting a ping on a number plate usually took next to no time.

Up here though, there was a distinct lack of Automatic Number Plate Recognition equipment, which slowed things down considerably.

Hamza regarded the building beside them. 'Reckon we can get a search warrant to get in?'

'Aye. Maybe,' Logan said.

'The text messages are pretty damning. And it could be argued that he threatened the victim's life,' Hamza pointed out. 'Actually, did we check if he has a record?'

'I did. He doesn't,' Logan said. 'Which I have to say, I found surprising.'

'Did you look and see if there are any notes on him on the database?'

Logan was eyeing up the front door of the warehouse, only half-listening. It was a heavy, solid bugger of a thing. A kick— even from feet his size—was unlikely to budge it.

'What? Oh. No,' he said, turning away from the workshop entrance. 'Meant to, but time ran away. Run a check when we're back in the office, will you? Anything historical will probably have fallen away by now, but worth a look.'

'Will do, sir.'

Logan nodded, then threw a glance over his shoulder at the door, like he might be able to catch it unawares. Annoyingly, it hadn't budged.

A few good wallops with an enforcer battering ram would wipe the smug look off the bloody thing's face—metaphorically speaking—but he didn't have one handy, and he was probably in enough trouble with the Detective Superintendent as it was.

'Shite,' he said, for the second time in as many minutes. 'I'm meant to phone Mitchell.'

'Want me to step away, sir?' Hamza asked.

Logan tutted. 'I said I'm meant to phone her, son. I didn't say I was going to.'

Hamza smirked. 'Ah. Right. Gotcha.'

'You got your speech sorted yet?'

'Speech?' The DS frowned, then the penny dropped. 'Oh. The Best Man speech? Aye. I've done it. Wrote it ages ago. It's just fifteen minutes of relentless piss-taking, really.'

Logan flinched. Hamza picked up on the meaning behind it right away.

'Ten minutes?' he said. Then, when Logan continued to look doubtful, 'Five minutes?'

'I always think five minutes is about right,' the DCI told him. 'People don't want to sit listening to us wittering on, do they?'

'Oh, I don't know, sir. A lot of people I've spoken to say the speeches are their favourite bit.'

That wasn't what Logan had been hoping to hear. 'Do they?' he grunted. 'Who've you been asking, like?'

'Everyone. Tyler's family, his friends from school. Sinead, obviously. People he trained with. I want to do a good job, so I thought it was important to do my homework. I've got hours of material. Literally hours.'

Logan stared at him in mute horror for several seconds, then quietly said, 'Fuck.'

'Sorry, sir?'

'Nothing. Doesn't matter. Do your fifteen minutes, son. I'm sure everyone will love it.'

'You think? Not too long? I wouldn't want people getting bored.'

'The existence of DC Neish may be many things, Detective Sergeant. I don't think boring is one of them. You say what you want to say about him. Take as long as you need.'

'No, you're right. Cheers, sir. I will.'

'Good lad,' Logan told him. 'But, obviously, don't go over twenty minutes, or I'll punch you to the ground myself.'

'Understood,' Hamza said. He nodded at the building beside them. 'Want me to get cracking on that warrant?'

'Aye. May as well. Got a feeling the bastard's not going to show face anytime soon.'

Logan's phone rang. He winced, dreading whose name would be on the screen, then relaxed when he saw whose it was.

'Ben. You're still in one piece, then?' he asked. 'I heard you'd put on one of your performances.'

'Aye. Worked a treat, as always,' Ben confirmed. 'But we just had a call, Jack. It's Ross Lyndsay, Fergus Forsyth's flatmate.'

'What about him?'

Logan listened as Ben recited the information he'd been given about the call.

'OK. That *is* interesting,' he remarked, once the DI had finished. 'Uniform there yet?'

'Not yet. They're en route, though.'

'Right. Good. Get onto them and tell them not to go in, and tell Lyndsay not to touch anything, either. In fact, tell him to go wait outside,' Logan instructed. He made a hand-gesture indicating DS Khaled should end the call he was just starting to make. 'Hamza and I are on our way.'

Chapter 35

Lana Lennon sat in silence, the tiny flitting movements of her eyes the only outward sign of the processing that was currently happening inside her head.

She hadn't believed them when they'd said that Clyde knew about the affair. 'How could he?' she'd asked. 'He'd have said something. He'd have blown his top.'

'There were texts,' Sinead had told her, but this had only made her even more sceptical.

'Texts? From Clyde? Clyde never sent texts!' she'd insisted.

They'd produced the printouts then. Laid bare the exchange between her husband and her lover. There had been a moment of disbelief, several seconds of denial, and then the silent processing had started.

Sinead and Tyler watched her, saying nothing, letting her reach whatever conclusion she needed to get to on her own. The shock was real—she'd had no idea that Clyde had known about the affair. Both detectives would've staked their careers on that.

'It doesn't... I mean...' Lana began, then she shut down again for another few moments, her internal processing resuming.

'We appreciate it must be a shock for you,' Tyler told her.

'A shock? Yes. Yes, it's a shock, all right.' She sounded numb. Muted. Her eyes were wide open, though, and Tyler couldn't remember the last time he'd seen her blink. 'I didn't... I spoke to him after he sent that message. He seemed fine. We went to bed together.'

'Went to bed?' Sinead asked, seeking clarification.

Lana did blink then, taken aback by the insinuation. 'Oh. God. No, not like that. It's been months since we last tried... Clyde has problems maintaining—' She shook her head, annoyed by her own over-sharing. 'I don't mean we were intimate, I just mean we both went to bed around the same time. There was no drama. No shouting. If he's angry about something, he's not one to hide it.'

'Maybe he was playing it cool,' Tyler said. 'If he was planning to kill Fergus the next day, he wouldn't have wanted you knowing that he knew about the affair.'

Lana was quick to shake her head. 'He can't hide things. Not like that. If something's bothering him, I can tell. The way he talks, or the things he says, or… or the way he moves. If he's annoyed, if I've done something to bother him, then I can tell. Even if he denies it. I can tell. He's quite transparent, really.'

'Most of them are,' Sinead said, earning herself a little dunt under the table from Tyler's knee. 'So, as far as you were concerned, Clyde had no idea about the affair that night?'

'None. I mean…' Lana gestured to the printouts. 'Clearly he did, but… God.' She brought a knuckle to her mouth and chewed on the skin, her eyes filling with tears. 'Why would he hide it? If he knew, why would he hide it, unless he was going to kill him?' She buried her face in her hands, her shoulders shaking. 'Oh, God. It was me, wasn't it? It was my fault? If he hadn't been with me, if we hadn't been together…'

'You shouldn't blame yourself, Lana,' Sinead soothed. 'You couldn't have known he'd react like this.'

'Yes. I should've. Of course, I should've. It's what he does. Flies off the handle. His temper, he… he can't control it. He just… he lashes out. He can't find the words, so he lashes out. It's instinctive. He doesn't even know he's doing it sometimes,' Lana said. She was babbling now, unable to stop the words coming even if she'd tried. 'You can see it in his face, that moment when he realises what he's done. That he's gone too far.'

'He hit you,' Sinead said. It wasn't a question, and Lana didn't waste their time by bothering to answer it.

'He'd cry, sometimes, then. Afterwards. He'd break down and cry.' She shook her head, and all those blinks she'd been holding back came one after the other. 'And... I'd hold him,' she whispered. 'I'd comfort him. I'd... fucking... *apologise* to him. *I'd* apologise to *him*. I'd tell him it was OK. Tell him he wasn't a bad person. Tell him it was my fault, that I'd try harder, that he shouldn't blame himself.'

Lana was collapsing before their eyes. Not literally. Not physically. Emotionally, though, she was crumbling away. Becoming rocks, then rubble, then dust to be carried off on the breeze, until there was no trace left of the person she'd been.

She bit the skin around her thumbnail again, and this time drew blood.

'And... and I brought someone else into that. I knew what he was, how he behaved, what he might do, and I got someone else involved! It's my fault. Fergus is dead. He's dead, and it's all my fault!'

'Again, Mrs Lennon, it isn't,' Tyler told her. 'Whoever killed Fergus—whether it was your husband, or someone else—that's on them. Not you. You're not to blame. Not for any of this. We've seen the texts. Fergus went into the relationship with his eyes open. He knew you were married. You made that clear. He pursued you, despite that. He was the one who really pushed for the relationship, not you.'

It seemed to just occur to Lana then that the detectives had pored over all of the private, intimate messages that she and Fergus had sent to each other. Her cheeks stung red, and the shame of it lowered her gaze to the table.

For a long time, she said nothing. She thought about it—the twitching of her lips and the slight intakes of breath suggesting words were about to come—but she remained silent for a full minute or more before finally settling on what she wanted to say.

'I was flattered, I suppose. I mean, I'm hardly a catch, am I? Not so much "past my best" as "never likely to get there",' she lamented. 'And he was so young. So full of life. And funny! God, but he was funny. He made everyone laugh, right from day one. Usually, when someone new starts, it's awkward for a bit. You know? You try to make them comfortable, but it takes a while for them to settle in. To find their place.'

'But not him?' Sinead asked.

Lana smiled and shook her head. 'No. No, you'd have thought he'd worked there all his life. He just... fit, you know? There was no awkwardness. None. He just turned up one day, and it was like he'd always been there. And when I first spoke to him, it was like... I knew him. Like I'd known him forever. There was none of that uncomfortable stuff when you don't know what to say to someone. It was just... easy. Familiar.'

'Would you say you hit it off right away, then?' Tyler asked.

'Oh, yes. Immediately,' Lana said. 'But, then again, he hit it off with everyone right away. Some of the younger teachers—women—you could see they were interested. Of course they were, he was... not handsome, exactly. That's not quite right. *Beautiful*. He was beautiful.'

More tears made their way down her cheeks, but more through awe than grief, like she was marvelling at some life-affirming sunrise, or getting her first glimpse of the Northern Lights.

'He was just so vibrant. And kind. He radiated kindness. That's why the kids all loved him. He had time for all of them. And he was so good with Bennet.'

'Bennet?' said Tyler, glancing down at the printed notes Sinead had brought into the interview.

'My son. He hated sports. PE was his least favourite subject. He used to be a bit overweight, but Fergus changed all that,' Lana explained.

'How did he do that?' asked Sinead.

'He put together a training schedule for him for outside school hours,' Lana said. 'They even went running together, sometimes. Bennet really looked up to him. He was like a big brother.' She crumbled again then, her hand shaking as she brought it to her mouth. 'And I've barely spoken to him since we heard. God. He must be so upset, and I've been so wrapped up in myself that I've barely said a word to him.'

258

'Did Bennet know anything about your relationship?' Tyler asked. 'You and Fergus, I mean.'

'No!' she retorted, visibly horrified by the suggestion. 'No, he had no idea. No, definitely not.'

'You did think the same about your husband,' Sinead gently reminded her, but Lana stood firm.

'No. He didn't know. He couldn't have. We were very careful to keep things secret.'

'Copsand knew,' Sinead said. 'Mrs Robertson, I mean. Or she suspected enough to point us towards you, anyway.'

Terror flashed across Lana's face, but it was closely followed by the realisation that it didn't really matter now. The worst possible outcome—by some margin—had already happened.

'Not Bennet, though. Bennet didn't know,' she said, trying to convince herself as much as the detectives. Perhaps, even more so. 'He couldn't have known. He couldn't have.'

A look passed between Tyler and Sinead, so brief and subtle that Lana missed it completely.

'How would he have felt if he had found out?' Tyler asked. 'Would he have been angry, do you think?'

'Angry? No. He'd have been bloody delighted!' Lana told him. 'He was always on at me to leave Clyde. And… we were talking about it. Fergus and I. We were making plans to go. Together. With Bennet. The three of us. We'd have had to tell Bennet then, obviously, but I think… I think he would've been happy.' She sniffed, rolled her eyes in embarrassment as the tears began to fall again, then managed to croak out a final, 'I think we all would've,' before her voice betrayed her completely.

She reached for her tea, which was now barely lukewarm, and hid behind her cup for a while as she struggled to compose herself.

'If Clyde found out you were planning to leave and take Bennet with you, do you think that could have driven him to kill Fergus?' Sinead asked. 'Hypothetically, I mean. I'm not asking you to say if you think that's what happened, just if you think that it's theoretically possible for Clyde to do something like that?'

'Do I think he could kill?' Lana whispered. She glanced at the mirror, then at the door, like she was terrified he might be standing there, watching and listening. 'I do. I know he could.'

Another look passed between Tyler and Sinead. Both detectives shifted their weight a fraction forward.

'What do you mean?' Sinead asked. 'How do you know?'

There was a hysterical note to Lana's voice when she replied, the words reverberating around inside the half-empty mug.

'Because of what he said,' she choked out. 'Because he told me he'd done it before.'

Chapter 36

Ross Lyndsay teetered on a pair of child-sized crutches, the foot of his strapped-up leg hovering an inch or two above the pavement outside his house.

He hopped in a half-circle at the sound of yet another car door closing, and jerked in fright at the sight of DCI Logan striding towards him, his coat billowing behind him in the wind like Dracula's cape.

In the hospital, the detective had seemed like a very large man indeed. Out here, in the open, he was a monster. A hulk. Had it not been for the condition of his leg, Ross's instinct would have been to make a run for it before he was eaten alive.

There were four uniformed officers within a hundred yards—one standing guard outside his house, while the others went door to door, asking the neighbours if they'd seen anything suspicious. Ross took little comfort from this, though. The detective was their boss, after all. If he decided to pick Ross up and throttle him, they were unlikely to intervene.

To the little man's surprise, the ogre in the overcoat was far more affable than he'd been on their two previous encounters.

'Jesus, can we get Mr Lyndsay a seat from somewhere? The man has a broken leg,' he said, scowling at the uniformed constable standing guard outside the front door.

With a nod, the officer turned to enter Ross's house, only to be abruptly halted by a barked order from the DCI.

'Not from in there! Think, man,' he said. 'Go ask a neighbour.'

The constable blushed, nodded again, then scurried off to knock on the door of the house across the driveway.

'Sorry about that,' Logan said. 'How's the leg?'

Ross's eyes narrowed with suspicion, sensing a trap but unable to work out what it might be. 'It's... sore.'

'I'll bet,' Logan said. 'We'll get you a seat. You remember DS Khaled?'

Ross gave a tilt of his head in Hamza's direction, just as the DS arrived at Logan's side. 'Uh, yes. Hello.'

'Mr Lyndsay,' Hamza said. 'How's the leg?'

'He says it's sore,' Logan said, answering for him.

'I'll bet,' Hamza replied.

'We're getting him a seat,' Logan said.

'Good stuff. Take the weight off a bit.'

'Aye,' Logan agreed. 'Take the weight off a bit.'

Ross looked between them both, convinced they were talking in some sort of code that he couldn't decipher. Before he could even try, the questions came.

'What happened?' Logan asked, indicating the house with a jerk of a thumb.

'What? Oh. I don't know,' Ross answered. 'I just... I got a taxi home from the hospital. The door was open. Or... not open. It was half-closed. Resting against the frame, sort of thing. Like, as if it had been opened, but then—'

'We get the picture,' Logan said. 'Someone had forced it?'

'Yes. Yes, someone had forced it,' Ross confirmed. 'I opened it, listened for a bit to see if anyone was there, then I went in.'

'And?' Hamza prompted.

'And... it was a mess. They'd trashed the place.'

'Who's they?' Logan asked.

Ross frowned and gave a half-chuckle, like this should be obvious. 'Well, I mean... the burglars.'

'The burglars?'

'Obviously. Who else burgles houses?'

'So, it was a burglary?' Logan asked. 'What did they take?'

Before Ross could reply, the constable arrived with a dining room chair and set it on the pavement beside him.

Several seconds passed while Ross made a meal of lowering himself into the seat, somehow almost breaking his other leg in the process.

Once he was safely installed on the seat, Logan asked the question again. 'These burglars, what did they take?'

'I don't know,' Ross admitted. 'I didn't really check. I phoned the police, then got a call back to go outside and wait. They could have taken anything.'

'Telly still there?' Logan asked.

'Yes. I think so. Yes.'

'Unlikely to be a burglary, then,' Logan said. 'Just you wait there and rest your leg, Mr Lyndsay. We'll go take a look. Would you like a cup of tea?'

The thought of the hot beverage made the little man realise how cold he was, and he shivered. 'Yes. That would be lovely.'

Logan turned on the constable, all scowls again. 'Have you no' even offered the man a cup of tea?' he barked.

'Um, no, sir,' the constable confirmed. 'Sorry.'

'What is this, Nazi Germany?' Logan demanded. 'Get back to that neighbour and get her to rustle you one up.'

The look that the constable fired at the house next door spoke volumes about the welcome he'd received on his previous visit. He didn't protest, though, and instead trudged sullenly back up the path, and gave the door a knock.

'Right, we'll leave you in this officer's capable hands,' Logan told Ross. He reached into his coat pocket, produced a pair of latex gloves, and snapped them over his shovel-like hands. 'DS Khaled? You're with me,' he announced, then they both headed up the driveway to Ross Lyndsay's front door, nudged it open, and vanished inside.

–

Lachlan stood in the doorway of the large but ramshackle house he shared with a few other Inverlochy Castle Hotel staff members, one eye welded shut with sleep, the other blinking furiously as it tried to figure out what the fuck was going on.

'Can I come in?'

It took Lachlan's sleep-fuddled brain a few seconds to get to grips with the question, then he grunted and stepped aside, making room for Bennet to come scurrying in.

Bennet was still in his school uniform, although he'd taken off his tie and unfastened the top button of his shirt.

Something about his presence there was ringing alarm bells for Lachlan. A klaxon rang in his head, warning him that…

Shit!

'What time is it?' he asked, suddenly wide-awake and on full-scale alert. 'Fuck! I'm meant to be on at three.'

'It's just after one,' Bennet said.

It took a few moments for Lachlan's panic levels to drop back down from DEFCON 1, then he closed the door and ushered Bennet through into the living room.

'Is everyone else out?' Bennet asked, taking a seat on a cast-off couch that sagged pitifully beneath his weight.

Lachlan looked around, blinking. The surge of adrenaline that had forced him fully awake was dwindling rapidly, and he seemed vague and confused as he tried to work out the answer to Bennet's question.

'Yes?' he said, unconvincingly. 'I don't… what time did you say it was?'

'Just after one.'

Lachlan shrugged. 'Then, yeah. I think so.' He moved an overflowing ashtray from the arm of one of the room's three mismatched armchairs, and took a seat. 'Why are you here? Shouldn't you be in school?'

'It'll be lunchtime now. Or near enough,' Bennet replied. His hands were clasped together, squashed between his thighs. 'Sorry. Did I wake you up?'

'Yeah,' Lachlan said. There was an accusation there, but then he dismissed it with a sigh and an 'it's fine. What's up?'

'Nothing.'

'Bollocks. There's something,' Lachlan insisted. 'You'd better not just be after a lift somewhere or something...'

Bennet said nothing. His thighs pressed more firmly inwards, squeezing his hands together like they were in prayer.

'Jesus. What is it? What's happened?' Lachlan asked.

Bennet met his gaze for a second, maybe less, then he jumped up off the couch again and made for the door. 'Sorry. I shouldn't have come. Sorry.'

'Whoa, whoa, hold on,' Lachlan urged, getting up to intercept. 'There's obviously something bothering you, mate. What is it? Is it your dad? Has he done something?'

Bennet shook his head. His eyes were constantly on the move, darting here, there, and everywhere, refusing to settle on any one thing.

'Talk to me, mate,' Lachlan encouraged. 'What is it? What's the matter?'

'You know that teacher? Fergus. PE. The one the police were asking about last night?'

Lachlan nodded slowly. 'Yeah. What about him?'

Bennet swallowed. Every part of his face twitched in turn, like it was fighting to stop him saying what he was about to say. Like it was trying to suppress the awful, terrible truth.

Somehow, though, the words made it out. 'There's something I need to tell you,' he whispered.

And then Lachlan staggered backwards and fell into another armchair as Bennet told him everything.

—

It wasn't a burglary. Not in the conventional sense, anyway.

There were three TVs in Ross Lyndsay's house—32-inchers in the bedrooms, and a bigger one hooked onto the wall in the living room. None had been taken.

The same went for the Sky box, the PlayStation, an iPad, and a collection of boxed action figures which, as far as Logan knew, might well have been worth a fortune.

The place had been well and truly trashed, though. Cushions had been torn open, their stuffing strewn across the room like innards and body parts on a medieval battlefield. Pictures had been taken down and smashed, light fittings hung from wires, and every drawer, cupboard, and cabinet in the place had been gone through in a hurry, their contents scattered and broken on the floor.

Mattresses had been sliced open. Furniture had been smashed. Carpets had been pulled up, and curtains pulled down throughout the whole house.

It was Fergus's bedroom that had taken the worst of it, though. Not an inch had been missed. Even the light and power sockets had been unscrewed and prised from the wall. A bedside alarm clock had been smashed, exposing its sparse innards.

'They were thorough, I'll give them that,' Logan remarked, turning slowly in the centre of the room.

Hamza stood by the door, taking a few photographs on his phone and scribbling a few notes. 'Aye, someone was on a mission, all right.'

'Vandalism, you think?' Logan asked.

'More likely someone was looking for something, I'd say,' Hamza replied, and Logan rocked back on his heels a little, pleased by this observation. He was good. He wouldn't stay Detective Sergeant for long.

'Aye. Well spotted,' Logan told him. 'Someone was on the hunt for something.'

'The question is *what*?' Hamza asked.

'And did they find it?' Logan wondered. He took another look around the room. 'Not in here, I don't think. I reckon they hit this room first. This is where they expected to find whatever it was. They were more thorough in here. The rest of the house was turned over quickly. They went to a lot of effort in here. And, given that they got to the point they were lifting lino in the kitchen, I reckon they left empty-handed.'

'Any ideas what they might have been after, sir?' Hamza asked.

'Aye. A pretty good one.' Logan indicated the light switch that dangled from the bedroom wall like a broken cuckoo from a clock. 'Something small enough to fit in there.'

It took Hamza a second or two, then it hit him. 'The key.'

'The key. That's my thinking, too,' Logan said. 'Someone turned this place upside down so they could get their hands on that key.'

'Must be pretty important.'

'Aye. To someone. We any closer to finding out what it opens?'

'Not sure, sir,' Hamza admitted. 'Tyler was running with that. Want me to phone him?'

Logan stood in silence for a while, taking a final look around the room. His gaze painted every surface, cataloguing the room and everything in it.

'No,' he said, once he was done. 'We'll check with him when we're back at the office. We'll let Scene of Crime in to check this place over. See if they can find anything that'll help us figure out who trashed the place. I assume they're on their way?'

'I'd have to check, but I think so, sir,' Hamza confirmed.

Logan grunted and ushered the DS towards the front door. 'Right, well, let's fuck off before Geoff Palmer gets here,' he said. He'd seen what he needed to see and didn't feel any need to stick around for the next part. 'His is the last bloody face I want to see.'

This wasn't quite true, he realised a moment later when he emerged from the house to find a sour-faced black woman in a pristinely white shirt and polis tie waiting for him by his car.

'Aw…shite,' he muttered, but not quite quietly enough.

'Yes. *Deep* shite, Detective Chief Inspector,' said Detective Superintendent Mitchell. 'And you're up to your neck in it.'

Chapter 37

Bennet stood by the door, contemplating making a break for it while he waited for Lachlan to say something. To say *anything*. To offer some sort of response to the bombshell Bennet had just dropped.

When he did finally speak, it was nothing especially constructive.

'Fucking hell, Benny,' he said. He was sitting on the arm of a chair now, the shock of the last few minutes having all but knocked his legs out from under him. 'I mean... fucking hell. That is... I mean... That is...'

Bennet wrapped his arms around himself and took a backwards step towards the exit. 'Sorry. I shouldn't have said anything. I shouldn't have told you,' he said.

'Too fucking right you shouldn't!' Lachlan said, then he raised a hand to stop the younger man leaving. 'Wait. Wait. Hold on. I just... give me a minute to process it, eh?'

Lachlan ran his hands through his hair, then down his face. He was awake now. Fully awake. Perhaps more awake than he'd ever been. Bennet's confession had been like an electric shock to the brain, driving away all drowsiness and bringing the world into pin-sharp focus.

'Have you told anyone else?' he asked.

Bennet shook his head. 'No. God. No. Of course not. I shouldn't have told you, either. I just... I had to tell someone. It was eating me up.'

'Aye. Aye, I can imagine,' Lachlan said. 'But, I mean... still, Benny. What the fuck were you thinking?'

'I wasn't. Not really,' Bennet admitted. There was a faint whistling sound as he inhaled through his nose, then he spat out the question he'd come here to ask. 'What should I do? Should I tell anyone?' He looked down at his feet, dreading the answers he was about to get. 'Should I tell the police?'

Lachlan groaned, ran his fingers through his hair a few more times, like he was trying to backcomb it, then nodded. 'You have to, don't you? They're bound to find out. They might already know, and be looking for you now, for all we know.'

Bennet shook his head. 'They're talking to my mum.'

'Shit. They're not blaming her, are they?'

'What? No!' Bennet said. It was clear, though, that this hadn't really occurred to him, and his brow creased in concern as he lowered himself back onto the couch. 'I don't think so, anyway. Why would they blame her? She didn't do anything!'

'You have to say something, Benny,' Lachlan urged.

Bennet shot a look to the ceiling, or to somewhere higher still. 'But... what'll happen?' he asked. 'If I tell them, what'll happen?'

'I don't know,' Lachlan admitted. 'But better you tell them than they find out some other way. It'll look better if you go to them, than if they have to come looking for you.'

'I'm scared,' Bennet whispered. 'About what'll happen.'

'I know, mate. I don't blame you. But it's the best way. In the long run.' Lachlan checked his watch. 'Listen, I need to start getting ready for work, but why don't you hold off here until school's over? Maybe go talk it over with your mum, then the two of you can go talk to the police together.'

'You're going to work?' Bennet asked.

'Well... aye. Coleen's already gunning for me. She doesn't need much of an excuse before my arse is out the window.'

'You won't tell anyone, will you?' Bennet asked, his eyes narrowing. 'You won't go running to the police?'

Lachlan glanced at the door. It was the only way out of the room, and it was directly behind Bennet, so Lachlan would have to pass him if he tried to leave.

'Course I won't,' Lachlan said. 'No offence, mate, but the last thing I want to do is get mixed up in it all. I mean, I'm always here if you want to talk… but, I'll be honest, it feels a bit out of my league, this.' He smiled. It was kind and wary at the same time, like he was dealing with an injured wild animal. 'Talk to your mum, though. Wait here until you think she'll be at home, then go tell her what you told me. She'll know what to do. She'll understand.'

She wouldn't, Bennet knew. Of course, she wouldn't. How could she? How could anyone? He barely understood it himself.

She'd hate him, once she knew what he was.

And what he'd done.

'It's going to be OK, Benny,' Lachlan assured him.

'You can't possibly know that,' Bennet replied. 'Nobody can.'

'No, mate, I suppose we can't,' Lachlan conceded, after a moment's pause. 'But honestly… what's the alternative?'

–

Detective Superintendent Mitchell, to her credit, had not immediately started tearing strips off Logan in front of Hamza and the Uniforms. Instead, she'd instructed him to walk with her, and then had set off along the street so she could deliver his bollocking in a marginally more private setting.

A bollocking from this senior officer was quite unlike the bollockings he'd received from the last one, of course.

Mitchell hadn't once cast aspersions on his parentage, insinuated that he enjoyed sexual intercourse with members of the animal kingdom, or labelled him as any part of the female reproductive system. Nor did Logan feel, at any point during the conversation, that the Detective Superintendent was one wrong word away from breaking his nose with a well-aimed head-butt, or punching his mouth clean off his face.

It was all quite refreshing, really.

But, while the delivery style may have been different, the general gist of it was the same. Logan had fucked up, and for that, there would be consequences.

'Is it my fault, Jack?' Mitchell asked, as they strolled side by side along the quiet residential street, nosy neighbours ducking out of sight when they passed, only to pop back up again at their windows the moment they had strolled on. 'Did I not make myself clear?'

The house, and the officers standing outside it, were some way behind them now. Logan had glanced back just once, and found Hamza and the Uniforms all pretending not to be watching.

'No. I mean yes. You did,' Logan said. And then, in the howling void of silence that followed, he added the missing, 'Ma'am.'

'I made it clear that DI Forde was to remain in Inverness?'

'You did, yes,' Logan reiterated.

'Well, that is funny,' Mitchell said. 'Because DI Forde isn't in Inverness. He's in Fort William. So if, like you say, I made my wishes clear, then either you misunderstood a simple instruction—which doesn't bode well for your future career prospects—or you deliberately disobeyed a direct order. This, also, does not bode well for your future career prospects.'

They reached a T-junction at the end of the road. Logan followed Mitchell's lead as she hung a right and proceeded in that direction, her hands tucked in behind her back.

Strolling along like that felt a bit like being back on the beat. So much so, in fact, that he automatically fell into step beside her.

How many miles had he covered like that over the years, he wondered? How much shoe leather had been worn away down dodgy back alleys and shady streets?

'So, which is it, Jack? Idiocy or mutiny?' Mitchell pressed, dragging him back to the here and now.

Logan screwed up his face. 'Bit of both,' he said.

If he'd hoped this might thaw the ice a bit, he was sadly mistaken.

'I really suggest you start taking this seriously, Detective Chief Inspector,' Mitchell warned. 'I didn't drive all the way down here to "banter".'

Just as well, too. In all the time he'd known her, Logan couldn't recall the DSup ever displaying much of a sense of humour. There were rumours that she'd been fun once, but that person had long-since been buried under the weight of rank and responsibility.

The primary school where Ross Lyndsay worked stood ahead on the left. Ross's lollipop hut was locked up, but a surly-looking man with silver hair and coal-black eyebrows was hobbling towards it across the school grounds, muttering below his breath.

'It's bad enough you disobeying my order, but then to not return my calls? To keep me out of the loop on the investigation? That's disciplinary-level stuff, Jack. All of it is, in fact. And you bloody well know that.'

'Aye. I should've called. I messed up,' Logan admitted. 'Ben… DI Forde… he was desperate to get stuck back into things. We were coming down here, and I didn't have the heart to tell him that he had to stay behind.'

Mitchell shot him a look that was a sharper comeback than any words she could have said.

'I know, I know, I should've just told him. I should've left him back in Inverness,' Logan continued. 'But he's been a godsend. We almost had a riot outside the station earlier, but Ben went out and calmed it all down.'

'A riot?' Mitchell said, stopping abruptly.

'Aye. But it was nothing, really,' Logan insisted. 'Like I say, Ben…'

His voice trailed away into silence as he realised his error.

'You sent Detective Inspector Forde—a man recovering from a cardiac condition so severe it required an extended stay in hospital—to deal with a riot?'

'It wasn't *that* recent…' Logan began, but another look from Mitchell made him think better of it. 'I take full responsibility, of course, but I didn't send him. He went by himself. I wasn't there at the time, so he was the senior officer.'

'Who shouldn't have been there in the first place,' Mitchell said.

A movement from across the road caught Logan's eye. He watched, only half-listening to the reprimands from the Detective Superintendent, as the silver-haired man unlocked the crossing patroller's shed and withdrew a long, high-vis coat.

'Shit!' Logan exclaimed, loudly enough to draw the man's attention and stop the Detective Superintendent in her tracks. 'Of course! What a bloody idiot.'

'I'm sorry?'

Logan tore his eyes from the man in the shed and turned his attention back to Mitchell. 'Are you firing me?'

'What?'

'Right now. Are you firing me right now?'

Mitchell took a step back, caught off guard by the question. 'There's a process that needs to be followed. You know that.'

Logan did know that. He was counting on it, in fact.

'Right. Well, why don't you head back up the road and get cracking on that?' he suggested. 'Then give me a shout when you've decided what you want to do.'

'You don't get to give out the orders here, Jack,' Mitchell reminded him. 'You get to listen while I—'

'Aye. Very good,' Logan interjected. 'Listen, you do what you have to do. There's just been a breakthrough on the case.'

'A breakthrough?' Mitchell echoed. 'How do you know?'

Logan grinned at her, then turned and strode away. 'Because I'm the one who just made it.'

—

DI Forde sat at his computer, reading over emails and enjoying what was, by anyone's definition, a good cup of tea.

Some early toxicology work had come through for the victim. The report suggested that Fergus dabbled lightly in both alcohol and cannabis, although the second one was such a faint trace he may have just spent time in the company of someone who partook of the occasional puff.

Another email had left him scratching his head. It was from the headteacher at Fergus's old school. They'd contacted him after getting his details from Lochaber High to try to get some background on Fergus and maybe identify his next of kin.

The message was a brief one. It read:

'I'm afraid I don't know a Fergus Forsyth, and have no record of one ever working here. Apologies.'

Ben took a sip of his tea and contemplated the message for a few moments, then he rattled off a reply, and this time attached a photo of the victim that LHS had provided.

Normally, they'd have sourced a few pictures from the victim's social media, too, but Fergus didn't appear to be on any. Not unusual for teachers, though. The last thing most of them wanted was their private lives being picked over by the kids in their charge.

He had just clicked send when two things happened simultaneously—the arrival of Tyler and Sinead, and the ringing of his desk phone.

The DI gave the junior detectives a quick wave and a nod, then picked up the phone and rattled off a third of a greeting, before the voice on the other end cut him off.

'Ben. It's me,' Logan said. The slight echo on the line and the rumble of an engine revealed he was driving. 'What's the latest?'

'Hello, Jack. The latest? Not a lot, really.' He explained about the toxicology report and the email from the headteacher. 'How about you? Find anything interesting up the road?'

'Just Mitchell,' Logan said.

'What do you mean?'

'She drove down to talk to me,' Logan said.

'Could she no' have just phoned?'

Ben could hear Logan shifting around in his seat. 'Aye, well, she wasn't having a lot of luck getting through,' the DCI said. 'But anyway, what's happening with the school kids and staff? They still out front?'

'No, long gone,' Ben said. 'Why?'

'I need to talk to someone at the school.'

'That works out nicely, then. I said someone would go in to update them this afternoon. You be back in time? It's about three now.'

Logan confirmed that he'd go straight there, then asked about Lana Lennon.

'Sinead and Tyler are just back in from talking to her right this minute,' Ben said, beckoning the detectives over. 'Here, I'll put you on speakerphone and you can ask them.'

'All right, boss?' asked Tyler, leaning so close to the phone it gave a screech of feedback when his voice looped back around at him via Logan's car.

'Aye. Fine,' Logan said. 'What's the story?'

'Do you mean with Lana Lennon?' Tyler asked.

'Naw. In Balamory,' Logan spat.

Tyler blinked. 'Boss?'

'Jesus fu—*Of course,* I mean with Lana Lennon. What did you get from her?'

Deciding that it was probably in everyone's best interests, Sinead took over from DC Neish. 'Nothing concrete, sir. She was quite open about the domestic violence, though. He's been hitting her for years. She's adamant she doesn't want to press charges, though.'

'Tell him about—' Tyler began, but Sinead nodded and held up a hand to silence him.

'There was something else, though. Lana said that Clyde claimed he'd been married before, but that his ex-wife was dead. Said he'd killed her.'

The only sound from the speakerphone was the rumbling of an engine and the faint whistling of wind, then Logan said, 'Jesus. Did she believe him?'

'She says no. Not until now, anyway. But given everything that's happened…'

'Get onto it,' Logan instructed. 'And talk Lana into pressing charges for the DV. Easy arrest warrant, and it means we can batter down his workshop door and see what he's hiding.'

'We sent her home about half an hour ago,' Sinead said. 'Escorted her up the road a little bit in case the press tried to follow her.'

'Shower of arseholes,' Logan muttered, in case anyone on the call wasn't already fully aware of his feelings on the loathsome, bottom-feeding, parasitic bastards. 'And did they?'

'No, sir. I think DI Forde singing Lady Gaga to a crowd of rioting school kids probably let most of them knock-off early,' Sinead reasoned. 'Not going to top that for a front page.'

'Fame at last,' Ben remarked, but Logan didn't share his sense of humour on the matter.

'They won't have gone far. They'll be around somewhere,' he insisted. 'Up to their elbows in someone else's shite, seeing what they can dig up. Do we have any word on Clyde's whereabouts yet?'

Sinead and Tyler both looked to DI Forde to provide the response on that one.

'Not a thing,' he said. 'Cameras on the trunk roads haven't picked him up, and he hasn't driven past any polis cars today. He's probably still local, but laying low somewhere.'

Logan cursed under his breath, too quietly for them to make out the actual words over the rumbling of the engine, but loud enough that they got the general idea.

'Extend the search. Get Mantits to authorise extra resource. I want the bastard found,' the DCI instructed. 'Tyler, Sinead.'

'Boss?'

'Get back onto Lana Lennon. Get as much information as you can from her about this supposed ex-wife of Clyde's. And get her to press charges for the DV. That'll make our lives easier.'

'I'll give her a phone,' Sinead said.

'No. Go to her house. Do it face to face. You're asking her to break the habit of a lifetime. She's covered for the bastard for years. A phone call's not going to cut it. Softly, softly,' Logan said. 'Then, if that doesn't work, play on her relationship with Fergus. Make her reflect on just what her husband is capable of. Whatever it takes to get us that arrest warrant.'

The thinning of Sinead's lips and the way she pulled back her hair suggested she wasn't entirely comfortable with the order, but she responded with a 'will do, sir,' and left it at that.

'Good. Hamza and I will swing by the station on my way to the school,' Logan said.

Ben checked his watch. 'You'll be cutting it fine for getting there before the last bell,' he said. 'Wouldn't you be better going straight there?'

'No, I need to pick something up,' Logan explained. 'The key Shona took from Fergus's stomach. Have it ready for me, will you?'

'The key, boss? You figured out what it opens?' asked Tyler.

'No,' Logan admitted. 'But I might just have thought of someone who can.'

Chapter 38

His name was Alan Dunne. To the pupils—and most of the staff—of Lochaber High School, though, he was better known as 'Janny'.

He sat behind a shonky desk in a room that was forty percent office, forty percent workshop, and twenty percent 'other'. The exact make-up of that 'other' was hard to define. It was part kitchen, part warehouse, part security station, and part cleaner's cupboard.

The janitor sat on a throne of boxes and paper towel bales, carefully studying the small sliver of metal that had been placed in a clearing on the desk before him.

'Any ideas?' Logan asked.

'Give us a minute.'

Alan struck Logan as a man clinging desperately to the end of his tether. He'd eyed the DCI with suspicion when they'd been introduced, and had sighed heavily no less than six times in the brief conversation that had followed, before graduating to full-scale eye-rolling when Logan had asked him to take a look at the key.

At first, Janny had given the evidence bag just the briefest of glances, before shaking his head and saying he had no idea. Logan had insisted he take more time, though, so the caretaker had begrudgingly led him to the office/workshop/other, and spent much of the time since then sitting staring at the thing in silence.

With yet another weary sigh, Alan hefted his own bunch of keys onto the desk. It was much larger than the already impressive bunch the janitor at the primary school in Invergarry had unlocked the lollipop hut with, and touched down on the desk with a heavy thunk.

Picking up the bag, he turned it over, checking the key from both sides. Then, he set it down again, and began rifling through his own bundle, fingers pecking away like hungry birds.

'No, no, no. No. No, no,' he muttered, dismissing the first few keys without a second thought.

'Could it be a locker or something?' Logan asked.

Janny stopped long enough to give him a snide look, then went back to his bunch of keys. There had to be a hundred or more of the things on the big metal loop, Logan thought. They were all shapes and sizes, from big old-fashioned iron things to those designed for tiny padlocks.

None of them were quite right, though, and as the caretaker continued on through the bundle, Logan felt his hopes begin to dwindle.

Sure enough, some minutes later, Alan finished comparing his own keys with the one in the evidence bag, but failed to find a match.

'Bugger it,' Logan grunted. 'You're sure you don't have one like it?'

'You watched me go through them, didn't you? You watched me go through them there, just then.'

Logan had indeed watched. Like a bloody hawk. There had been a few close calls, but nothing similar enough to warrant any further investigation.

'Aye. Shite. I thought, maybe...' It was his turn to sigh this time, although far less forcefully than the janitor had been doing for the past half hour. 'Never mind. Worth a try.'

'Sorry I couldn't have been more help,' Alan said, getting to his feet, even as he slid the bag across the desk. 'Now I've fallen behind, thanks to all this. So, if you don't mind...'

The janitor was a big man, yet he seemed to have been afflicted by Small Man Syndrome, making him more aggressive than there was any need to be. Logan thought about pointing this out to him, but bit his tongue. What would be the point?

Besides, if he had to spend his days fixing the messes caused by several hundred teenagers, he'd probably be a right crabbit bastard, too.

'Well, if you think of anything else,' the DCI said, pocketing the evidence bag.

'I won't,' Alan insisted.

Logan smiled through gritted teeth. 'Well, if you do...'

'I won't, though, will I? I've checked all my keys. You just watched me. And a right waste of bloody time it was, too. If it's not there, then...'

He blinked. Frowned. Shot a look at Logan's pocket where the key had been stashed.

'What?' Logan asked. 'What is it?'

'Forsyth...' the caretaker said, rolling the name around inside his mouth. 'He was PE, wasn't he?'

'That's right. Why?'

Alan stepped past the detective without a word, then raised a hand, crooked a finger, and beckoned for him to follow.

—

Tyler smiled and nodded, his hands gripping the wheel, his mind miles away. Beside him, Sinead spoke about seating plans for the wedding, the deposit for the photographer, the music they'd play, and the food they'd eat.

They'd gone over all this before. So she had told him, anyway. He had vague memories of discussions not unlike this one, but was unable to recollect many of the details. He knew his own responsibilities for the day—turn up and follow instructions—and sort of glazed over the rest of it when Sinead brought it up.

It wasn't deliberate. He tried very hard to listen and get involved. He'd even offered a couple of opinions, although both had been wrong.

The truth of it was, though, he didn't care about any of it. Not about who sat where, or who ate what, or what they danced to and when. All that stuff was just window dressing. It was the side-salad that came with restaurant meals that he never touched.

All he cared about was a vow. A kiss. Her hand in his. Nothing else mattered. Not one bit.

Well, apart from the karaoke he'd suggested, but that had been shot down in flames very quickly.

He was idly tapping a rhythm on the steering wheel, thinking about which of the *X-Men* he'd most like to be, when a name cut through the haze.

'Wait, what?' he asked, shooting her a glance. 'What did you say?'

'Which bit?' Sinead asked.

'Just then. A second ago. You said about inviting…?'

'Oh. Yeah. I just… I feel bad for him.'

'Who?'

'Hoon.'

'Hoon?!' Tyler cried. A passing car blared its horn as he drifted across to the wrong side of the road, and he hurriedly jerked the wheel to the left. 'As in *Hoon* Hoon? As in psychopathic ex-Detective Superintendent Hoon? That Hoon?'

'I just… he's had a rough time. I think it would be nice.'

'For who? Not us! Not anyone else present. He's insane!'

'I thought you liked him,' Sinead said.

Tyler did a double-take, and this time almost steered them into the verge at the side of the road. 'What? Why?! How have I given you that impression? He's a terrifying lunatic.'

'I know. I just… last time we were down here. The Glenfinnan Monument case. You seemed to have a good time with him.'

'He could've got me fired!' Tyler reminded her. 'Or killed!'

'You told me you had fun,' Sinead countered.

Tyler ran out of steam a bit then. 'I mean… I suppose it was *kind* of fun, yes. Kicking in doors and all that. But it doesn't change the fact that he's deranged. And that he hates me.'

'He doesn't hate you,' Sinead said. 'He told Jack he liked you.'

Tyler shook his head. 'No, he didn't. Who, Hoon? No. Told the boss? No way. Nuh-uh. No chance.' He flexed his fingers on

281

the wheel, then blew out his cheeks. 'What did he say, like?' he asked, clicking the indicators and turning onto the street that led to the Lennons' house.

A small white van shot towards them, forcing Tyler to wrench the wheel to the left and swerve the car up onto the pavement.

'Ooh, fuck,' he ejected, as the van flew past, a wild-eyed older man wrestling with the wheel.

'Was that…?' Sinead asked, spinning in her seat in time to see the van go careening around the corner. 'That was him. That was Clyde Lennon!'

The brakes squealed as Tyler stamped down on them. Up ahead, the front door of the house stood ajar, Lana's car parked up in the driveway.

'Shit,' Sinead hissed, a sinking feeling forming in her gut. She unclipped her seatbelt and threw open the door. 'Get after Clyde. Don't let him get away.'

'You be all right?' Tyler asked.

'Fine. Just go. I'll call it in,' Sinead said, jumping out of the car. She hesitated, not yet closing the door. 'And please… be careful.'

'I always am,' Tyler said, checking his mirrors before clicking the indicator.

Sinead considered him sitting there in the driver's seat, listening to the fading roar of the van engine. 'Yeah, well,' she said. 'Maybe not *that* careful…'

—

Logan was led through the corridors of the school, past classrooms and cloakrooms, until they reached a set of swing doors that led through to an empty changing room with a dozen or so bags hanging from hooks, and similar numbers of clothing piles bundled untidily on the benches.

From another door at the far end of the room came the squeaking of trainers on polished wood, and the thack-slap of basketballs being bounced with neither skill nor enthusiasm.

'Through here,' the janny urged, barrelling through the other door without bothering to knock.

Almost thirty children filled the hall. Most of them seemed ridiculously small and far too young to be in secondary school. First Years, Logan assumed, although none of them looked like they had growth spurts looming in their immediate futures, and they may well have been Primary Fours out on a day trip.

The few who had been successfully managing to bounce their basketballs lost control of them as they turned to look at Janny and his giant new friend. A young female teacher in grey joggies and a yellow t-shirt shot the newcomers an inquisitive look from the back of the hall, but made no move to intercept.

Logan got the impression that you didn't question the caretaker. If he turned up on some mission to faff about with the lights, or board up some broken window, you kept your mouth shut and you let him get on with it. The school was his world, and everyone else was just a pain in the arse who happened to be passing through it.

The janny stopped by a dented metal storage cabinet, and Logan's eyes were drawn to the keyhole in the handle. Before he could figure out if the lock was the right size for the key, Alan opened both doors, negating the need to bother sizing it up.

The sagging shelves inside held different-coloured sports bibs, tubes of tennis balls and shuttlecocks, and various other bits of equipment that were likely necessary for the running of the department. Nothing obviously untoward, or even worthy of closer examination.

'Here. What about this?' the caretaker asked, gruffly indicating a drawer down near the bottom of the cabinet, on the right-hand side.

The front was only a few inches high, the stainless steel scuffed and scratched from years of use, and probably a good few months of misuse, too. The janitor gave it a tug, shaking the whole cabinet as the locking mechanism thunked against the metal frame.

'Been locked for months. No bugger knew where the key was,' he explained.

'What's in it?' Logan asked, eyeing up the keyhole. It was about the right size and shape for the key in his pocket.

'Not much,' the other man said with a shrug. 'Nothing they didn't have others of, or haven't been able to do without. I've been meaning to try to get it open, but... well.'

'Always something more important to do,' Logan said. He nodded. 'Aye. I know the feeling.'

He took the evidence bag from his coat pocket, unsealed it and removed the key, then hesitated for a moment with it pointed at the lock. If this worked—if this opened—it could change everything. Fergus Forsyth had gone to quite the extreme to hide it, and Logan might finally be about to find out why.

He slid the key into the lock.

He turned it.

Click.

Yes!

'Right, then,' he announced, wheeling around to face the class of basketball-challenged youngsters. He clapped his hands a couple of times, getting their attention before the echo had finished its first lap of the hall. 'Class dismissed.'

Chapter 39

Sinead phoned in to the station as she ran towards the house, told Ben about Tyler being off in pursuit of Clyde's van, and requested backup at the Lennon house.

He told her to wait outside. She told him that she couldn't do that, then hung up and hurried up the path, stopping at the front door of the house just long enough to knock and announce her presence.

'Mrs Lennon? It's Sinead Bell. I'm coming in.'

She pushed through into the hallway, a sense of dread slowing her movements and honing her focus. There was music playing in the kitchen, some upbeat 80s number, half-buried beneath the excitedly mundane witterings of a radio DJ.

The kitchen door creaked as Sinead nudged it open, braced for what she might find inside.

Nothing. The room was empty, the back door closed.

A tap was running, the water rumbling like distant cannon-fire against the curved metal base of the sink. Sinead left it, and turned her attention to the other doors in the hallway.

'Lana,' she called, but no answer came.

She stopped at the bottom of the staircase, listened for any sound up there, then opted for one of the other doors on the ground floor. The first was a small dining room, barely large enough for the table and four chairs that clustered together in it.

One of the chairs had been pushed back until the back legs touched the skirting of the wall behind it. A notebook stood open on the table, revealing the beginning of an apology letter composed in Mrs Lennon's familiar fastidious handwriting.

A slim metal pen lay on the floor, halfway between the table and two glass-panelled doors that led through into the living room. Both were open.

The music in the kitchen became something slower and more solemn as Sinead shuffled around the furniture and approached the doors. Other than the music and the thunder of the tap, the house remained silent. Still.

Empty, perhaps.

Empty, she hoped.

But empty, it was not.

—

Tyler reached the junction where the A86 met the A82, and had a decision to make. Left would take him back down the road towards Fort William. Right would lead north, up past the Commando Memorial, and onwards to Skye, or Inverness, or any one of a number of possible escape routes.

Where would Clyde go? South would be familiar. South would also make Tyler's life a lot easier, as the cavalry would likely be tearing up that road in the next few minutes, perfectly positioned to intercept.

He groaned. Nothing was ever that easy.

'Fuck it,' he said.

North it was.

He hit the sirens, indicated, waited for the traffic to slow, then pulled away to the right and powered up the steep climb at a nippy-but-sensible fifty miles per hour, forcing the cars ahead to pull in at the layby right before the memorial turn-off.

There were a few straights ahead. Prime overtaking territory. If Clyde had gone this way—and Tyler was sure he would have, because this was the way that made the detective's life more difficult—then he could be flying on up the road already. With a clear-ish road, the wind at his back, and a total disregard for the speed limit, Clyde could be close to Letterfinlay by now. It would take some fast driving to catch the bastard now.

Tyler edged the accelerator pedal down, and the Audi crept smoothly up to sixty. He had just hit the first of the long straights when his phone rang over the car audio, and Hamza's name appeared on his screen.

'Ham. Not a great time,' Tyler said, after thumbing the answer button on the steering wheel.

'Aye, I heard. Where are you?'

'Headed north. I just passed the Commando Memorial.'

'Have you got eyes on him?'

'No. Had to make a call. He might've headed down the road to the Fort, but—'

There was a thunk and the wheel jerked in his hands, swerving the car towards the centre of the road. Tyler swore, tightened his grip, and brought the car back under control.

'What happened? What was that?' Hamza asked.

'Fucking pothole,' Tyler said.

'Take it easy. Don't take any risks. If he gets away, he gets away.'

'Oh, he won't be getting away,' Tyler replied. 'I'm nearly doing sixty.'

There was a lengthy pause from the other end of the line. Tyler had just started to wonder if the signal had dropped when Hamza's voice returned.

'Sixty? Is that it?'

'What do you mean, "is that it?"' Tyler spat. 'Sixty's fast.'

'Aye, if you're an old woman,' Hamza told him. 'I bet he's no' doing sixty.'

'Well, maybe he'll crash, then! And, anyway, I bet he doesn't feel sick on the twisty bits.'

'All right, all right,' Hamza said. 'You're there, I'm not, you make the judgement call.'

'I will,' Tyler assured him. 'I am.'

'Uniform's still knocking around in Invergarry. I'll get them to head south and try to intercept.'

The call ended, leaving Tyler alone with the screaming of the sirens and the mid-tempo thrumming of the car's engine.

Sixty was plenty.

Sixty was fast.

It certainly felt bloody fast, anyway, and that was before the twisty bits.

But Clyde Lennon wouldn't be sticking to the limit. Not with everything he stood to lose.

'Fuck it. What's the worst that could happen?' Tyler muttered, then he floored the pedal, and the Audi roared like a beast uncaged.

–

The first thing Sinead noticed was the hammer. It lay on the floor just inside the living room, one side clawed, one side blunt, both sides bloodied and wet.

She saw a shoe next, abandoned and alone.

A foot. A leg.

A body.

It had to be a body. Not a person. Not any more. There were too many injuries. Too much blood. The damage to the head and face so significant that it could've been anyone lying there. Any*thing*, almost.

But it wasn't just anyone, Sinead knew. It was Lana Lennon.

What was left of her.

She checked for a pulse she knew she wouldn't find, but to her amazement found one. Weak, feeble, but there.

And suddenly, panic kicked in. The overwhelming sense that this woman's life was now in her hands. That everything that happened next was her responsibility. Her fault. Her burden to carry.

She didn't fight the panic, but let it flare all the way up to maximum for a few seconds, then pushed it aside and forgot about it. Not forever—it would come back someday when she least expected it, she knew—but she was rid of it for now, and that was all that mattered.

Dropping to her knees, she did her best to clear the blood and mucus from Lana's airways. The English teacher's face was like nothing Sinead had ever seen, not even in the shitty horror films Tyler had made her watch after she'd subjected him to a double bill of both *Mamma Mias*.

Her cheeks were concave. Her jaw was shattered. Her nose was... gone, battered back into the pulpy mess of her skull.

With some effort, she rolled Lana into the recovery position, then whipped out her phone and started calling for an ambulance.

'It's OK, Lana. You're going to be OK,' she soothed.

There was no way the woman could hear—please, God, don't let her be conscious—but that didn't matter. The words were designed to calm Sinead herself, more than anything.

She requested the ambulance, hung up, and checked Lana's vitals again. The pulse was still there. Her chest was moving, though her breathing was faint and laboured. Given the beating she'd taken, though, it was a miracle she was alive at all.

And then, Sinead heard it.

The creak of a floorboard behind her.

Before she could react, a hand caught her by the hair and yanked her backwards, and Sinead cried out in pain and in fright as she was dragged, off-balance, to the floor.

Chapter 40

The snap of Logan's rubber gloves rang out like a gunshot in the empty gym hall. He could hear the excited chattering of the boys and girls in their respective changing rooms, as they speculated wildly about the abrupt end to the lesson, and the man who had brought it about.

Once the gloves were on, Logan gave an experimental flex of his fingers, then hooked both index fingers around the outer edges of the drawer, where it was least likely he'd disturb any fingerprints, and eased it open.

The metal drawer did not slide out easily, and the slow, drawn-out squeal it gave relegated 'fingers down a blackboard' to Logan's second least favourite noise.

With a bit of tugging, some side-to-side jigging, and a few encouraging swear words, the drawer finally opened enough to reveal its contents.

Which were precisely fuck all.

'What? No,' Logan muttered, yanking harder until he could see all the way to the back of the drawer. The back half, to his dismay, held exactly the same as the front half. 'You've got to be kidding me,' he said a little louder this time, as he shoved his hand inside and swept it around the edges, in case something might be tucked away there.

There wasn't.

He wasn't sure if the drawer was meant to come all the way out, but he gave it a big enough tug that it screeched free of its fittings, leaving him holding it in one oversized hand.

This only served to confirm the emptiness of it, which did nothing to ease the rate at which his mood was darkening.

'It can't be fucking empty!' he announced, refusing to believe the evidence of his own eyes, and his outrage at the very suggestion of it boomed around the hall. 'Why would it be empty?'

He turned the drawer over in his hands, checking the bottom, then fiddling about at the catches in case some secret compartment was revealed.

Setting it down, he dropped to his knees and peered into the gap that the drawer had left. He thrust a hand in, felt along the top in the hope of finding something taped there, but came away disappointed.

'How can it be fucking empty?' he demanded, scowling down at the drawer sitting on the scuffed gym hall floor. 'What's the point?'

His resentment got the better of him, and he gave it a kick. It skidded a foot or so across the floor, then stopped with a clack and a rattle.

Odd.

Logan squatted beside it, but didn't pick it up yet. He eyed it from a variety of angles first, like a bare-knuckle fighter sizing up an opponent, and only then lifted it off the floor.

He gave it a shake, and heard the same rattling sound as before. With a bit of experimentation, he narrowed the sound down to the front panel, close to where the keyhole was.

His heart sunk a bit then, assuming the sound was coming from the locking mechanism, but a bit more shoogling and shaking revealed it was coming from elsewhere in the front.

He tipped the drawer from side to side, and listened to something sliding around. The front was made of a single piece of metal, bent around the locking mechanism to form a slim rectangular box, with a gap of a few millimetres where the back didn't quite meet the drawer's base.

On the side where the sound was coming from, the metal was scratched and a little bent. Logan took his keys from his pocket, and wedged the long blade of his front door key into the gap.

The thin sheet of the drawer front's metal bent outwards like folding cardboard. As soon as the gap was big enough, a small black object slid out and clattered against the back of the drawer.

'Now, that's more like it,' Logan said, as his eyes fell on a key of another kind.

There, propped against the back of the drawer, was a USB thumb drive.

—

'What the fuck are you doing? What have you done?'

Sinead twisted on the floor, rolling herself upright, her hands raised defensively in front of her. The grip on her hair had been released as soon as she'd fallen, and she now stood looking down at a young man in school uniform, kneeling at Lana's side.

'Mum? Is that…? Is that my mum? What did you do? God! Mum! What did you do to her?'

'Bennet. Bennet, it's OK. It's OK, calm down,' Sinead urged. 'I'm with the police. The ambulance is on the way.'

He had his hands on her, and was giving her a shake, like all the gore and the damage might just fall off her onto the carpet. His fingers were already slick with blood, his black jumper shiny, his white shirt turned red.

'What did you do?' he wailed. 'Mum! Mum! Please, Mum! Please, Mum!'

Sinead put a hand on his shoulder. He drove an elbow back, trying to shrug her off, but she moved her grip to his upper arms, and gently steered him back.

'Give her some space, Bennet. Let her breathe,' she instructed. 'It's going to be OK, the ambulance is coming. The ambulance is on its way.'

He fell back so he was sitting on the floor, all snot, and tears, and blood. His body shook with big violent trembles he couldn't possibly hope to control. He hadn't been able to take his eyes off his mum since entering the room, but he turned away now, like she was the last thing on Earth he wanted to look at.

'This is your fault! If you hadn't come here... if you hadn't dragged her into all this...!'

'Calm down, Bennet,' Sinead told him. 'OK? Just calm down. We're going to get her help. We're going to get her seen to.'

Bennet's eyes fell on the hammer lying there on the floor, wet with his mother's blood.

Sinead moved, but too late. Bennet scrambled for the hammer before Sinead could stop him. He snatched it up and backed away a few paces towards the door.

'This is... is this my dad's?' he asked, turning it over in his hands. His voice was flat. Level. Almost indifferent.

'Put it down, Bennet,' Sinead instructed. 'Put the hammer down. It's evidence.'

'Evidence?' he said, like the word was some strange made-up one she was trying to bamboozle him with. He looked from the hammer to his mum, then back to Sinead.

'Put it down, Bennet,' Sinead instructed.

He didn't.

His fingers tightened around the rubber grip.

Far off in the distance, a siren wailed.

—

Tyler was almost enjoying this. If you ignored the rising nausea, the growing panic, and the nagging suspicion that he might shit himself at any moment, it was actually quite fun.

The flashing lights and sirens helped, of course. He wouldn't dream of overtaking so close to a bend, for example, were it not for the car ahead slowing and pulling in to the left. He dropped a gear, found the clutch's biting point, then powered smoothly past, the engine not just giving him the power he needed, but urging him to demand more, to push it harder, to go faster, faster, *faster*!

The last time he'd driven like this had been... when? Back in his Uniform days? Even then, high-speed pursuits had been few and far between, and he'd hated them when they'd happened.

Now, though, with the Audi chewing up the straights and hugging the corners, he thought about opening a window and letting the wind blow through his hair, and wondered why he didn't do this more often.

There was a bend ahead, coming up fast. He knew this part of the route well. The long curve to the right dead ahead would lead to another straight section of road, then a sharp left turn that would require a bit of thought on the braking.

If nothing was coming, he'd be able to swing out onto the wrong side of the road and follow the racing line, reducing his need to slow down. If there was traffic coming the other way, he'd have to drop down a couple of gears, stick to the left, and make up time on the next straight.

There was a house just a little past the corner. A man and a woman stood in the garden, waving both arms above their heads, trying to attract his attention as he sped towards them.

Tyler rounded the bend, and saw a car coming up fast on the wrong side of the road.

Close.

Too close.

He hit the brakes, foot all the way to the floor.

He gripped the wheel so tightly the mounting nut groaned, like the whole thing might come off in his hands.

There was a bus on one side of the road, the overtaking car on the other. Someone's brakes squealed. Someone's horn blared. Someone screamed.

That last one was probably him.

The car shuddered under the weight of the braking. He was doing fifty now. Forty. The approaching car easily matching that.

No one was stopping. No one had time. No one had a chance.

They were going to hit, and hit hard.

Tyler wrenched the wheel to the left. Noises filled the inside of the car, none of them good. Crunches, creaks, thumps, and cracks. The piercing monotone of his horn crying out for help.

He saw a fence, briefly, then it was lost beneath his front wheels, and all he could see was bushes, and bracken, and trees, and a steep drop into a field below.

The wheel bucked and spun, far too violently for him to hold onto. He released his grip, screamed some more, and braced himself for the—

BANG!

The airbags deployed, filling the cabin. The car stopped moving forwards and started moving upwards, instead. Coins and pens and other debris floated in the space between the deflating balloons of the airbags, as if gravity had been turned off. He could reach out and touch them, he thought, time slowing enough that he could marvel at the way they hung there. He could reach out and pluck them right out of the air.

Time rushed back to its regular speed, and the second impact came. It came suddenly and without warning. It came with a fanfare of breaking glass and rending metal, as the car finished its forward flip and smashed, roof-first against an embankment of heather, crumpling the pillars and filling the air with diamond-like fragments of windscreen.

The engine gave a final cough and a wheeze, and smoke billowed in through the vents. The metal carcass of the car groaned as it settled into its resting place, back wheels thunk-thunk-thunking as they slowed to a stop.

And then, the only sounds from the car were the pinging of cooling metal, and the solemn single note fanfare of the horn ringing out across the wilderness.

–

Bennet stood in the driveway, blinking like he'd just woken up. The sound of a siren echoed off the house behind him, as a police car pulled sharply in off the road and came to a stop just a few feet ahead.

He watched, saying nothing, as two officers jumped out—one male, one female. They both stared at him for a moment, wide-eyed with horror, and then the female officer took charge.

'Sir? I'm going to ask you to put down the hammer,' she said.

Her words sounded far-off and distant, and it took Bennet a few moments to make sense of them. He looked down at his hand, at the hammer, at the blood. He could feel it on him, the blood, its warmth cooling in the early-evening air.

'Drop the hammer, sir,' the woman said again. She couldn't have been much older than he was. Twenty-two or twenty-three, maybe. She was trying to sound confident, but he could see through her charade. She was scared. Scared of him.

Just like the one in the house had been.

The male officer was talking into the radio on his shoulder, too quietly for Bennet to make out what he was saying.

Not that it mattered now.

Not that he cared.

'Sir, I'm not going to tell you again. Drop the hammer, or—'

Bennet dropped the hammer. He wasn't sure if it was deliberate, or accidental. The blood had made his fingers slippy.

The female officer was on him in an instant, gripping his arm, twisting it painfully behind his back. He felt a cable tie loop around it and tighten, binding one wrist to the other. He turned his head, and the woman in the uniform flinched when she saw his face, and heard the cold, matter-of-fact rumble of his voice.

'She's in there,' he said, twitching his head in the direction of the front door. 'I think... I think she's dead.'

–

Hamza regarded the USB drive in the evidence bag, turned it over a couple of times, then raised his gaze to where Logan stood on the other side of his desk.

'Where'd you get this, sir?'

'The key in Fergus Forsyth's stomach? I found what it opened,' Logan announced. 'That was inside.'

'Bloody hell. Nice one, sir,' Hamza said, sitting up in his chair. 'What's on it?'

'I've got no idea. Thought I'd leave that to you to find out. He went out of his way to hide it, so I'm hoping it's something interesting.'

'Good find, Jack,' Ben called over from his desk. 'We'll make a real detective of you yet.'

'Aye, well, let's no' get ahead of ourselves,' Logan said. 'I still prefer kicking in doors and shouting at people.'

Hamza reached into his desk drawer, removed a pair of blue rubber gloves from a box, then began to peel open the evidence bag.

'Tyler and Sinead back with Lana Lennon yet?' Logan asked, looking around at the empty chairs of the Detective Constables. 'Any joy getting her to press charges?'

Hamza shot Ben a look, kicking the question up the chain of command. Logan spotted it, and his brow shifted like tectonic plates before an earthquake.

'What is it?' he demanded, looking from the DS to the DI. 'What's happened?'

'Lana Lennon's been attacked,' Ben explained. 'She's in a bad way. They saw Clyde Lennon leaving the house. Tyler's giving chase.'

'Tyler?' Logan said, his voice rising half an octave. 'Giving chase? You can't be serious? Has that useless bastard even got a real driving licence?'

'Uniform's on the way to the house, and moving to intercept the suspect,' Hamza said. 'Last I heard from Tyler, he was heading north on the A82.'

'What do you mean, *last you heard from him*?' Logan demanded. 'Where is he now?'

'We, eh…' Hamza deferred to Ben again with another imploring look.

'We don't know, Jack,' Ben said. 'We can't get hold of him.' He cleared his throat and glanced away, unable to hold the DCI's stare. 'We can't get hold of either of them.'

Chapter 41

Pain.

No, worse than that. *Agony*.

That was what Tyler had been braced for.

It hadn't hit him yet. It would, of course. It would strike any second now. He'd find his legs broken. Or his arms shattered. Or his ribs sticking out through his back.

Any second now, it would kick in.

Any second.

'Fucking Nora! You all right, mate?'

Tyler turned in the direction of the voice, but slowly so his head didn't fall off.

An upside-down man was squatting by the window. He looked happy. Or maybe sad. It was hard to tell with his mouth at that angle.

Did he know he was upside down, Tyler wondered? Should he tell him?

'What?' he heard himself asking.

He could speak, then. That was good. It meant he still had a mouth, and all the other apparatus involved.

'I said, are you all right?' the man asked. 'Are you hurt?'

'Not yet. But it's coming,' Tyler said.

The man's expression changed. Into what, it was hard to say.

'What do you mean?'

'What do *you* mean?' Tyler retorted, then he hit him with the awful truth of his predicament. 'You're upside down.'

The man turned away, said, 'I think he must've banged his head or something' then turned back again. 'Can you get out?'

Tyler had just started to ask, 'Of what?' when the brain-fog lifted enough for him to make a little more sense of his situation. 'Oh. Shit,' he remarked, looking around at his surroundings. 'Am I still in the car?'

'You are, yes. We've called for help. You probably shouldn't move.'

Tyler fumbled for the seatbelt catch, heard but didn't fully comprehend the warning from the other man that he probably shouldn't do that, then he fell head-first onto the roof of the car, and almost broke his neck.

'Fuck! Who put that there?' he demanded, although it wasn't immediately clear what he was referring to.

After a bit of sprackling, significantly more swearing, and a gravity-assisted sideways topple, he managed to focus enough to conclude that the doors were too fucked to ever open again, and that he might have to spend the rest of his life here inside this upturned vehicle.

Fortunately, that particular panic passed quickly, when a woman in stout Wellingtons opened the boot, and beckoned for him to crawl out that way.

He emerged, coughing, and blinking, and stumbling on the uneven marshy ground. The woman was talking to him, but there was a delay between the sound leaving her mouth and it reaching his ears, and it took him several seconds to realise he was the one she was talking to.

'What?' he asked, interrupting her halfway through a sentence. It didn't throw her off for long.

'I just said we've reported it umpteen times. Council. Police. Anyone who we thought might do something about it. I mean, it's ridiculous how often it happens. Ridiculous. How many's that now, Ian?'

'A dozen, easily.'

'A dozen, *easily*. And that's just since we moved in. How long ago was that, Ian?'

'Three years, give or take.'

'Three years, give or take,' the woman echoed. 'A dozen in that time. Easily.' She shook her head, visibly disgusted by whatever the hell she was banging on about.

Tyler dabbed at his head, expecting to find blood there. His fingers came away clean, and he almost didn't know whether to be relieved or disappointed.

'This is a first, though,' the woman continued. 'Two in ten minutes. Too bloody fast for the corner, that's the problem. There should be a sign. One each side. "Slow. Corner". Something like that.'

Tyler stopped searching for injuries, as the jumble of words tumbling from the woman's mouth fell into an order that made some sort of sense.

'Wait, what? Two what in ten minutes?'

'Accidents,' the woman said. She gestured down the slope to the field below.

A line had been churned through the grass—a long brown scar through the greenery.

And there, at the end of it, lying on its side, surrounded by three older men and a disinterested sheepdog, was a van.

—

They found Sinead in the living room. On the floor, next to Lana Lennon.

'Is the ambulance here?' the Detective Constable demanded, rising to her feet. 'Her pulse is weakening. She needs the hospital.'

'It's on its way,' the female constable replied, her gaze fixed on the horror-show that was Lana Lennon's face. 'Jesus Christ. What happened? Was it the kid?'

'No. I don't know. I don't think so,' Sinead said. 'Did you get him? I sent him outside to get you.'

'He… he had a hammer,' the constable said.

'I know. It was here when I came in, he picked it up and wouldn't let it go,' Sinead said. 'He didn't go for you with it, did he?'

'No. No, he dropped it. Eventually. He's in the car.' Her eyes drifted back to the woman on the floor. 'But… Jesus. Who does that to someone? Who could actually do that to another human being?'

Sinead didn't look down at Lana. She didn't need to see the face again. It was burned in now. She'd be seeing it for years to come.

'Someone angry,' she said. 'Someone very, *very* angry.'

—

Clyde Lennon had not escaped his crash as lightly as Tyler had, but things could certainly have been a lot worse for him. There was some blood. Not a lot, but some. It trickled from a cut on his forehead, and would have been covered by his hair, had his hairline not receded as far as it had.

The impact of his crash had been less. Unlike Tyler's dramatic end-over-end flip, Clyde's van had remained on four wheels for most of its off-road descent, before hitting a bump and rolling onto its right-hand side as it reached the bottom.

The design of the van meant the storage area at the back was inaccessible from the front, so Clyde's only way out was through the passenger door, which was directly above him. Neither of the older men watching on, nor the sheepdog, were making any attempt to help him, and he was battling unsuccessfully to clamber out on his own when Tyler stumbled the last few steps down the hillside.

The DC's legs still weren't quite working properly, and he could only stop his descent by thudding against the back doors of the van. This hurt more than the crash had, and he stood there, stunned into silence for several seconds, the men and the dog all watching him to see what he was going to do next.

Shaking away the cobwebs, Tyler made his way around to the front of the van, leaning on the roof for support.

At the front, his eyes met those of the man inside through the windscreen.

'Clyde Lennon,' Tyler began. He patted himself down, searching for his warrant card, before concluding he must've dropped it in the car. 'Fuck it,' he slurred, too far gone at this point to care. His finger gave a squeak as he pressed it against the glass, pointing to the man inside. 'You're nicked!'

—

Logan jumped from the Beamer, elbowed his way through the crowd of nosy bastards that had formed beside the queue of traffic, and reached the front in time to see Tyler depositing Clyde Lennon into the back of a police van.

'Boss!' Tyler gasped when he saw Logan barging through the onlookers. His legs gave way beneath him, and Logan caught him with a lunge and a grab.

'You're all right, son,' the DCI told him.

'Sorry, boss,' Tyler said, forcing his legs to support him again. 'Just a bit shaky.'

Logan released his grip, but kept his hands close in case he needed to catch the DC again. 'You look like shite. What happened?'

'Am I bleeding?' Tyler asked. He turned, showing himself from every angle. 'I feel like I should be bleeding.'

'No. You're fine. You just… you're no' a good colour.'

'Bit racist, boss,' Tyler said, his voice a little slurred. He inhaled slowly through his nose, then shook his head. 'It's not racist. I don't know why I said that.'

'What the hell happened?' Logan asked. 'Did you hit your head or something?'

'Why does everyone keep asking me that?' Tyler wondered. 'No. I mean, aye. Maybe. It all happened so fast. One minute, I was… wait. Where did that bastard in the other car go? The one that nearly hit me?'

Logan looked around them. There was a bus stopped a little further back in the Fort William direction, and dozens of cars stopped in both directions behind a couple of polis vehicles, including the one that now held Clyde Lennon.

'Ah, fuck it. I'll have his plate on my dashcam,' Tyler announced. 'We'll get him. Or her. Might be a her. I didn't notice. Not sexist that, is it?'

'You're talking even more shite than usual, son,' Logan pointed out. 'What actually happened?'

It was then that Logan noticed the fence of the house beside them. Or the relative lack of fence, at least. What was left of it was spread across quite a considerable area that stretched from the road, down the hillside, and all the way to...

'Your car!' Logan exclaimed. 'That's your car.'

'Where?' Tyler asked, then he shook his head for about the fifth time that minute. 'Oh. Down there. Aye. It's upside down.' He frowned, just a little. 'I think. It is, isn't it? Upside down.'

'What the hell happened?' Logan demanded.

'Same as always bloody happens,' said a sturdy-looking woman in a flat-cap and Wellies. 'They come off the big straight too quickly for the bend and lose control. A dozen times it's happened, easily. And that's just in the last three years, since we moved in.'

'We've been on at the council,' a man beside her said, but Logan managed to tune out the rest of his rant, and turned his attention back to DC Neish.

'How the hell did you walk away from that?' he asked.

'Women's intuition, boss,' Tyler said, winking and tapping the side of his head.

Logan regarded him in silence for a few seconds, then called over to the closest Uniform. 'Call ahead to the hospital, will you? Tell them I'm bringing one in.'

'Will do, sir,' the Uniform confirmed.

'I don't need the hospital, boss,' Tyler said. 'Unless...' He dabbed at his head. 'Am I bleeding?'

'No, you aren't bleeding, son,' Logan told him, taking him by the elbow. 'But best get you checked out, eh?'

Tyler puffed out his cheeks, then relented with a nod. 'We'll maybe need to take your car, boss. Mine's upside down.'

'Aye, we'll take mine,' Logan said, guiding Tyler through the crowd, and clearing a path with a barked, 'Out of the road, you rubbernecking bastards.'

'Go easy on the twisty bits, eh, boss?' Tyler said, as Logan opened the passenger door and poured him inside. 'My stomach doesn't cope well with them.'

'Aye. I'll take my time,' Logan assured him.

He started to close the door, but Tyler held a hand out and blocked it. 'Have you heard from Sinead?'

'Aye. She rang into the office when I was on my way up here. She's with Lana Lennon. We'll probably meet them at the hospital.'

'Hospital?' Tyler said, pouncing on the word, the haze that had been clouding his eyes clearing instantly. 'Why? Is she hurt?'

'Aye. Badly battered, by the sounds of thing,' Logan confirmed. 'Claw hammer. Real mess.'

'What? No!'

Logan realised the misunderstanding when Tyler's face all but collapsed in on itself.

'Shit. No. Lana Lennon was attacked, I mean,' he said. 'Sinead's fine.'

'Christ! Don't do that, boss!' Tyler ejected, running both hands through his hair. 'Jesus!'

'Sorry, I thought you meant... Sinead's fine,' Logan assured him. 'Arm in.'

Tyler frowned, stared at his extended arm for a few seconds like it belonged to someone else, then set both hands down in his lap, letting Logan close the door.

He didn't speak again until the DCI was in the car beside him, and they both had their seatbelts on.

'I got him, though, boss. Didn't I?'

'You did, son. You got him. Good work.'

Tyler smiled shakily. He swallowed, his eyes watering. 'Cheers, boss,' he said.

And then, bending forwards, he vomited onto the floor.

Chapter 42

Hamza regarded his laptop like it had betrayed him in some way.

It had recognised the USB almost immediately, spent a few seconds whirring and grinding as it added it to the list of available drives, then presented him with a pop-up window demanding the security key.

'Bollocks. It's locked.'

'How do you mean?' asked Ben, peering over the top of his glasses.

'The thumb drive. It's protected.'

'What… like a password?' Ben asked.

Hamza almost delved into the technical details, then decided it was easier just to nod. 'Yeah. Basically a password.'

'Can't you, you know, hack it? Or whatever it is they do?'

Hamza almost laughed. DI Forde—and Logan, too, to an extent—seemed to be labouring under the illusion that he was some grand master of computer code, when in reality he just knew his way around a couple of different operating systems, understood some basic HTML, and was a certified power user of the Microsoft Office suite. Deciphering an encryption keychain was not really in his skillset.

'Afraid not, sir,' Hamza had to admit. 'Now, if it was a spreadsheet, or a *OneNote* notebook, then I could…' He sat forward sharply. 'Wait. Notebook.'

'You want a notebook?' Ben asked. 'Stationery cupboard. But go canny, for God's sake, or Mantits will—'

'No, I don't mean me. Fergus Forsyth. The notebook Sinead found in his drawer,' Hamza said. 'I think I might have just figured out what that code's for.'

Logan sat in the cramped A&E waiting room at Belford Hospital, the smell of vomit still stuck halfway up his nostrils, and refusing to leave. Tyler sat stiffly upright in the chair beside him, insisting that all this was unnecessary, and regularly reminding the DCI that they had a murder to solve.

'I'm just saying, boss, it's a waste of time. I'm fine,' Tyler said.

'Aye, well, my bloody passenger footwell would beg to differ,' Logan grunted.

'It was the shock, that was all. I'm right as rain now, look.'

He raised both arms from the chair, almost like he was levitating, then dropped them back down again and pulled a face that suggested he'd proved some sort of point.

'See?'

'What was that meant to be showing me?' Logan asked.

'Just that I'm fine. Nothing's broken. I might have a few bruises in the morning, but… look. Legs, too.'

He raised one leg, then the other, bending them at the knee, then kicking them out again, much to the consternation of an elderly woman with one red, weeping eye, who sat directly across from him.

'Sorry,' Tyler told her, setting both feet on the floor.

'He's been in an accident,' Logan explained. 'He's no' trying to kick you in the face.'

'Aye, you'd soon know if I was!' Tyler said. He started to laugh, then saw the woman's look of horror. 'Not that I would. Kick you in the face, I mean. That'd be out of order.'

Both detectives watched as the old woman got up, moved four chairs to the left, then sat down again and pretended they weren't there.

'Jesus, I think maybe you've got a bleed on the brain or something,' Logan muttered. 'What did you say that for?'

'I don't really know, boss. Think maybe I'm still amped up on adrenaline, or something,' Tyler said. 'But, honestly, I'm fine. We don't have to stick around here. We should get back to the office.'

Logan leaned his head back against the wall behind him, and fixed his gaze dead ahead, to where posters promoting various mental health and stopping smoking helplines filled the wall.

'I ever tell you about Stanley Burns?' he asked.

Tyler shook his head. 'Don't think so, boss. Who is he?'

'Old colleague of mine. We used to get paired up from time to time back in my Uniform days.'

'What, did he drive the stagecoach?' Tyler asked with a grin. Logan shut him down with a look. 'Sorry, boss.'

'He did do a lot of the driving, actually. In the car, I mean, no' on horseback,' Logan continued. 'Great driver. Really knew his way around a motor. Used to teach the advanced driving classes to new recruits sometimes, in fact. High-speed stuff. Pursuit. That sort of thing.'

'Bet he was a nutter, wasn't he?'

'Actually, no. Nice guy. And sensible, too. You're right, though. You'd think any bugger who enjoys driving that fast is going to be a bit of a headcase, but not Stanley. No, Stanley only went fast when he knew it was safe. He didn't take chances, or unnecessary risks. Even sitting in the passenger seat when he went tearing up the motorway doing a ton, you felt safe. Like… I don't know. Invulnerable.' Logan's lips pulled together into a thin line. 'He was a good guy, Stanley. Two kids, he had. Lovely wife. Mairi, her name was. Real family man.'

'What happened to him?' Tyler asked.

Logan turned his head just enough to meet the DC's eye. 'Hm?'

'I'm assuming something bad happened, and there's a big moral to the story coming,' Tyler said. 'Like, he had an accident, didn't get checked out, and then died a week later, or something.'

Logan shook his head. 'No. He was fine. Retired a few years ago,' the DCI explained. 'Lives in Motherwell now, I think.'

'So… what was the story about, then?'

'Nothing,' Logan said, crossing his arms. 'I just wanted you to shut the fuck up for thirty seconds.'

Down at the far end of the waiting room, the old woman tutted at the bad language, and mumbled something about young people today.

She then looked up hopefully as the door opened, before recoiling when she saw a blood-splattered young woman come barrelling through the doors.

'Hey! You all right?' Sinead asked, hurrying over to stand before Tyler. 'I just heard what happened.'

'Fine. I keep telling everyone, I'm fine,' Tyler said. He looked Sinead up and down. 'But, Jesus, what happened to you?'

She looked down at herself, said, 'shite', loudly enough to earn a muttered reprimand from the old lady, and suddenly looked like she'd rather be anywhere but in those clothes. 'Didn't realise it was this bad. I'd better get changed.'

'That from the attack?' Logan asked, being careful not to use any names, what with the disapproving pensioner earwigging in.

'It is, sir, aye.'

'In a bad way, then?'

'Very. They're working on her now, but... even if she survives...'

Logan nodded. From what he'd heard via Hamza and Ben, Lana Lennon's injuries would be life-changing, at best. She wouldn't be standing in front of a classroom for a while, if ever.

'You OK?' Tyler asked.

Sinead smiled, but said nothing. Tyler took her hand and squeezed it.

'Some day, eh?' he said.

'Aye,' she agreed. 'Some day. I assume... *the suspect* got away?'

Tyler puffed up his chest and raised an eyebrow. 'You know what they say about people who assume, Sinead. They ass... what is it? They ass you and me? That can't be it. Is that what they say? Why would they say that?'

'Jesus Christ, son,' Logan sighed. 'You had a big moment in the palm of your hand there, and you threw it away. No, he caught the bugger.'

'Caught him?' Sinead asked, equal parts surprised and confused by this. 'But I thought... I thought you crashed?'

'He did,' Logan said.

'But so did the other guy,' Tyler added.

This did not make Sinead any less confused. 'So... what? You crashed into each other?'

'No. Two separate crashes,' Tyler explained.

'In the same place,' Logan added.

'I mean, what are the chances?' asked Tyler. 'But, anyway. The point is, I caught him. They're keeping him in a van out front until the docs are ready to check him over. The boss is insisting they take me in first, though.'

Sinead shot Logan a grateful look, which he dismissed with a shake of his head.

'Is he hurt?' she asked.

'Only his pride!' Tyler said, smiling proudly.

'And his head,' Logan reminded him.

'Oh. Aye. And his head.'

Logan slapped his hands on his thighs, then stood up. 'Right then, Sinead, what size are you?'

Sinead frowned. 'Sir?'

'There's that clothes shop just down there on the High Street. Across from the church. I'll go get you a change of clobber, then you can sit here and make sure this eejit doesn't make a run for it.'

'I'm fine, boss. Honestly! I don't need to be here.'

'Aye, you do,' Sinead told him. She scowled at him for a few seconds, making sure he knew not to argue, then turned back to the DCI. 'Eh, you sure you're OK doing that, sir?'

'Can hardly have you sitting around looking like you've just escaped the Texas Chainsaw Massacre, can we?'

'Well, no. But I'll need everything,' Sinead said. She fixed him with a look that emphasised this point. 'Like... everything.'

Logan shifted a little uncomfortably on the balls of his feet. 'What...? You mean, like... everything?'

'Aye,' Sinead confirmed. '*Everything.*'

'I mean… aye. Whatever. That's fine,' Logan said, his voice going a little gruffer and a little deeper, as if it was trying to assert his masculinity. 'I can get you everything. That's no problem, at all. It's no' like it's the first time I've bought women's underwear.'

He felt the look from DC Neish burning into the side of his face from below. Common sense urged him not to look down, but he didn't listen, and found Tyler staring up at him with a grin that couldn't believe its bloody luck.

'Don't you worry, boss,' he beamed. 'Your secret's safe with us.'

–

One mildly humiliating shopping spree later, Logan returned to the Incident Room carrying a bag of bloodied clothing, and the faint but lingering smell of the contents of DC Neish's stomach.

Hamza and Ben both rose from their chairs as he entered, and he could see right away that there had been a development.

'Well?' he asked, not beating around the bush. 'What's happened?'

Both the DI and the DS started talking at the same time, before Hamza relented and let Ben go first.

'We had a very interesting call while you were gone, Jack. From one…' Ben consulted his notebook. '…Lachlan Byres. Says he's a friend of Bennet Lennon's. They work together at the castle.'

'And?' Logan prompted, as he dropped the bag of clothes onto the Exhibits desk, and began to shrug off his coat.

'Apparently, Bennet was round his house earlier this afternoon, between twelve and one. He told Lachlan he had something he needed to get off his chest.'

Logan paused with his coat half-off. '*And?*' he said again.

'He confessed.'

'Confessed?'

'To the whole thing. Killing Fergus. Cutting his head off—we'll find it in his dad's workshop, apparently. I've got Uniform heading over there with a battering ram now. Hamza was about to head out and meet them.'

'I'll do it,' Logan said, pulling his coat back up onto his shoulders. 'Why would the boy kill him, though? I thought he liked him? I thought all the kids loved him?'

'Bennet told his pal that Fergus was blackmailing him.'

'*Blackmail*? What about?'

'He didn't know,' Ben said. He pointed to Hamza. 'However…'

'Got into that USB stick, sir,' the DS said, taking his cue. 'It's, eh… it's pictures. And video. Of Bennet and Fergus. Together.'

'What, shagging?'

'That and more, sir, aye.'

Logan lowered himself onto the edge of the closest available desk. His eyes darted left and right, like he was reading something floating in the air in front of him.

'Jesus,' he uttered. 'How old is he? Bennet?'

'Seventeen, sir,' Hamza said. 'But timestamps on the files go back about eighteen months. It's been going on for a while.'

'Christ Almighty. How are we just finding out about this now?' Logan groaned.

'Seems like Fergus was good at covering his tracks,' Ben said. 'One of the numbers he was in regular contact with—the ones we couldn't identify—it was Bennet's. Looks like he deleted all calls and messages that passed between them.'

'When?' Logan asked.

'When what?'

'When did he delete them? Is there a way of finding that out?'

Hamza shook his head. 'Not that I know of, no. Why?'

'If he deleted them as he went along, that's one thing. If he deleted them all right before he died, that's either one hell of a coincidence, or it tells us something.'

'Tells us what, sir?'

'I've got no bloody idea,' Logan admitted. 'But it definitely tells us something.'

'Maybe Bennet deleted them?' Hamza suggested.

'Then why leave him with the phone in the first place?' Ben wondered. 'It's going to take time to delete all traces of yourself from someone's phone, especially when contact was that frequent.'

'Ben's right. Much easier just to take the phone and dump it somewhere. Makes no sense to leave it on the body.' Logan stood up again, and checked his watch. 'The school will be shut, but get onto someone there. Track them down. See if they have a record of phone numbers for the kids. That other number on the list that's missing from Fergus's phone…'

'You think he's been at it with another pupil?' Hamza asked.

'Possibly, aye. Worth checking, anyway. Where's Bennet now?'

'Holding cell downstairs,' Ben said. 'We're keeping an eye on him. He's had quite a shock.'

'Aye, well, he's about to get another one,' Logan said. 'Prep an interview room, and we'll have a crack at him when I get back.' He shoved his hands deep into the pockets of his coat, like he was bracing himself for some oncoming storm. 'I'm off to look for a head.'

Chapter 43

Logan stood back from the action and watched two Uniforms batter the living shit out of the door to Clyde Lennon's workshop.

He wasn't the only one watching. Half a dozen journalists had assembled at the front of the building, before a cordon had been put up, forcing them back far enough that Logan could pretend they weren't there.

The door was solid and managed to withstand quite a few strikes from the battering ram, before the lock finally realised it was on to a loser, and relented with a crack.

The Uniforms, their job done, shuffled sideways out of the way, leaving the path clear for Logan to enter the workshop.

The cold was the first thing he noticed. It rolled out of the gloom to meet him as he stepped through the open doorway and into a room that felt needlessly large.

The workshop part—four workbenches with an assortment of power saws and other attachments—took up less than a quarter of the space. A couple of tables, chairs, and various other pieces of furniture took up maybe the same again. They were all at various stages of completion, some barely skeletons, others awaiting just a final sanding or a polish.

The rest of the room was empty. Bare. Wasted space. The light from the high windows fell there, painting vaguely rectangular shapes onto the otherwise featureless floor.

The smell of the place was rich and, unsurprisingly, woody. Pine, and oak, and oils, and stains, with just a hint of something smoky and burnt around the edges. It made him think, not of somewhere industrial, but of smoking rooms in rich men's clubs.

Of academics in cluttered libraries. Of old canal boats, or hunting lodges hidden deep in the woods.

His feet squeaked on the rubbery tiles as he pushed further into the room. The floor was clean. Impeccably so, in fact. He'd have expected sawdust—he knew from experience that the stuff got everywhere—but the floor had been swept, so not a hint of it remained.

The same could not be said for the workbenches. Wood shavings and sawdust were piled up on those, spread unevenly across the flat parts, and heaped in every corner on every bench.

Every bench but one. Logan was drawn to it, and to the jagged teeth of the circular saw that stuck up through a slot in the surface. There was no sawdust anywhere on this bench. There was no mess of any kind, in fact. Were it not for the scrapes and scoring on the wood, and a few flecks of rust on the saw blade, the workbench could've been brand new.

As it was, someone had evidently gone to a lot of effort to clean it up. Kneeling, Logan shone his torch into the narrow gap between the bottom of the bench and the floor. A small scattering of sawdust under there had escaped the brush or the vacuum cleaner. Not much, but some.

Standing again, he tried to shift the bench, but it was a heavy bugger of a thing, and it went precisely nowhere.

'Give us a hand in here, will you?' he called, beckoning in a couple of Uniforms.

He supplied them both with gloves, ordered them to join him at one end, and—with a lot of heaving and shuffling—they managed to swing one end of the bench almost a full foot to the right.

'Thanks. Wait outside, will you? I'll shout if I need you again,' Logan said, then he brought up a hand and blocked the path of a constable who almost went traipsing through the sawdust that had just been unveiled on the floor. 'That way. Go around. Pay attention.'

'Eh, sorry, sir,' the officer squeaked, then he and his mate scurried off to wait out front.

Logan knelt on the floor, picked up some of the sawdust, and ran it through his fingers. It was, to all intents and purposes, sawdust. Nothing special. No reddish stains or bloody marks. No scraps of flesh, or chunks of bone. It was sawdust, nothing more.

'Bollocks,' he muttered, letting it fall back to the floor.

The lad who'd called to report Bennet's confession—Lachlan—had said Bennet had told him the head was somewhere in the workshop, but he hadn't been able to give them anything more to go on than that.

There were a few cupboards and drawers in the workbenches. Logan checked through them, finding nothing but drill bits, chisels, and other accessories in the drawers, and various hand tools in the cupboards.

One cupboard, in the largest of the benches, refused to open. He tried the handle a few times, tugging hard, just in case the door was merely stuck, then concluded that, no, it was definitely locked.

He spent about three seconds looking around for a key, another two seconds considering his options, and then grabbed a drill from one of the other cupboards, and bored a hole right through the locking mechanism.

A strong smell came wafting out as he opened the door, and he buried his mouth and nose into the crook of his arm before he had a chance to process what it was.

Inside, wood stain leaked from a freshly-drilled hole in a tin, and pooled in a puddle on the cupboard floor. Logan rummaged around, but found only half a dozen or so containers of stains, oils, and other fluids. There was no head, though. Not unless it had been liquidised.

He tried the furniture next. Only one piece—a bedside cabinet—was a potential hiding place, and even then it would make for a tight fit. He braced himself for a moment, before pulling the cabinet door open.

Empty.

'Shite.'

He was rapidly running out of places where a human head might feasibly be stuffed. The ceiling was high and solid, with no liftable tiles or air vents that might offer somewhere to hide body parts.

There was a neatly stacked pile of wood leaning up against one wall. Logan dismantled part of the stack, hoping that it might reveal a hidden hollow in the middle with a head inside, but no such bloody luck.

Where, then? It wasn't in the workshop, so where was it? Had it already been moved? Had it already been taken?

Logan turned slowly on the spot, waiting for inspiration to strike. It did, a moment later, in the form of a toilet door.

'Well, now,' he said, the words carrying across the empty space. 'I wonder...'

The bathroom was notably less clean than the rest of the place. It was ridiculously small, given the size of the rest of the building, with a wall-mounted sink the DCI wouldn't be able to fit both hands in at the same time, and an ancient-looking toilet connected to a large cistern mounted high up on the wall.

There were two air fresheners hanging in the room, one on the back of the door, the other in the bowl of the toilet. They made the air taste cloyingly sweet, and Logan held his breath as he checked in the plastic bin behind the door, and peeked into the gap between the toilet and the wall.

Nothing.

He stood up then, looked down into the chipped, skid-marked bowl, and reached for the chain that hung from the cistern.

A quick pull led to an impressive flush. Logan watched the water foaming as it swirled around, reddish-pink bubbles popping as they hurtled around the U-bend. He raised his gaze to the cistern on the wall.

'Shitting blood, my arse.'

Chapter 44

Bennet had declined a solicitor, but given his age, and the seriousness of the charges they may well be bringing against him, Logan had insisted one be brought in.

She was a new face to Logan's team—mid-forties, once-dark hair now flecked with grey, and a look of bemused horror on her face that suggested she had no idea how she'd ended up with this gig, and that she would be writing a stern letter to HR about it at the earliest possible opportunity.

She had tried to discuss things with Bennet, but the boy had remained tight-lipped and was busily pretending that she didn't exist.

Eventually, because it was getting late, and she had a home to go to, the solicitor had relented and given the nod for the interview to go ahead.

Ben had done the introductions and recited the spiel for the recording, then had assumed the role of 'Good Cop' by letting Bennet know that his mum was in a stable condition in hospital, and promising to keep him updated of any developments.

'Must've been a shock for you,' Logan cut-in. 'Seeing her lying there like that.'

Bennet nodded furtively, his hands clasped in front of him so they hid the lower half of his face.

'What do you think happened?' the DCI pressed.

'Dunno.'

'No idea?'

Bennet rubbed his hands back and forth across his top lip, before mumbling, 'My dad.'

'What about him?'

'Well, he did it, didn't he?'

Logan shrugged. 'Did he? What makes you say that?'

More rubbing. A nervous tic. He was going to wear his lip away, at this rate. 'His hammer was there.'

'A hammer's a hammer, Bennet.'

'It was his.'

'How do you know?'

'I just... I just know.'

'But *how* do you just know?' Logan asked. 'We've looked it over. It's no' like he put a sticker with his name on it. It's just a hammer. There's no way of knowing who it belonged to. Not that I could see, anyway. How about you, Detective Inspector?'

'Just looked like any old hammer to me,' Ben confirmed. 'We could maybe have got prints off it, but, well, Bennet went and grabbed it on us, so that's out the window.'

Logan nodded sadly. 'Aye. Shame, that. A more cynical man might think you did that on purpose,' he said to the teenager across the table. 'Same with getting your mother's blood on you. What better way to hide traces of it than by covering yourself in the stuff?'

Bennet screwed his eyes shut, and spoke in a whisper. 'I didn't do it! I came in and found her there! That policewoman, she'll tell you.'

'She did, aye,' Logan confirmed. 'She said you came in while she was tending to your mum.'

'See! See, I told you!'

'She couldn't say where you came from, though,' Logan continued. 'Or even say for sure that you weren't in the house the whole time. You appeared out of nowhere and grabbed her by the hair.'

'I thought she was attacking her. I thought she'd hurt Mum.'

'No, you didn't, Bennet. Be honest,' Logan urged. 'You knew she didn't attack your mum, because you did. You tried to kill her. Just like you killed Fergus.'

Bennet's eyes opened wide. He shook his head, smearing a shiny slick of snot across his clasped fingers. 'What? No. No, I wouldn't. I didn't. He was... why would I? Why would I do that?'

'We spoke to Lachlan, son,' Ben said. 'He told us everything. Everything you said.'

'What? No,' the boy said, snorting out a laugh like it might counteract the look of betrayal on his face. 'No, he... I don't...'

'And we found the footage. The photos and videos,' Logan said. 'The two of you. You and Fergus. Together.'

Bennet's head snapped down. His hands came up to shield his eyes, and to block their judgemental gazes.

'To clarify for your sake,' Logan said, turning to the solicitor, 'since you don't seem to be asking any questions, the footage is of a sexual nature.'

'Oh!' the solicitor ejected. She was visibly shocked by this, like it was some *Sixth Sense* style twist to the tale she hadn't seen coming. 'Right. I see. I mean, I haven't seen, obviously. I don't really want to...'

She glanced down at her notepad, and Logan imagined she might have the words 'be a good lawyer' written there to remind herself.

'And it's definitely him? Them, I mean?' she asked, once she'd looked back up again.

'It is,' Ben confirmed. 'From what we can tell from the time... thingies in the video data, it dates back to shortly after Bennet's sixteenth birthday. Although, given Fergus's role as a teacher...'

'Of course,' the solicitor said.

'It wasn't like that,' Bennet protested. 'He wasn't taking advantage. It just... it just happened.'

'He just happened to give you oral sex in the school changing room?' Logan asked, and Bennet's cheeks burned until they were almost purple. The DCI leaned forward, his tone becoming softer and less confrontational. 'You were barely sixteen years old, son. He was an adult. He was your teacher. He's meant to look out for you.'

'He did! He always did! He loved me. He told me! He told me he loved me!'

'Whatever he felt about you, Bennet...' Logan shook his head. 'It wasn't love. Not even close. He was a predator. He preyed on you, and God knows who else.'

'Nobody else! There wasn't anyone else! It was just me and him.'

'And your mum,' Logan said.

Bennet's forehead became a series of raised ridges. His eyes flitted between both detectives, never settling on one for more than a second.

'What?' he croaked. 'What are you talking about?'

'You telling me you don't know?' Logan asked.

'About what? What about my mum? What are you saying?' the boy demanded, each word shriller than the last.

'Fergus and your mum were having a relationship.'

'Jesus Christ!' exclaimed the solicitor. Clearly, she hadn't seen that one coming, either. She shrunk beneath the glares of the men across the table, said, 'sorry', then leaned sideways when Bennet jumped to his feet.

'No. No, that's bullshit. That's not true,' Bennet spat. 'You're lying. He wouldn't do that. You're lying. You're all lying!'

'It's true, son,' Ben said. 'I'm sorry.'

'Don't be sorry, Detective Inspector. He knows full bloody well,' Logan barked. 'Don't you, Bennet? That's why you attacked her, isn't it? That's why you tried to kill her with that hammer.'

'No! No, it wasn't me! I told you, it wasn't me! It was my dad!'

'Oh, aye, because you know for sure it was his hammer,' Logan said. 'How can you possibly know that, Bennet? What's the difference between that and any other bloody hammer out there?'

'I just know!'

'You can't. How can you possibly know?'

'*Because I got it from his toolbox!*'

As the sentence faded, the only sound in the room was the faint creak of Logan's chair as he leaned back in it.

'You got it from his toolbox,' the DCI said. It wasn't a question, just a reiteration of what the boy had screamed, in case the microphone had peaked and the statement had been lost.

Bennet was breathing heavily, but the emotions that had driven him onto his feet were being swiftly replaced by the sense that he'd said the wrong thing. Logan could see it on his face, the realisation that he'd made a serious error of judgement. Any moment now, the backtracking would begin.

'Not… I didn't mean then. Not today. I didn't mean I got it from the toolbox today,' he said.

'Take a seat, son,' Ben urged. 'Nobody's going anywhere for a while yet. Might as well get comfy.'

Bennet danced his weight from foot to foot, looked at the solicitor, then at the door, then at his own reflection in the big mirror on the wall.

Then he wrapped an arm around himself, pulled his chair back into place, and flopped down onto the unforgiving plastic.

'I didn't kill her,' he insisted.

'But you did kill Fergus?'

'No! No, I…' He wheeled round to face his solicitor. 'Can you *say* something? Or do something? Please?'

The woman beside him squirmed, like a reluctant audience member who'd just been singled out by a performer on the stage. 'Like what?' she asked.

'Well, I don't know, do I? But don't just sit there!' Bennet yelped. 'Tell them I didn't do it!'

'That's not really my role,' the solicitor explained.

'Jesus fucking Christ! I didn't kill anyone! I took the hammer from the toolbox ages ago. I kept it under my bed, just in case.'

'Just in case what?' Logan asked.

There was a silence. A lengthy one. Bennet looked up at the ceiling, one leg bouncing so hard it made the whole table vibrate.

'In case he ever tried to use it on us,' he said, in a low, guttural whisper. 'Or… or in case I ever had to use it on him.'

'Your dad, you mean?' asked Ben.

'Yeah. My dad.'

'How did it get from under your bed to the living room?' Logan asked.

Bennet shrugged. 'I don't know. He must've taken it.'

'So, he knew it was there? Kind of defeats the point of you hiding it, doesn't it?'

'No. He… I mean, maybe. I don't know. He must have. Yeah. He must have.'

There was a knock at the door. The solicitor's gaze went to it immediately, like she was excited for some new, unexpected twist.

It came as something of a disappointment, then, when rather than some big reveal taking place, Logan quietly announced to the recording that he was leaving the room, stepped outside, and pulled the door closed behind him.

They all sat in silence for a few seconds, then the door opened again and Logan poked his head through the gap. 'I think we'll take a break there for a while, Bennet,' he said. 'We've just brought your dad in. I reckon it's about time we heard his side of the story, don't you?'

He waited for Ben to get up and follow him out of the room, then sent Uniform in to escort Bennet back to the cells.

'We should get onto the PF about holding him,' Ben said, once he, Logan, and Hamza had watched the boy and his bewildered-looking legal counsel be led away.

'He's over sixteen,' Logan replied, then he sighed. 'Aye. No. Better run it by them. In enough hot water with Mitchell as it is.'

'What for?' Ben asked.

Shite, Logan thought.

'Nothing. Doesn't matter,' he said, then he turned abruptly to Hamza and changed the subject. 'Tyler and Sinead back, then?'

'No, sir. Not yet. No word.'

Logan glanced at the door of the second interview room. 'But Clyde Lennon's here? I gave strict instructions that Tyler was to be seen first.'

'Aye, but you're no' in charge of the NHS, are you, Jack? Unlike us poor buggers, they don't have to answer to you,' Ben pointed out. 'Anyway, they do triangles.'

'Triangles?' Logan asked, his brow furrowing. 'What are you talking about, *triangles*?'

'You know what I mean. When they see you based on how serious your condition is.'

There was silence for a moment, as the other two men processed this.

'You mean "triage"?' Logan eventually guessed.

'Oh. Is that it? You knew what I meant,' Ben said. 'Maybe they thought Clyde Lennon's condition was more serious than Tyler's.'

'Aye,' Logan nodded, and looked along the corridor in the direction of the empty Incident Room. 'I suppose it must be that.'

Chapter 45

Tyler lay on his back on a hospital bed, two padded foam blocks squashing his head, his body held rigid on a spinal board. His right shoulder blade was itchy. It had been itchy for quite some time now, and all attempts to ignore it had thus far been met with failure.

The Velcro strap across his forehead also itched, but it was nowhere near as bad, and was just providing a sort of backing harmony for the main, out of reach trouble area on his back.

He needed to pee quite badly. This had also been going on for a while. Sinead was allowed to feed him sips of water through a straw, but he had declined her last few offers, for fear of what might happen if any more liquid entered his body.

Worse than any of that was the boredom. It had been two hours since the CAT scan that the doctors had insisted he have. The scan images had to be sent up to Inverness, apparently, so someone could read them up there. Given the length of time they were taking, he was starting to think they'd sent them up the road by bus.

It was the hope that was the real killer, though. He was in one of five or six curtained off areas in the hospital's A&E department, and the three-metre wide corridor on the other side of the curtain apparently got more foot traffic than Princes Street on Hogmanay. The first few dozen times he'd heard footsteps squeaking closer, he'd felt a little surge of hope that they were coming to extract him from this bloody contraption.

The next few dozen times, the surge became a flurry.

Now, he barely even registered the footsteps at all.

His spirits were sagging, his willpower was fading, and his bladder was on red alert.

There was only one thing for it.

'I spy, with my little eye,' he began. 'Something beginning with... c.'

'Crappy clothes?' Sinead guessed.

Tyler snorted. 'I thought the boss did all right!'

'Aye, you would,' Sinead said, looking down at her mismatched outfit. She hoiked at the back of her baggy jeans, adjusting the waistband of the men's boxer shorts that Logan admitted he'd bought in a moment of panic. 'I look like Vanilla Ice.'

'Was he the "Stop! Hammer Time!" guy?'

Sinead shrugged. 'God knows. Bit before my time.'

'Aye, me too,' Tyler said. 'Anyway, no. It's not "crappy clothes".'

Sinead clicked her tongue against the roof of her mouth as she considered the possibilities.

'Cows?'

'No. Where are the cows in this cubicle?'

'Cubicle!'

'No. Good try, though.'

'Castle? Is it a castle? I bet it's a castle.'

'You're not even trying now,' Tyler told her. 'You're not taking it seriously.'

He felt her join him on the bed. Not fully—there wasn't room for that—but partly. She turned her chair and leaned out from it, contorting herself into a position so that her head was next to his. Or next to the padded bracing that was clamped around his, at least.

Her hand slipped around Tyler's and squeezed, and he felt himself relax.

Then he remembered how close he was to wetting himself, and tensed again as best he could.

'This make it easier?' he asked her.

'Definitely,' she said. 'I can see what you see now.'

'Shite, isn't it?'

'Definitely no cows,' she said. 'They should put a telly up there.'

'What if it fell down?'

Sinead smiled. 'I'd be OK. I could move.'

'And I'd pretty much welcome death at this point, so it's a win-win,' Tyler said.

He felt Sinead turn to look at him, and caught a suggestion of movement out of the corner of his eye. 'Is it uncomfortable?' she asked.

'What, this old thing? Nah,' Tyler said. 'I was thinking I might get one for home, actually. I wonder if they do them in blue.'

'That'd bring out your eyes.'

'I know. That's why I suggested it,' Tyler said.

'You could wear it to the wedding,' Sinead suggested. 'Imagine everyone's face if you rocked up at the altar wearing that.'

Tyler made a strangled choking sort of sound. 'Oh, don't make me laugh,' he begged. 'I'll piss myself. I mean it. I'm one wrong move away.'

The cubicle curtain swished open, revealing the young female doctor who had insisted on the scan, and an older man who looked like he hadn't slept for more than half an hour in the last thirty-six.

'Good news, Mr Neish. No damage done,' the doctor announced. 'The scan shows no injuries.'

'Oh, thank God,' Sinead said, sitting up.

'I told you there was nothing to worry about,' Tyler said. He shot a hopeful look at the female doctor, who now loomed above him. 'Can I get out of this thing?'

'You absolutely can. Right now,' she replied, already hauling at the Velcro that held him in place.

The relief was immediate. He sat up, wrenched an arm up his back, and groaned with pleasure as he clawed at the itch on his shoulder blade, his fingers just long enough to hit the spot.

'Aw, man. That's good. That's so good,' he muttered, his eyes shut, and his tongue practically hanging out of his mouth. 'You've no idea how good that is.'

'I think you're painting a pretty vivid picture,' Sinead told him. She stood, stole a brief look at the older man who hadn't yet said anything, then turned her attention to the doctor. 'So, is that us? Can we go?'

'Soon. Yes. There's just a couple of things to discuss first,' the doctor said, returning Sinead's smile. There was something plastic about it, though. Something not quite right.

Sinead looked at the older man again. Another doctor, according to his lanyard. *Senior Consultant.*

'What is it?' Sinead asked.

The consultant replied before the younger doctor had a chance to. 'I appreciate you're colleagues, but I think it's probably best if we speak to Mr Neish on his own.'

'We're engaged,' Sinead said. 'We're getting married next week.'

'Oh,' the consultant said. He looked at Tyler as if awaiting some sort of confirmation. 'Right. Well, then, if Mr Neish is happy for us to go ahead…'

'Aye. You can say anything. What's wrong?' Tyler asked, swinging his legs down so he was sitting on the edge of the bed.

'Right. Well. OK, then. I'm Doctor Nisbet. I'm a consultant here at the Belford. And, well, I'm afraid something has come up on your scan. I'd like to arrange some more tests.'

Tyler felt Sinead's gaze turn on him. Felt it burning there.

'I thought you said it was clear?'

'It was. Kind of. There were no spinal injuries, which was the main purpose for the scan,' the consultant explained. 'But I'm afraid… well.' He smiled, but it wasn't a real smile. Not by a long shot. It was an apology, plain and simple. 'I'm afraid it may have shown up something else.'

Chapter 46

Clyde Lennon was one of the least pleasant individuals DCI Jack Logan had ever met. And, given the standard of the competition, this was really saying something.

He sat across the table from Logan and Ben now, rolling his tongue around and around in his mouth like he was chasing a soor ploom. He had his arms folded and his head tilted back so he was peering along the length of his nose at the detectives, clearly as unimpressed by them as they were by him.

'Just to reiterate, Mr Lennon, you've declined legal representation,' Ben said.

'Don't need it. Ain't done nothing wrong.'

'A growing pile of evidence would beg to differ with that,' Logan told him.

'You've got nothing on me, or you'd have charged me already,' Clyde spat back. He grinned, showing his yellowing teeth. 'See? I don't need a lawyer. I know your tricks.'

'That's no great surprise,' Logan said. 'Given the number of run-ins you've had with the polis over the years.'

'I've never been charged with nothing.'

'No, not charged, but we have our own internal database where we log details of complaints. Even those that have been withdrawn by the victim. And, I must say, your entry is longer than most,' Logan said. 'You're a violent man, aren't you, Mr Lennon?'

'I can handle myself, if that's what you mean.'

Logan consulted the paperwork spread out in front of him. 'Aye. You certainly seem to be able to handle yourself against women and children, all right. Good for you. That must take some guts.'

'I've never been charged—'

'How did it feel finding out your wife was cheating on you, Clyde?' Logan asked. 'Did that make you angry?'

Clyde licked his lips, unfolded then refolded his arms, but said nothing.

'I bet it made you furious,' Logan continued. 'The thought of the two of them. Together. Going at it.'

'Younger man like that,' Ben added.

'Probably at it for hours,' said Logan.

Ben sighed longingly. 'Oh, for half that energy.'

'I know what you're trying to do,' Clyde sneered. 'You're trying to get me riled up, so I'll say that I killed that fucking teacher. Well, I didn't. All right? I didn't know anything about any affair.'

'Aye, you did,' Logan said. 'We've got the texts to prove it.'

'Texts? What texts? What are you on about, texts?' Clyde demanded. 'Texts from who?'

'These texts,' Logan said, giving Ben the nod. He watched as the DI took the printouts from a folder and set them out on the desktop, facing the suspect. 'Ring any bells?'

Clyde leaned forwards and regarded the printouts with a mix of suspicion and contempt. 'No. What are these?'

'Don't piss us about, Clyde. They're texts sent between you and Fergus Forsyth the night before he died.'

'I've never sent a text in my life! Check my phone bills. Or my phone. Check them. You'll see. I don't text. Ever,' Clyde insisted. 'Why would I start with him? If I've got something to say, I'll fucking say it face to face. Anyway, where would I even get his number from?'

'These messages were sent to and from your phone,' Logan said, but there was something about Clyde Lennon's outrage that had sprinkled the first few seeds of doubt. 'Are you saying you didn't send them?'

'Give the man a fucking prize,' Clyde retorted. 'Yes. That's what I'm saying. I didn't send them. I didn't know anything about no affair until that fella phoned me today.'

Logan interlocked his fingers and leaned closer. 'What fella?'

'Journalist. Said he'd heard about the affair from teachers at the school. Wanted a fucking quote, or something. Asked me how I felt about it.'

Logan's hands clasped more tightly together until they were almost one big fist. 'What journalist?' he asked through gritted teeth.

'I don't know. *The Mirror*, or something. Cheeky bastard. Asked if I'd killed that PE teacher.'

'And what did you say?' Ben asked.

'I told him just what I'm telling you now,' Clyde spat. 'No, I didn't. But if I'd found out he was shagging my wife, then I would have done.'

'Is that why you attacked Lana?' Logan asked.

A blink. A frown. Another seed of doubt sown.

He didn't know. The bastard didn't know.

'What do you mean?' Clyde asked Logan. Then, when no reply came, he tried Ben. 'What's he on about? What's he saying?'

'You know what he's saying, son,' Ben said, sticking gamely to the plan. 'You attacked her with a hammer. We saw you fleeing the house. We gave chase. Don't tell me that crash has done damage to the old memory banks?'

'Attacked with a hammer? What? When? I don't know anything about... is she dead?'

'You'll be sorry to hear, but no, she's not. We're hoping to get a statement from her soon, in fact,' Ben told him. 'So, you might want to get in first and give us your side.'

'Oh, thank Christ,' Clyde said, practically laughing with relief. 'She'll tell you, then, won't she? She'll tell you it wasn't me.'

'Or she'll tell us it was,' Ben said.

'Nah. She won't.'

'Why not?' the DI asked. 'Because you've got her too scared?'

'Because it wasn't me!' Clyde spat.

'Then why run from the house?' Logan asked.

Clyde sat back, his scowl returning. 'Because I knew this would happen, didn't I? Soon as I found out she'd been shagging that teacher, I knew you lot would put two and two together and come up with five, like you always do. You'd say I did it. You'd try to pin it on me, get yourself looking good for the bosses. So, I went back to the house, grabbed some stuff from upstairs, and fucked off, sharpish.'

'Wee bit too sharpish, eh?' Ben said. 'Could've been nasty, you losing control of your van like that.'

'Yeah, well, I heard one of you lot chasing me, didn't I? Giving it all *wee-woo*, *wee-woo*. Put the wind up me.'

Logan wasn't ready to move on to the car chase. Not yet. 'And you didn't go into the living room?' he asked.

'No, I came in, went upstairs, put a bag together, and left,' Clyde said. 'Why? Is that where…? Fuck me. Seriously? She was in there? Jesus. Does Bennet know?'

'He does,' Logan confirmed.

'Bet he fucking blames me, too, doesn't he?'

'Why wouldn't he?'

'She's fucking poisoned that boy against me. It's what they do, women,' Clyde spat. 'You're divorced, ain't you? You got kids?'

Logan made no move to answer the question.

'Bet your missus has done the same to you. Poisoned them against you. Twisted things to make you look like the bad bastard.' Clyde shook his head in disgust. 'They're all the same. Lana, my ex, yours. They're all the bloody same.'

'Speaking of your ex-wife, Mr Lennon. Lana told us earlier that you claim to have killed her. That right?'

'What? No. I never said that,' Clyde said.

That wasn't true. Logan could see it written in every one of the man's movements. He was a piss-poor liar. One of the worst the DCI had seen.

'I don't believe you,' Logan said. 'We checked up, and your ex—Beverley—she is dead. Wasn't you, of course. Aneurysm. But

332

Lana wasn't to know that, was she? Why would you say that to someone, Clyde? To keep her scared? To keep her in line?'

'She's talking shit,' Clyde insisted, even less convincingly. 'And this is all a waste of time. You've got nothing to tie me to the teacher's murder. You're just trying to noise me up, in the hope you can find a way to pin it on me. You've got nothing.'

Logan raised an index finger. He'd been waiting for just the right moment, and here it was now, presenting itself.

'Far from it, Clyde. We've got something very interesting indeed.' He addressed the next part to Ben. 'You heard the phrase, "a smoking gun", Detective Inspector?'

'Aye. Aye, I'm familiar with it, Detective Chief Inspector,' Ben said, neither man taking their eyes off Clyde.

'Would you say what we've got is the equivalent of a smoking gun?'

'I'd say it's better than a smoking gun,' Ben said. 'I'd say it's two smoking guns. I'd say it's a whole smoking arsenal, in fact.'

'What the fuck are you going on about?' Clyde demanded.

Logan placed a glossy printout on the table between them. 'Can you tell me what that is, Clyde?' he asked.

The suspect flicked his eyes down at the image. 'It's a toilet.'

'Have another look,' Logan urged. 'See if it looks familiar.'

Clyde held his gaze for a few seconds, then relented and looked down at the photograph. Both detectives saw the moment the recognition hit. 'It's my toilet. In the workshop.'

'Well spotted,' Logan said, placing another photograph down. 'And that's the cistern for said toilet. Correct?'

'Aye,' Clyde confirmed, a little more wary now.

'I loved those old wall-mounted numbers,' Ben said. 'Held a lot of water. Gave you a proper flush. Everything in the pan, gone in one. None of this three or four flushes you have to do these days. Big cisterns. Plenty of space in them.'

'You can say that again, Detective Inspector,' Logan agreed.

'What the fuck are you pair talking about?' Clyde asked. 'Toilets, cisterns... what?'

Clyde Lennon was a bad liar. Truly awful. One of the worst Logan had ever seen.

Which is why the DCI knew he was telling the truth now. He had no idea what was coming next, and Logan almost felt sorry for him as he placed the final photo down on the table.

'We found this in your workshop toilet cistern, Clyde,' he said.

Across the table, the other man tilted his head, trying to figure out what he was looking at. Then the colour dropped out of his face—just drained away, all in one go.

'Is that...? Fuck. Is that...?'

'It is,' Logan confirmed.

'Fuck. *Fuck!*'

'Maybe you wouldn't mind explaining how Fergus Forsyth's head ended up in your workshop toilet, Mr Lennon?' Ben asked. 'Because me and him? We're dying to find out.'

Clyde was still staring at the photograph like he couldn't tear his eyes away. His tongue did laps of the inside of his mouth again, back to chasing that boiled sweet. 'I think...' he began, then he swallowed hard. 'I think I want that solicitor, after all.'

Chapter 47

Tyler sat in the passenger seat of Sinead's car, staring ahead at the windscreen wipers, which swished back and forth, fending off the rain shower that had started on the drive over from the hospital.

Night had drawn in, and the flecks of rain outside the wipers' reach blurred the lights from the police station, giving them a magical, Christmas-like aura.

Neither of them noticed.

'We should push it back,' Sinead said. 'The wedding.'

'We're not pushing it back,' Tyler said.

'Just for a month or two. Until we get the results. Until we know.'

'We're not pushing it back,' Tyler insisted. 'Unless... unless you want to?'

'No! No, of course not. Of course, I don't.'

Tyler gave a nod, the decision made. 'Right. That's settled, then. We don't push it back.'

'OK. Good. But... we can. If you want to.'

'I don't want to. I want us to get married like we planned. And then...'

'We'll go from there,' Sinead said, finding an end to the sentence that had eluded him.

'Exactly. Aye. Then, we'll go from there,' he said.

She took his hand. Held it. Kissed it. Rubbed it against her cheek.

'You OK?' he asked.

'Fine. You know. Ish. You?'

'Ish,' Tyler said. He blew out his cheeks, then nodded at the building ahead of them. 'We should go in.'

'You sure you're going to be OK?'

Tyler nodded. 'But we don't say anything. Not until we know. And even then, not until after the wedding. All right? Like we agreed.'

'If that's what you want.'

'It is. It could still be clear. The biopsy. It could...' Tyler sighed. 'They'll have to know, obviously, but just... just not yet, eh? And... shite. I'll have to tell my mum, too. Won't I?'

'You will. *We* will.'

She gave him a smile. They kissed, and they held each other in the dark.

'Ceiling,' she told him.

Tyler blinked. 'Eh?'

'I–Spy. It was "ceiling",' she said, then she unclipped her belt and her door. 'Now, come on,' she told him, giving his hand one final squeeze. 'Let's go inside.'

–

'Where the hell have you been, you malingering bastard?' Logan asked, when Tyler and Sinead came striding, side by side, through the double doors of the Incident Room.

'They had me in a neck brace, boss. One of them spinal board things,' Tyler said, not missing a beat. 'Had to wait for the all-clear from Inverness, then I spent about forty-five minutes pissing like a racehorse when they eventually took it off.'

'Everything all right, son?' Ben asked.

'Aye. Aye. Everything's fine. No harm done,' Tyler said, all teeth and smiles.

'I can't figure it out,' Ben remarked. 'With everything that's happened to you over the last couple of years, and given there's been no permanent damage done, either you're cursed, or you're blessed. I'm just no' sure what one.'

'Bit of both, maybe, boss,' Tyler said. He clapped his hands and rubbed them together. 'Who's on for tea?'

There was a moment of suspicious silence.

'Tea? You're actually offering to make tea?' Hamza asked.

'Aye. I always make tea.'

'You never bloody offer, though,' Logan pointed out. He glanced from Tyler to Sinead. 'What is it? What happened?'

'Nothing happened, boss!' Tyler laughed. 'I just... after being strapped down like that, it's good to be up and about.' He looked around at the other men, who all looked back with narrowed eyes. 'Look, if you don't want tea...'

'Well, now, we never said that,' Ben pointed out. 'Since you're offering, I'll have a coffee.'

'Coffee? At this time of night, boss?' Tyler asked.

'Aye, but I reckon we're going to need it,' Ben replied. 'Hurry up and get the kettle on, and we'll go over everything. But, needless to say, I think we've got a long bloody night ahead of us.'

–

It felt oddly comforting to be sat together around the Big Board. Even here, seventy miles from home, there was a real sense of familiarity to it. Of camaraderie. Tyler had even enjoyed the ribbing he'd got about the quality of his tea, and the poor selection of biscuits he'd been able to snaffle from CID's not-so-secret stash.

He and Sinead sat close together, their chairs rolled over from their desks so that Hamza sat on one side, and Ben on the other. Logan stood at the board, recapping a quite impressive list of developments that had occurred that day.

'So... to be clear, sir,' Sinead said, once Logan had finished giving his thoughts. 'We've got the texts from Clyde Lennon, he came running out of the house after Lana had been battered, and we found the victim's severed head in his toilet cistern...'

'That's all correct, aye.'

'But you don't think he did it?' Sinead concluded. 'Like... any of it?'

'That's right.'

'Like... *any* of it? At all?'

'He's a bloody awful liar,' Logan explained. 'He's no' got the self-control. Whatever he's thinking or feeling, you can see it all over his face. When we told him about Lana, and when he saw the head, that was real shock. He had no knowledge of either one.'

'He could've been faking it,' Hamza suggested.

'He's no' that smart. Trust me,' Logan said. 'You get to know the difference, even with the clever ones. There's always some wee giveaway somewhere. But that clown? He's as transparent as a fucking window pane. If he was lying, we'd know. Which means, he isn't. Which means—'

'He didn't do it,' Sinead said.

'The son, then?' Tyler suggested. He looked around at the others. 'I mean, it's got to be, hasn't it? He confessed to his mate, there's all the video stuff. He could've sent the texts from his dad's phone, then deleted them. He'd have had access.'

'Battering his own mum, though?' Hamza said. 'That's pretty extreme.'

'Jealousy?' Sinead reasoned. 'If he found out about the rela-tionship. Lana and Fergus, I mean.'

'Still, a claw hammer to your own mum,' Hamza said, wincing. 'I mean, aye, mother-*in-law*, maybe...'

'He could've been in the house when I got there,' Sinead said. 'I didn't hear him come in.'

'There we go, then!' Tyler announced. 'Fergus is blackmailing him with the videos, so Bennet kills him. He hates his dad, so he tries to frame him for it, then when he finds out his mum has been shagging Fergus, too, he goes mental and caves her head in with a hammer.' He held his hands out as if to welcome some inevitable praise. 'Case closed.'

'No,' Logan intoned.

Tyler's arms flopped back down at his sides. 'No? How no'?'

'Because none of that feels right,' Logan said. He had his back to the team now and was studying the Big Board. 'You get blackmail in these teacher–student relationships, but it's generally the other way around. If it came out, Fergus Forsyth stood to lose a hell of a lot more than Bennet Lennon ever would. Career would be ruined. He might end up charged. Bennet's a smart enough kid, he'd have known that. And then there's the key.'

'What about it, boss?'

Logan kept his feet planted, but turned and looked back over his shoulder. 'Well, he ate it, didn't he? That doesn't strike me as a man threatening to use it.'

'You think he swallowed it because he *didn't* want word of the relationship to get out?' Hamza asked. 'Hiding it from who, though? Bennet?'

'More likely hiding it from whoever did Fergus's and Ross Lyndsay's house over. I think they were looking for the key, or maybe the USB drive itself.'

Ben's phone gave a bleep. He picked it up, glanced at the screen, then set it down again.

'Swallowing something's a bit of a desperate hiding place, is it not?' he asked.

'It is,' Logan agreed. 'So, what does that tell us?'

There was a moment of silence, before Tyler chipped in.

'He was in a rush?'

'Panicking, maybe,' Hamza offered. 'Like, he knew someone was coming for it, and it was the only place he thought he could keep it safe.'

'Thoughts, Sinead?' Logan prompted.

Sinead blinked and sat up straighter in her chair. 'Sorry, sir. Eh… yeah. What they said.'

'You seem distracted, Detective Constable. Am I boring you?' the DCI intoned.

'No, sir. Sorry, sir. Just…' She very deliberately did not look at Tyler. '…a bit tired, sir.'

'Told you, you should've had the coffee,' Ben said.

'Stay focused,' Logan told her, then he turned his attention back to the board. 'So, our theory is, Fergus Forsyth made recordings of his sexual encounters with Bennet Lennon for the duration of their relationship, and kept them hidden. Either he made these for his own gratification, or some other purpose we're not aware of. Someone got wind of them, wanted to get hold of them, and so Fergus was forced to hide the key in the most readily available hiding place—his own stomach.'

'Who would want to get hold of the footage?' Sinead asked, making an extra effort to get involved.

'You tell me,' Logan prompted.

'Well… either someone who wanted to ruin Fergus's reputation, or protect Bennet's?'

'Or someone who wanted to do both, maybe?' Tyler said. 'That could take us back to Clyde again.'

'Or even Lana,' Hamza suggested. 'If she found out that the man she was in love with was having it away with her teenage son, I can't imagine she'd be overly impressed.'

'True, but there's nothing to suggest she knew anything about what was going on between Fergus and Bennet,' Logan said. 'She was still talking about them all running away together, and getting away from her arsehole of a husband. Besides, there's no way she could have lifted the body by herself.'

Ben's phone gave another bleep. He held it at arm's length, and started patting himself down, searching for his glasses.

'So, we're ruling Lana out?' Hamza asked.

'For now,' Logan said.

'Which leaves Clyde, Bennet, or some other bugger entirely,' Ben remarked, still searching for his specs.

'Or both!' said Tyler. 'They could've been working together.' The initial burst of enthusiasm that had come with the idea quickly began to wane when he realised quite how unlikely that was. 'Or, you know, they might not have been. And probably weren't.'

'Don't worry. There's no such thing as a bad idea, son,' Logan said.

'Except that,' Ben added.

'Aye,' the DCI agreed. 'Except that one you just had. Otherwise, there's no such thing as a bad idea.'

'Haha. Aye,' said Tyler, making a passable attempt at laughter. 'Sure thing, boss.'

Logan regarded him in silence for a few seconds, then did the same to Sinead. His eyes narrowed, then he shook his head and turned back to the board. 'In all seriousness, son, it wasn't a terrible idea. I just don't see it. It doesn't fit what we've got.'

He rocked on his heels, considering the information pinned up on the Big Board. The texts that Clyde Lennon denied all knowledge of. The body's location, with all its implications of revenge and retribution, not to mention its connection to Lana and Fergus's secret rendezvous. The head shoved unceremoniously in a toilet cistern in Clyde's workshop.

Based on those things alone, they had a case against Lana's husband. If he'd found out about what was happening between Fergus and Bennet, he'd have even more of a reason to get violent.

Had he gone to confront Fergus about that, and not the affair with Lana? Had things escalated from there?

But then, why would the body be at the Well of the Seven Heads? Too big a coincidence, if it wasn't connected to Lana.

He ran through a few more possibilities. What if Lana had killed Fergus, with the help of Bennet, or Clyde? How would that play out?

Maybe she and Bennet both found out they were sleeping with the same man, took their revenge, then jealousy drove Bennet to attack his mother afterwards.

It was possible. Plausible, even.

He just wasn't feeling it. He had a nose for bullshit, and Lana Lennon had been nothing but convincing in all their conversations. She hadn't known Fergus was dead. She hadn't suspected anything was going on between him and her son.

She had trusted Fergus. Implicitly. From almost the moment she'd met him, she'd said.

'She felt like she'd known him forever,' Logan muttered.

'Boss?'

Logan turned from the board, something stirring at the back of his mind. Not a thought, exactly. Not yet. But a spark of one.

'Lana Lennon. She said... when she spoke about Fergus, she said it was like she'd known him for years. Like, he was familiar.' He sucked in his cheeks, thought for a moment, then shook his head, tentatively at first, then with more conviction. 'No. No, that would mean...'

He sat on the edge of a desk, eyes drawing maps on the floor as that spark became a thought that led to dozens more, all flashing up, rapid-fire.

The others said nothing. They knew better than to interrupt when Logan was like this. Derail his train of thought at a time like this, and you'd be left picking yourself up out of the wreckage.

'What if...?' he muttered. 'What if we're looking at it all wrong?'

'Wouldn't be the first time, boss,' Tyler pointed out, then he bit his lip to stop himself saying any more.

'How do you mean, Jack?' Ben asked, then he patted the top of his head, found his glasses there, and pulled them down with a self-reprimanding tut.

'What are the chances of Fergus Forsyth just happening to get into relationships with both Lana and Bennet Lennon at the same time?' Logan asked. 'I mean, he's a young guy, good-looking. Plenty of opportunities, but he jumps into bed with a woman twice his age who he has nothing whatsoever in common with, and then starts having sex with her sixteen-year-old son, and recording it all for posterity.'

'It's definitely odd, sir,' Hamza said.

'Unless he had another motive,' Logan reasoned. He pointed to the photograph of Clyde Lennon. 'Revenge.'

There was near-silence as the other detectives considered this, the only sound coming from DI Forde muttering to himself as he tried to get into his email.

'We've had revenge as a motive from the start,' Logan said. 'Given where the body was stuffed. But what if Fergus was the one looking for revenge on Clyde Lennon? Stealing his wife. Grooming his son.'

'Why would he want revenge on Clyde, though, sir?' Hamza asked.

Logan sucked air in through his teeth. 'I think… I think I might know the answer to that,' he said. 'I just wish I didn't.'

'Jesus Christ, Jack!' Ben exclaimed, jumping to his feet more quickly than he'd likely done in years. He thrust his phone out, almost like he wanted to be rid of the thing. 'Email just arrived. I think you're going to want to see it.'

Chapter 48

'You get something to eat, Mr Lennon?' Logan asked once the tape had been restarted. 'We treating you all right?'

'Not really,' Clyde said. 'Food's shit. And cold.' He gestured to the notepad of the grey-haired solicitor who had been dragged away from his family to sit in on the interview. 'Put that down, will you? Food was cold. And shit.'

'I don't think that's really relevant, Mr Lennon,' the solicitor said. He was more switched on than the other one, Logan thought, but shared the same desire not to be here.

'This shouldn't take too much longer,' Logan said. 'We just have a few more questions, and then you can get some rest.'

Clyde beckoned across the table, inviting the detectives to come at him. 'Well, come on. Let's have it.'

'Did you ever meet Fergus Forsyth?'

'No.'

'Ever see a picture of him?' Logan asked.

'Why the fuck would I have seen a picture of him?'

'On the school website, maybe?'

Clyde sighed. 'I'm hardly pissing about looking at school websites, am I?'

'So, to be clear, you're saying you don't know what Fergus Forsyth looked like?'

'Yeah,' Clyde sneered. 'That's what I'm saying.'

Logan side-eyed Ben, who picked up on the signal and opened the folder he'd brought in with him. 'I'm going to show you a photograph of Fergus Forsyth now, Mr Lennon,' the DI said. 'I'd like you to take a moment to look at it before responding.'

The slow shhhkt of the photograph being slid across the table seemed deafening in the hush of the interview room. He could sense Tyler and Hamza on the other side of the mirror, watching with breath held to see if his theory was right.

He hoped it wasn't. He hoped he was wrong. He really did.

But he wouldn't be. He wasn't.

The email had all but confirmed it.

'What the fuck is this?' Clyde demanded, eyes snapping up from the picture on the desk. He repeated the question immediately, his voice rising to a shout. 'What the fuck is this?! What are you showing me?'

'Do you recognise the person in that photograph, Mr Lennon?' Logan asked.

'Yes! Of course. But that's not him. He's not Fergus!'

'That's Fergus Forsyth, Mr Lennon,' Logan insisted.

'Bollocks it is!' Clyde spat. He slapped his hand down on the photograph, covering most of the face.

'Then who is it?' Logan asked. 'Who is the man in the photo?'

'That's Kenny,' Clyde bellowed. His voice cracked and he spread his fingers, unmasking enough of the face so that he could look into its eyes. When he spoke again, it was in a whisper. 'That's my son.'

–

'Bloody hell,' Hamza said, his voice low to reduce the risk of it travelling through the glass. 'That's mental. So Fergus was at it with his own step-mum and... what? Half-brother?'

When he got no response from Tyler, he gave him a dunt with an elbow.

'What?' Tyler asked, rousing. 'Oh. Aye. Crazy stuff.'

'You all right, mate?' Hamza asked.

Tyler nodded, a little too keenly. 'Aye. Aye, grand. Grand.'

'Not having cold feet, are you? About the wedding?'

'No!' Tyler said, a little too loudly.

Both detectives stepped back and waited for any sign that they'd been heard. Other than the briefest of dirty looks from DCI Logan, they seemed to get away with it.

'No, nothing like that,' Tyler continued more quietly this time.

'Good, because you've got no idea how much time and effort has gone into that bloody speech,' Hamza told him. 'And then there's your stag night. I've got it all figured out down to—'

Tyler motioned to the glass. 'Maybe we should…'

Hamza leaned back a little, thrown off-balance by this uncharacteristic display of a work ethic.

'Oh. Aye. Yeah. Good point,' he said.

'We'll talk later,' Tyler told him, as they both turned their attention to the glass, and watched events playing out in the adjoining room.

'Yeah,' said Hamza, his gaze flitting sideways for just a moment. 'We'll do that.'

–

Clyde Lennon's earlier aggression had been replaced over the last few moments by a sort of stunned confusion. Had he not been sitting, he'd likely be wandering around in circles, Logan imagined, not quite sure where he was going, or what he was supposed to be doing when he got there.

But he was answering their questions. That, right now, was all that really mattered.

'Like… I don't know. Before Bennet was born. So… how long's that? Eighteen years? Maybe twenty since I saw him last,' he said. He picked up the photograph. 'He was just a boy.'

Once Logan had made the connection, the resemblance had been… not obvious, exactly, but definitely there to see. There was some similarity across the eyes, and the shape of the nose. The shape of the hairlines were similar, although age meant that Clyde's now started further back on the head.

Fergus looked like Bennet, too, if you were paying attention. Again, it was mostly the eyes, although something about the shape of the head matched, too.

No wonder Lana had instantly thought him so familiar.

'We tracked down his previous employer,' Ben said. 'The headteacher there was new to the school, and so he didn't recognise the name Fergus Forsyth. Some of the other staff, did, though. Apparently, Kenny changed it about a year after his mother passed away. Officially, like. Driver's licence, passport, the full thing.'

'Why? Why would he do that?' Clyde asked. 'He loved his mum. She made bloody sure of that. Made sure he'd always pick her over me. Why would he pretend to be someone else?'

'We think it was all done to get at you, Mr Lennon,' Logan explained. 'We think Fergus—Kenny—moved up here specifically to target you through your wife. And through Bennet.'

'Bennet? What's he got to do with anything?' Clyde asked, some of that old fire returning. 'He was just his teacher.'

Logan told him the truth of it. Watched the disbelief become horror, then grief, then another surge of rage that saw him twist and wrench at the photograph, trying and failing to tear it in half, before he finally hurled it to the floor.

'I feel sick. I feel sick! I want to be sick!' Clyde wailed.

The solicitor edged his chair away. 'I think my client might need a break.'

'No! I don't want a fucking break! I want to know everything. Tell me everything!' Clyde insisted. 'God, I knew it! I fucking knew she was poisoning him against me. Didn't I say that? That's what they do, women. They lie, and they twist things, and they make it seem like you're the bad bastard! I wanted to see him, you know? Tried, time and time again. But she wouldn't let me. Wouldn't have it. Bitch moved house half a dozen times so I wouldn't find them. What sort of life's that for a kid? Eh? No wonder he was fucking demented! She did this! That bitch of a mother of his. She did it!'

He pulled at his thinning hair and gnashed his teeth, shock and grief threatening to consume him completely. He was breathing like an animal now, his chest rising and falling like his lungs were doubling in size with each frantic inhalation.

'Well, know what? Good fucking riddance!' he spat, kicking out at the crumpled photograph on the floor. 'You sick, twisted piece of shit! Good fucking riddance to you! I've only got one son now. One!'

Logan and Ben swapped looks. This was it, then. The big moment.

'Aye, Mr Lennon,' Logan said. 'About that...'

Chapter 49

'Lachlan.'

The young man scrubbing away at the big soup pot in one of the castle's kitchen sinks didn't respond at first. It took a second shout before he paid attention, then turned to find his supervisor standing in the kitchen doorway with a large man in a long coat.

'Yeah?' he asked.

'This police officer would like a word.'

Lachlan smiled, nodded, then set the pot on the draining board and slipped both hands into the sink. 'Sure,' he said. 'Give me a second to get cleaned up.'

He scrubbed his hands, started to dry them on a towel, and carried it with him as he followed his boss and the detective through to a garishly decorated room just off the main foyer. It had been described to him as 'the small drawing room' but it was big enough to hold four couches, six matching armchairs, and a grand piano.

Logan had felt nothing but contempt for the whole place as he'd pulled up outside, and this had only increased as he was being led through it. He hated all its prissiness and pomp, detested how it celebrated wealth and excess, and the way it rubbed it right in your face.

Oh, sure, it was no doubt lovely, if you liked that sort of thing, but he felt about as home in it as a squirrel in a spaceship, and he could almost hear his mother's voice warning him no' to bloody touch anything, for fear that he might break it.

It was the sort of place that thought it was better than him.

Then again, it was probably right.

'Are you the fella I spoke to on the phone?' Lachlan asked, once they'd been shut in the room together.

'No. That was a colleague of mine,' Logan told him. He gestured to a scuffed leather couch that probably cost more than his whole house. 'Take a seat, son.'

'I'd better not,' Lachlan said. 'They go mental.'

'I won't tell them, if you don't,' Logan said. He pointed, a little more forcefully this time. 'Take a seat.'

Lachlan rubbed his hands around inside the towel, then shrugged and perched himself right at the front of the couch. 'Did you get him?' he asked. 'Bennet, I mean. Did you bring him in?'

'We did,' Logan confirmed.

'And? Did he tell you what he'd told me?'

'He did.'

Lachlan made a show of exhaling. 'Oh. Thank God for that. I couldn't not say, you know? When he told me what he'd done, I couldn't not—'

'Cut the shite, Ewan.'

Lachlan froze. Blinked. Swallowed. 'Sorry?'

'We know that's your real name. We know who you are, son,' Logan told him. He plink–plinked a couple of the high notes on the piano, not taking his eye off the young man in the stained kitchen whites. 'You and Kenny were both mentioned on your mum's funeral notice. We know Clyde Lennon's your dad.'

'I don't... I don't know what you're talking about.'

'Aye, you do,' Logan replied. He shrugged. 'It came as a shock to your old man, right enough. He had no idea. He knew about Kenny, obviously, but not you. Your mum never told him. Can't say I blame her, he's hardly the sort of role model you'd want around for your kids.'

There was a portrait on the wall above the piano of a man who looked almost the size of one. It looked old, no doubt valuable. Logan gave it a nudge with a finger, making it squint.

'Whose idea was it to come up here and bring your dad's life crumbling down around him? Kenny's?' Logan asked. 'Yours?'

When he got no answer, he gave a little wave of his hand. 'Doesn't matter, I suppose. All went wrong in the end, didn't it? He lost his bottle. He wanted out. But you couldn't have that, could you? You wanted to follow-through. You wanted to make your dad pay.'

'No.' Lachlan shook his head. 'I don't… this isn't…' He forced a grin, but it was far too broad, and nowhere near convincing enough. 'I'm sorry, I really don't know what you're talking about.'

Logan picked up a delicate jar of potpourri, sniffed it, then shook his head in disgust and set it back down again.

'Like I said, Ewan,' the DCI grunted. 'Aye, you do. We found Fergus's motorbike in the shed out back at yours. We have your fingerprints on it.'

'Bollocks, I wiped it all down!'

Lachlan stopped then. He closed his eyes, just for a moment. Something changed about his face, some muscles tightening, others relaxing, his expression shifting as he realised his mistake.

'What happened, do you think?' Logan asked. 'With your brother. Did he actually fall for her, like he told her? Clyde's wife, I mean. Was he really planning to run away with her?'

'I don't… I'm not…'

'How did he think that was going to work out? Considering what he was doing with Bennet—his own brother. *Your* own brother. How did he think he could possibly get away with it?'

'*Because he's a fucking idiot!*' Lachlan hissed. Panic flashed across his face, and he added, 'was', like his use of the incorrect tense was the incriminating part of his outburst. 'I mean…'

'So that was it, right enough? It was true?' Logan said. 'He fell for her. He started out using her to get back at Clyde, but he actually fell in love with her? Jesus Christ. But, you couldn't allow that, could you, Ewan? Couldn't have him deviating from the plan. So, you killed him. You killed your own brother.'

Lachlan hadn't moved from the couch, but his gaze flitted momentarily to the drawing room door.

'And you thought it through, too,' Logan said. 'You sent those texts between their phones, made it look like your dad had found

351

out about the affair. You used his workshop. Left Fergus's body in a place you knew would further point the finger. Planted your own brother's head in the cistern of his bloody toilet, all so you could punish him.'

'No. No, it's not like that. That's not—'

'Bennet came to you today to tell you about his relationship with Fergus. He was scared it might come out. He thought he could trust you. He thought of you like a brother, ironically,' Logan said. 'But then you went to his house, and you attacked his mother. You knew Clyde's hammer was under Bennet's bed, so you used that to make it look like Clyde did it. Like he battered his wife.'

'He did batter her,' Lachlan said. 'He battered my mum, and Kenny, and Bennet. It's what he does. It's what he's always done. It's who he is!'

'Oh, we know. And you wanted to get your own back on him. To punish him.'

'No! I mean… I mean…' Lachlan stammered. '*He* did. Kenny. It was his idea. It was all him. It was his idea to start the affair with Lana. And then, when he realised Bennet was into him, he pushed that, too. It was him who wanted to make Clyde pay. Not me. Not me, I didn't even know him! I didn't care.'

Logan dismissed that with a shake of his head. 'You cared enough to kill your own flesh and blood, son, so if…'

The penny dropped then. The lad was telling the truth. He didn't know Clyde. He didn't hate him enough to want to destroy him, or to kill his own brother.

His hatred was reserved for someone else.

'Bennet,' Logan said, and Lachlan's eyes narrowed at the sound of that word. 'Your brother was out to punish Clyde, but you weren't. You wanted to punish Bennet. You hated him. He got to have your dad, warts and all, and what did you get? Bounced here, there, and everywhere around the country. A dozen addresses in as many years. He got to have the life you didn't, and even though he was miserable in it, you were jealous of him.'

Lachlan opened and closed his mouth, snapping his bottom teeth against the top like a piranha chewing its food. 'He had no fucking idea what he had,' he muttered. 'He had no clue how good he had it. Money. A nice house. Both parents.'

'Jesus Christ, you said yourself, the poor bastard was getting knocked around.'

'What, and you think we weren't?' Lachlan cried. 'You think we didn't get slaps from her boyfriends, or people she brought home, or... or... fucking touched up by creepy old men because she'd shot all the rent money up her arm? You think that was better?'

He launched himself to his feet, every part of him now shaking with rage and burning with the shame of it.

'You don't know! You have no idea the shit we went through!' he spat. 'There was this one place we stayed, way back, when I was four, or five, or... I don't know. Kenny slept on this horrible, manky couch in the living room, but I had to sleep in her bed with her—in her bed.'

He looked past Logan at one of the room's big bay windows. It was dark outside now, and three different versions of himself stood shoulder to shoulder in the panes of glass.

'Every night she'd have a different guy come in,' he hissed, 'and every night she'd tell me to look away, to cover my ears, to be a good boy, to shut up, shut up, *shut up, you little shit, and just stop fucking crying*!'

He whipped a hand out from under the towel, and pointed to the door with the kitchen knife he'd stashed there, his face all screwed up with rage.

'And... what? Bennet thinks he has it bad? A couple of slaps? A few fucking raised voices? He has no appreciation of what he had. He has no idea what it's like to suffer! Not like I did! Not like me!'

For a moment, Logan was lost for words. He couldn't imagine it. Wouldn't. Couldn't stomach the thought of it. Was it any wonder the poor bastard had ended up like this?

The old floorboards creaked beneath the detective's feet, and Lachlan brought the knife around to hold him at bay.

'Fucking stay there! I mean it!' he warned. 'Yes. You're right. I wanted to hurt Bennet. I wanted him to feel like I had. I wanted him to lose everything. His dad. His mum. His whole fucking life. Everything.'

'And Fergus—Kenny—just got in your way,' Logan said. 'So you killed him.'

Lachlan ground his teeth together, pushing back against his emotions. 'He shouldn't have changed the plan. We were meant to be a team. We were meant to have each other's backs. He was meant to be my big brother.'

Logan attempted another shuffled step closer, but the floorboards betrayed him again and a warning look flashed across Lachlan's face, forcing the detective to stay rooted to the spot.

'I'm sorry, son. I really am. I can't imagine what it was like, going through everything you did. Living with that. There's only one person who could possibly understand, and... well, he's no longer with us, is he?'

Tears raced each other down Lachlan's cheeks. The knife shook, the point swaying in a figure of eight in front of Logan's face.

'He... I had to. He wasn't going to let me... he was going to...'

'Give me the knife, son,' Logan urged, holding a hand out. 'Give me the knife, and we can talk. That's all. We can just sit here and we can talk.'

'Oh, fuck off! You just want me to put it down so you can arrest me!'

'I am going to have to arrest you. I won't lie to you about that. But I mean it, son. We can talk,' Logan insisted. 'We can take some time, and we can just talk.'

'Don't lie! Don't lie to me! Everyone always fucking lies to me!'

Lachlan lunged, thrusting the knife forward, the blade glinting in the twinkling glow of eight gaudy wall lights that probably cost more than Logan made in a year.

Logan didn't move quickly. He didn't have to. He'd been waiting for that moment since before they'd entered the room, the knife nowhere near as well hidden by the towel as Lachlan had clearly thought it was.

He took a half-step to the right, caught the lad by the wrist, then twisted until the blade went clattering to the floor.

Lachlan's momentum carried him on, and he slammed into Logan. Being much larger, heavier, and braced for the impact, Logan didn't move a step. Instead, he put his arms around the boy, and held him in close, listening to his sobbing.

'You're all right, son,' Logan told him. They stood there together, a disappointment of a father and an unwanted son. 'You're all right.'

Chapter 50

Logan felt pretty pleased with himself when Sinead stepped out of her auntie's house and saw the car for the first time. The look on her face made all the bargaining worthwhile.

'Told you I'd get something nice, didn't I?' he crowed. 'Leave it with me, that's what I said.'

'Is that a Bentley?' Sinead asked, clopping her way up the path in heels she didn't look entirely comfortable walking in.

Logan regarded the car with a blank expression. 'Eh... aye. Maybe. Nice, though, eh? Whatever it is.' He gave her an appraising up and down look as she stepped through the gate and joined him on the path. 'You look beautiful.'

Sinead looked one-part delighted, three-parts mortified. She smoothed down the front of her already pristinely smooth white dress, and gave an embarrassed shrug. 'Cheers, sir.'

Logan laughed. 'I think we can dispense with the formalities today of all days, Detective Constable. Don't you?'

'Aye. If you say so, sir,' she said. 'You scrub up all right yourself.'

Logan adjusted his bow tie and gave his kilt a wee swish. 'Aye, well, high time this old thing had an airing.'

'Is that the kilt you're referring to, or...'

'Get your mind out of the gutter, Detective Constable. Of course, I mean the kilt,' he told her. 'Mind you, it's no' half bloody draughty under here,' he added, then he opened the car door and gestured for her to get in. 'M'lady.'

Sinead hoiked the dress up past her knees in a decidedly unladylike manner, put one foot in the car, then turned back to the house. 'Harris!'

There was some thumping and clattering, and a shout of 'Coming!' from inside, then Harris appeared in a kilt, untucked shirt, and bright yellow sports socks.

'You need to hurry up! You're meant to be there before me!'

'Just you go, Sinead!' her aunt called from inside. 'We'll be ready in two minutes. Circle around a couple of times, and we'll wait for you outside.'

'We can't be late, they've got another wedding booked in after mine!' Sinead called back.

'We'll be there! Go! Go!'

Sinead rolled her eyes, and looked to Logan for reassurance.

'They'll be there. It'll be grand,' he told her. 'There's nothing to worry about.'

She got in, smoothed herself down again, then gave Logan the nod to close the door. He had just thunked it into place when his phone rang, flashing Ben Forde's name up on the screen.

'Ben. Hello. We're on our way,' Logan said, walking around to the other side of the car. The heels of his rented brogues scuffed on the road as he stopped at the back of the car. 'Whoa, whoa, whoa, slow down,' he urged. 'What do you mean, "Tyler's gone"?'

'What do you mean, *what do I mean*? He's gone, Jack!' Ben replied. 'He was here ten minutes ago, but now he's gone.'

Logan shot a sideways look at the car beside him, then lowered his voice. 'Have you phoned him?'

'Of course, we've bloody phoned him. He's no' answering.'

'Jesus Christ! What's he thinking?' Logan grunted.

'Look, we've got it in hand,' Ben said. 'Me, Hamza, Hoon, and a few others are looking for him. He can't have got far.'

'Hoon?' Logan almost shrieked. 'The fuck's Hoon doing there?'

'Says he was invited,' Ben said.

'Hoon? Bob Hoon?'

Ben tutted. 'Hardly the bloody priority right now, is it?' he said. 'Just... keep Sinead away until we've got him back, all right? Circle around.'

'Aye,' Logan sighed. 'Aye. Fine. Text me as soon as it's safe.'

'Will do.'

'And give the bastard a thick ear from me,' Logan added, then he hung up the phone and shoved it into his sporran.

He spent a few seconds finding just the right nonchalant expression to affix to his face, then continued around the car and climbed into the back alongside Sinead.

'Everything all right?' she asked.

'What? Oh. Aye. Aye! Just, you know, usual wedding logistics,' he said, pulling on his seatbelt. 'By the way, do you know Hoon's coming to your wedding?'

'Yeah. We invited him,' Sinead said.

'What, on purpose?'

Sinead smiled. 'I don't know, I just… I sort of feel sorry for him.'

'Jesus, don't tell him that,' Logan warned. 'He'll burn the venue to the ground with every bugger in it.'

'Noted,' Sinead said. She looked through the window at the house she'd just left. 'And I suppose… we never know what's around the corner, do we? Life's too short, isn't it? To hold grudges, I mean.'

Logan ran his tongue across the back of his teeth. He thought of another young woman in another white dress.

'So, eh, that us off, then?'

'It is! That's us on the way for the big day!' Logan said. 'In your own time, driver.' He leaned forward and lowered his voice, just a little. 'But, eh, maybe take us the scenic route, eh?'

—

Ben and a small group of guests had assembled out the front of the Highland Archive Centre—a relatively new building that had been aiming for 'modern architectural triumph' but had instead landed somewhere between 'school gym hall' and 'young offender's institution'.

The sun had put in an uncharacteristically timely appearance that morning, and there had been a real sense that the day was going to be perfect, up until the point the groom had vanished into thin air.

Now, the DI stood on the grass, directing the search like it was a full-scale missing persons operation.

'We need to do this quickly, but quietly,' he instructed, addressing the group of mostly polis guests gathered in a knot around him. 'We don't want anyone else knowing he's buggered off if we can help it. We find him, we slap sense into him if he's having cold feet, and we bring him back before anyone misses him.'

'He can't have got far,' Hamza said. 'He said he was just going to the toilet.'

'You did check there, aye?' asked Dave Davidson. 'He's not just having a really big shite?'

'I checked. And he's not,' Hamza said.

'Right. We spread out, we keep in contact, and we find him. Quickly,' Ben instructed. He looked around the group. 'Anyone got any questions?'

Hoon's hand went up. Unlike the other men, he wasn't wearing a kilt, and had instead rocked up in a shiny grey suit and black shirt, neither of which had seen an ironing board in quite some time. He seemed substantially more hungover than the others, too, despite being the only one among them not to have been at the stag do the night before.

He didn't wait to be invited before speaking. 'Aye. Just a quick one,' he said, looking around at the group. 'Who the fuck is it we're actually looking for?'

–

Logan sat in the back of the car, tapping a rhythm on a bare knee with one hand, and checking his phone with the other in the hope of seeing a text from Ben telling him everything was sorted.

No such luck.

'You sure everything's all right?' Sinead asked.

Logan clicked the button on the side of the phone, turning the screen dark. 'Aye. Fine. Just… I told Shona we'd meet at the centre. Just making sure she made it OK.'

'High time you made your move there,' Sinead said.

'It's no' my love life that's the centre of discussion today, thanks very much,' Logan replied.

'I'm just saying. You'd be good together,' Sinead said. She shrugged. 'You need someone who understands, don't you? What it's like. Someone who gets it. And she does.'

Logan grunted. 'Aye,' he admitted. 'She does.'

'Well, then.'

'Again, let's focus on your relationship status for the day, eh?'

'Fine, fine. Today. I can't promise not to come back to the subject, though.'

'Aye, well, I can't promise no' to have you transferred elsewhere,' Logan told her, and they both smiled.

'Come on, what would you do without me?'

'I'd have my feet up in front of the bloody telly right now, for one thing,' Logan said. He gave his sporran a pat. 'And I wouldn't have had so many sleepless nights trying to write this bloody speech.'

She put a hand on his arm. 'Thank you,' she said. 'For this. For everything.'

Logan rested his own hand on hers for a moment, then tutted and shook his head, trying very hard not to show too much emotion. 'Och, away you go. It's nothing,' he said. 'It's my pleasure. Honestly. It's my honour, in fact.' He gave her hand a squeeze. 'I never knew them, but I know your parents would be proud.'

'Don't,' Sinead croaked, taking her hand away and waving it in front of her face. 'I've got mascara on. I can't go in looking like Alice Cooper. Quick, talk about something else.'

Logan racked his brains. 'Eh… you see the football?'

'No.'

'No, nor me. Tedious fucking game,' he said. 'Eh… oh! Lana Lennon's awake. Did you hear?'

'No! Is she? When?'

'Last night. Mantits sent a text. She's in a bad way—it'll be a long road to any sort of recovery—but he reckons she'll be fit enough for us to interview in a couple of weeks. Thought maybe you'd want to do it?'

'I'd be up for it, aye,' Sinead said. She looked out of the side window as Eden Court Theatre rolled past for about the fourth time. 'Poor Mrs Lennon.'

'She's already identified Lachlan—or Ewan, or whatever—as her attacker, though. And her and Bennet are both pressing charges against Clyde, I'm told. Should have a solid case against the bastard.'

'Good,' Sinead said. 'Hope he gets locked up.'

'He will,' Logan confirmed. 'And no' a moment too bloody soon.'

–

Bob Hoon ducked beneath the branches of the trees that lined the River Ness, unzipped his fly, and groaned with relief as his bladder drained out onto the grass. He shook, bent his knees, tucked everything away again, then swore under his breath when he spotted the splashes on his shoes.

He had just finished wiping them up and down on his calves when he spotted a man he knew best as 'that prick with the hair', leaning on a railing overlooking the river's edge.

'Aw, fuck's sake,' Hoon grunted. He glanced back through the trees, hoping he'd see someone else there who could deal with it, but found no one. 'Great. Where'd the fucking Super Friends all go when you need them?' he grumbled, then he set off along the bank and stopped a few feet from where Tyler sat. 'Haw. Fannybaws. You know they're all looking for you up there?'

Tyler, who had been slouched over on the railing, stood upright at the sound of Hoon's voice. He turned, squinting in the sun, looked the former Detective Superintendent up and down, then glanced furtively back up through the trees. 'Aye. I suppose they must be by now.'

'Right. Well, come on, then,' Hoon said. 'Pull your finger out your arse, and let's go.'

'I can't,' Tyler said, his shoulders stooping again.

'What? How no'? Leg caught in a fucking bear trap or something?' Hoon asked. 'No? Well, fucking get a shifty on, then.'

Tyler rubbed his forehead, his fingers sliding back and forth like they were trying to rub away a stain. 'I just… it's complicated.'

'Complicated my arse,' Hoon said. 'You stand there, you say, "I fucking do", ideally without the swearing, but that's up to you, and then you get pissed, eat cake, and fuck off to a nice hotel for some rumpy pumpy. Where's the complicated bit?'

'It's not that,' Tyler said. 'It's… there's more to consider.'

Hoon started counting on his fingers. 'Pissed. Cake. Rumpy pumpy,' he said. 'No, pretty sure that covers the lot. Now, come on, or do I have to fucking drag you in there by the hair? Because I will, but it's no' a good fucking look for your first day of married life.'

'I've got cancer.'

Hoon hesitated. This, in itself, spoke volumes.

'Cancer?' he asked, once he'd recovered.

Tyler nodded. 'I haven't… we haven't said anything. To anyone. Fuck. I don't know why I'm telling you, of all people.'

'Probably my warm and open personality.'

'Ha. Aye. Probably,' Tyler replied.

Hoon sniffed, shrugged, then took a step closer. 'Where is it?'

Tyler indicated downwards with a point. 'Down there.'

'What? Your feet?'

'No! Not my feet!' Tyler said. He shot another furtive glance up into the trees, and lowered his voice. 'My bollocks.'

'Oh. Right. Aye. I did wonder, right enough. I mean, who gets fucking feet cancer?' Hoon said. 'Was it a lump, or…?'

'No. Scan. I hadn't been, you know, checking.'

'Fuck me, seriously? I have a crafty feel about sixteen times a day. I thought that was just the standard for all men?' He looked away for a moment, then sighed. 'Look, son, I'm no' exactly the world's best at this sort of thing, but what's the worst that can happen?'

Tyler blinked. 'Well... I could die. That's not great.'

'Fuck, aye. I suppose so,' Hoon conceded. 'Jesus. Fair enough. You're right. Might as well just throw yourself in the water and be fucking done with it.'

'What?'

'Your missus. Or your almost missus, or whatever... you mind if I have a crack at her? In a few months, I mean. Once she's over the shock. I'd leave it a bit, I'm no' a fucking monster.'

Tyler turned to face him. 'What? No! Jesus!'

'Well, you're no' going to be here, are you?'

'There's a very high survival rate, actually!' Tyler spat. 'Over ninety-five percent, if they catch it early enough.'

'Aye, but they probably got to you too late,' Hoon said. 'Tragic, really.'

'No, actually. It's still quite early days!'

'Then what are you whinging about then, you hypochondriac fuckballoon?' Hoon barked. 'Quit moping about here watching men having a piss—'

'I wasn't watching, you just turned up!'

'—and get in there, say your bit, then drink, dance, and get your leg over. You might want to save the last bit for the hotel, but you'll have my utmost fucking respect if you don't.'

Tyler looked up through the trees again, and this time let his gaze linger there for a while.

'We might not be able to have kids, they said. The treatment... it can affect that.'

'Kids are all arseholes, anyway,' Hoon pointed out. 'You're better off without the sticky-handed, snottery-nosed wee fucks cramping your style.'

'We wanted them, though. Kids. Not right now, I mean... but we spoke about it. Someday, we did.'

'And does she know?' Hoon asked. He flicked his gaze down to Tyler's sporran. 'About the lads?'

'Aye. She knows everything.'

'And is she all dolled up to get married?'

Tyler shrugged. 'Yeah. Yeah, I think so.'

'Then there's your fucking answer, son,' Hoon said. 'She knows. Everything. And she still wants to marry you. I mean, personally, I think she needs her fucking head examined. Cancer's the least of your fucking concerns, if you ask me.'

Tyler chuckled. 'Aye.'

'No, I fucking mean it,' Hoon said. 'In a more just fucking world, she should be way out of your reach. If you were punching any higher above your weight you'd need a pair of stilts and a fucking oxygen mask.'

'Aye, well—' Tyler began, but Hoon wasn't done. Not by a long shot.

'No, but seriously. I mean, I didn't want to say anything, but fit lassie like that? Wi' a flaccid wee shitenugget like you? It's a fucking outrage, quite frankly. Seriously. It's a bloody sin. And she's going to realise that, sooner or later. Maybe even today. So, I suggest you get up there and put a fucking ring on her finger before whatever basement-dweller witchcraft you've managed to do on her wears off, and she sees you for the living clusterfuck of a man that you really are.'

Tyler straightened up, pushed his shoulders back, took a deep breath. Then he gave a nod and held out a hand. 'Thanks, Bob. I needed that.'

Hoon took the offered hand and tightened his grip just enough to make Tyler's eyes widen. 'No bother, son. Any time,' he said. 'But please, for both our fucking sakes, call me, "sir".'

–

'Oh, thank Christ,' Logan muttered, scanning the message on his phone. 'Driver, full steam ahead. We've got a wedding to go to.'

'Find him then, did they?' Sinead asked.

Logan blinked. 'Eh?'

She jabbed a thumb back over her shoulder. 'It's a car, not a soundproof booth,' she said. 'He OK?'

'He's fine,' Logan said. 'I mean, he'll no' be once I get my hands on him, but... aye. He's fine. They're all waiting.'

Sinead took a deep breath in, held it, then blew it back out again. 'Right. Well, I suppose this is it, then.'

'I suppose it is,' Logan confirmed. 'You OK?'

Sinead smiled. 'I'm... great. I really am.'

'Good. Good,' Logan said, patting her hand as she hooked it under his arm. 'And, eh, you're right, by the way.'

'I generally am,' Sinead told him. 'About anything in particular, or...?'

'Holding grudges. Life being too short,' Logan said. 'I'm, eh, I'm going to phone Maddie. She might not talk to me, but I'll leave a message. Just, you know, congratulations. Hope she's happy. That sort of thing.'

'Building bridges.'

'Aye,' Logan said. 'Building bridges.'

The car slowed as they approached the venue. Harris waved excitedly, now fully dressed and with the unrulier parts of his hair stuck flat to his head with a combination of gel, hairspray, and his auntie's saliva.

'Here we go, then,' Sinead breathed.

'Here we go.'

The car stopped outside the centre.

'Right, wait there, I'll let you out,' Logan said, opening his door.

'By the way,' Sinead said, stopping him in his tracks. 'You do know you have to dance tonight, right? It's traditional.'

'Me? Dance?' Logan asked. Then, he grinned, winked, and threw open the door. 'Just you try and bloody stop me!'

Epilogue

Olivia Maximuke woke late, made some disparaging comments at the sun that shone in through her too-thin curtains, then peeled her eyelids all the way open with the assistance of one of her thumbs.

She'd been on the phone dealing with 'work stuff' until after two, then had lain there on her bed until sleep had finally turned up to claim her just before six.

The four hours inbetween had been spent alternately scrolling the internet on her phone, stressing out, and holding her breath every time a car passed on the street outside.

Some digging over the past few days had brought up a few small mentions in local newspapers about the body found in the freezer a couple of months back.

Body.

Singular, where it should have been plural.

It was being put down as another victim of the Iceman. Which it was, she knew. She had no involvement in that man's murder. She was blameless. She was in no way responsible for his prolonged, agonising death.

Not directly, anyway.

But there should have been a second body in there with him. One that she would have been responsible for.

One who knew exactly what she'd done to him.

Or, what she'd tried to do, and failed.

She heard the front door close, and was out of bed in a flash. Edging aside the curtain, she looked down at the path and saw the top of her mum's head as she set off on another jog. Father

Conrad was waiting out on the street, knees pumping up and down as he ran on the spot.

They exchanged high-fives by the gate, then both set off down the street, and were almost immediately hidden by the trees of the garden next door.

'Crazy,' Olivia remarked, still not quite able to get her head around her mother's change of lifestyle.

She approved, of course. Her mum was out of the house more often—she'd even started spin classes, the thought of which had made Olivia laugh so hard she'd been left gasping for air—but she was far more fun when she was around than she used to be. She made breakfast on school days, and was always around for dinner. The chances of her drinking herself into an early grave had fallen sharply, too.

And it was nice to see her happy. She was still relying on a man to provide it, which was not unusual for her, but Father Conrad seemed like a good guy, despite the Jesus stuff. He didn't seem to be after anything, which was rare.

Olivia steeled herself, pulled the curtains all the way apart, then rapid-fired her eyelids as she tried to adjust to the sudden blinding brightness.

Once the worst of it had passed, she turned from the window to find some clothes to put on.

And that was when she saw it.

The note.

It was on her bedside table—a single sheet of paper folded in half and stood upright like a tent.

A word was written on it, the letters formed shakily, as if by an unsteady hand: 'Malyshka.'

She ran to the bedroom door and hauled her chest of drawers in front of it, blocking entry to anyone who might try to get inside.

Only then did she turn back to the folded tent of paper.

Only then did she pick it up, ease it open, read the one-word message scrawled haphazardly inside.

'Soon,' it read.

Soon.

CANELOCRIME

Do you love crime fiction and are always on the lookout for brilliant authors?

Canelo Crime is home to some of the most exciting novels around. Thousands of readers are already enjoying our compulsive stories. Are you ready to find your new favourite writer?

Find out more and sign up to our newsletter at canelocrime.com